THE LURE OF BABYLON

So he carried me away in the spirit into the wilderness: and I saw a woman sit upon a scarlet coloured beast, full of names of blasphemy, having seven heads and ten horns.

And the woman was arrayed in purple and scarlet colour, and decked with gold and precious stones and pearls, having a golden cup in her hand full of abominations and filthiness of her fornication:

And upon her forehead was a name written: "Mystery, Babylon the great, the mother of harlots and abominations of the earth."

And I saw the woman drunken with the blood of the saints, and with the blood of the martyrs of Jesus: and when I saw her, I wondered with great admiration.

Revelation 17:3–6

Michael E. Schiefelbein

THE LURE OF BABYLON

SEVEN PROTESTANT NOVELISTS AND BRITAIN'S ROMAN CATHOLIC REVIVAL

Mercer
University
Press
2001

To my mother, Mary Schiefelbein Warner,
and to the memory of my father, Sylvester J. Schiefelbein

ISBN 0-86554-720-3
MUP/H540

© 2001 Mercer University Press
6316 Peake Road
Macon, Georgia 31210-3960
All rights reserved
First Edition.

∞The paper used in this publication meets the minimum
requirements of American National Standard for Information
Sciences—Permanence of Paper for Printed Library Materials, ANSI
Z39.48-1992.

Library of Congress Cataloging-in-Publication Data

Schielelbein, Michael E.
The lure of Babylon : seven Protestant novelists and Britain's Roman
Catholic revival / by Michael Schiefelbein.
p. cm.
Includes bibliographical references and index.
ISBN 0-86554-720-3
1. English fiction—19th century—History and criticism. 2.
Christianity and literature—Great Britain—History—19th century. 3.
English fiction—Protestant authors--History and criticism. 4.
Catholic Church—Great Britain—History—19th century. 5.
Protestantism and literature—History—19th century. 6. Christian
fiction, English—History and criticism. 7. Religious fiction,
English—History and criticism. 8. Catholic Church—In literature. I.
Title.

PR868.R5 S35 2001
823'.809382—dc21

2001018332

TABLE OF CONTENTS

0165624

ACKNOWLEDGMENTS

MY THANKS ARE due to many people who contributed to this study. Deirdre David introduced me to the Victorian novel in a graduate course at the University of Maryland and provided me with excellent guidance on a dissertation that contained the seeds of this study. David Paroissien, a kind and attentive editor, made helpful suggestions for revising an article on Little Nell adapted in chapter three. In a thoughtful response to my query about untapped areas for research, Deborah Thomas encouraged me to pursue the subject of Catholicism. My classmate Donald E. Hall, inspirational in his professional accomplishments, patiently advised me on pursuing a publisher. Anonymous readers for *Religion and Literature* offered good suggestions for revising the article on Mary Shelley that appears as chapter two, and Mercer University Press's anonymous readers provided helpful comments for the book's final revisions.

Special thanks to my friends and colleagues in the Department of Literature and Languages at Christian Brothers University, who listened with interest as I described the progress of my work. Ann Marie Wranovix deserves special recognition in this regard. My warmest thanks also to Steve Klinkerman, who time and time again listened to me think out loud about the chapters in this book and who has encouraged me in countless ways over the years. Finally, I recognize with great love and devotion my parents, Mary Schiefelbein Warner and Sylvester Schiefelbein, whose deeply lived Catholicism introduced me to the subject of this book and whose personal sacrifices made possible the academic foundation upon which it is built.

Also deserving acknowledgement are the journals that granted permission for reprinting articles in this book: *Dickens Quarterly* for "Little Nell, Catholicism, and Dickens's Investigation of Death," which appeared in volume 8, number 2 (Fall 1992); *Victorian Newsletter* for "Crucifixes and Madonnas: George Eliot's Fascination with Catholicism in *Romola*," which appeared in a slightly different version in number 88 (Fall 1995), and for "'Blighted' by a 'Upas-Shadow': Catholicism's Function for Kingsley in *Westward Ho!*," which appeared in number 94 (Fall 1998); *Christianity and Literature* for "A Catholic Baptism for Lucy Snowe," which appeared in volume 45, numbers 3–4 (1997); and the University of Notre Dame's *Religion and Literature* for "The Lessons of True Religion: Mary Shelley's Tribute to Catholicism in *Valperga*, which appeared in volume 30, issue 2 (Summer 1998).

INTRODUCTION

ROMAN CATHOLIC REVIVAL
AND THE BRITISH CULTURAL IMAGINATION

HOW DOES A novelist both reflect the imagination of his or her culture and transform it through art? In what sense does a particular artistic transformation reveal the needs of the novelist? These questions suggest the theoretical basis of this study, but its real starting point is a group of enlightened novelists whose work reveals the intense anti-Catholic prejudices pervasive in nineteenth-century Britain. The critical reputation of these novelists has survived the test of time. This is particularly true of Walter Scott, Mary Shelley, Charles Dickens, Charlotte Brontë, and George Eliot; however, the other two authors studied here, Frances Trollope and Charles Kingsley, also continue to inspire critical attention. (For example, the fiction of Trollope, best remembered for her *Domestic Manners of the Americans*, has recently been reassessed in light of feminist concerns.)[1]

Amazingly, despite the plethora of criticism on most of these authors, very little of it explores the link between their work and a significant cultural phenomenon. In the words of D. G. Paz, author of *Popular*

---

[1] See the following works by Helen Heineman: *Frances Trollope* (Boston: Twayne, 1984); *Mrs. Trollope: The Triumphant Feminine in the Nineteenth Century* (Athens: Ohio University Press, 1979); and *Restless Angels: The Friendship of Six Victorian Women* (Athens: Ohio University Press, 1983). See also the recent biography by Pamela Neville-Sington, *Fanny Trollope: The Life and Adventures of a Clever Woman* (New York: Viking, 1998).

Catholicism in Mid-Victorian England, "[t]he fear and loathing of Roman Catholicism was a major part of the nineteenth-century cultural context."[2] In the imagination of nineteenth-century England, fed by commonplace epithets, the Romish Church loomed as the Whore of Babylon, whose papal pimp was the Anti-Christ himself. Popery was disseminated by crafty Jesuits who insinuated their way into the lives of unsuspecting Protestants. The confessional gave lecherous priests access to the secrets and even to the bodies of young girls and deprived husbands of exclusive spiritual authority over their wives.[3] Similarly, the convent threatened patriarchal authority over daughters and over women in general: within the walls of nunneries, subversive females established perverted communities without men, imprisoning girls for exploitation and abuse. Popery was anti-Protestant and therefore anti-English, its goal to replace enlightened, constitutional government with blind obedience to the Pope and his priestly agents in a reestablished Papal State maintained by superstition and idolatry. In short, popery threatened the body politic and, indeed, the very soul of England.

Although these sentiments emerged from an anti-Catholic tradition in England that began with the Reformation, it was only in the nineteenth century that such sentiments truly crystallized in the British imagination, generating an urgent national impulse for political and social suppression of the Romish religion and its practitioners. One reason was a new and growing Catholic voice in England. The discreet, aristocratic Old Catholics of previous generations, merely a dying remnant by the nineteenth century, were giving way to a rising middle class of Catholics from Ireland. In the early 1800s, charismatic Irish barristers like Daniel O'Connell fought for the repeal of prohibitions that prevented Britain's Catholics from serving in Parliament or running for public office.

As an attempt to appease Irish unrest, the Catholic Emancipation Act was finally passed in 1829, but not without public appeal to England's anti-Catholic lore. In his parliamentary speech of 1825, the Duke of York reminded his colleagues that Roman Catholics "refused to submit to our

---

[2] D. G. Paz, *Popular Anti-Catholicism in Mid-Victorian England* (Stanford: Stanford University Press, 1992) 12.

[3] See Frank H. Wallis's discussion of these and the following myths in chaps. 2 and 7 of *Popular Anti-Catholicism in Mid-Victorian Britain: Texts and Studies in Religion*, vol. 60 (Lewiston: Edwin Mellen Press, 1993).

rules" and "denied any authority of the civil power over their church."[4] Then, in their "1828 Address to the Protestants of Great Britain," the Grand Orange Lodge declared that "[i]n the present era, our religion is menaced by the attacks of Popery," and that with Catholic Emancipation, "[t]he liberty of these realms, our religion, and our monarchy would again be placed under Papal darkness and despotic oppression."[5] Even the Emancipation Bill itself perpetuated suspicion toward Catholics, prohibiting them from enjoying certain offices, prohibiting ordained Catholics from serving in Parliament, and requiring those who were elected to office to deny papal authority in civil affairs. The bill also restricted them from wearing religious garb or performing religious ceremonies in public. It especially targeted religious communities, providing for the "gradual Suppression and final Prohibition" of the Jesuits and all other male religious orders and declaring that any Jesuit entering Britain in the future would be banished.[6]

Even more vituperative anti-Catholic rhetoric met the proposal to endow permanently the Catholic seminary in Maynooth, Ireland, in 1845. Sir Robert Peel introduced the proposal in order to end rancorous annual debates about a policy put in place by the Irish Parliament and to curry the favor of the Irish clergy on behalf of the British government. Behind a petition campaign that secured over a million signatures were formal denouncements of Maynooth's popery. The people of Worthing, Sussex, called the seminary "a hot-bed of error, sedition, and persecution, and a mainspring to all anarchy and confusion reigning in Ireland," while residents of Lympsham, Somerset, blasted the proposed bill because it "emboldened the Roman Catholics," condoned popish beliefs that were "utterly repugnant to the word of God," and threatened to bring Divine wrath upon England for "promot[ing] idolatry which God abhors."[7]

---

[4] From *Hansard* 13, 138-42, 25 April 1825, in Edward R. Norman, *Anti-Catholicism in Victorian England* (London: George Allen & Unwin, 1968) 127.

[5] "1828 Address to the Protestants of Great Britain," from R. M. Sibbett, *Orangeism in Ireland and throughout the Empire*, vol. 2: 29-31 in Norman, *Anti-Catholicism*, 129–30.

[6] An Act for the Relief of His Majesty's Roman Catholic Citizens, 1829, in Norman, *Anti-Catholicism*, 138.

[7] As quoted in Wallis, *Popular Anti-Catholicism*, 118.

The bill passed, but the strong popular sentiment against it never subsided, flaring once again during an effort to repeal the bill in 1851. During this period, anti-Catholic rhetoric reached new heights of sensationalism in periodicals like the *Record*, which declared that when Maynooth's priests were "burning the true Protestants at the stake for obstinate heretics, they naturally will expect that these Liberals, who now humour them out of charity, will be cajoled or frightened into their willing tools, and that they may see them heaping faggots upon their victims and dancing around the flames."[8]

Along with a new Catholic voice in England came a growing Catholic population. The influx of Irish Catholics throughout the nineteenth century gave a face to a religion that had been all too easy to ignore in the eighteenth century. Whereas in 1780 there was an estimated Catholic population of 69,376, in 1851—after decades of Irish immigration during industrial expansion and then during the potato famine—that population had grown to about 900,000,[9] and most members of this population—over 727,000—were Irish-born.[10]

Britain's views toward Ireland were always colored by anti-Catholic sentiment like that fostered by the *Times* in one of its many pronouncements on papism in Ireland: "[I]t is impossible for the most bigoted slave of Rome to read the letters, the speeches, and the pastorals of the Irish Bishops without internally congratulating himself that he is not placed under their temporal jurisdiction."[11]

Such opinions were aroused especially by Irish Catholics when they settled in England and segregated themselves from mainstream Protestant culture, which they often viewed with hostility. Alarmed by the growing Irish population, sectarian journals like the *Bulwark*, which once declared "how near to savages the Popish Irish are,"[12] perpetuated anti-Catholic stereotypes linking Irish poverty and crime with papism. In the meantime, the famous anti-Catholic agitator William Murphy provoked rioting among the Irish by declaring that "Catholic priests were

---

[8] *Record* 7, June 1852, 4 in Wallis, *Popular Anti-Catholicism*, 125.

[9] Alan D. Gilbert, *Religion and Society in Industrial England: Church, Chapel, and Social Change, 1740–1914* (London: Longman, 1976) 46.

[10] Wallis, *Popular Anti-Catholicism*, 212.

[11] *Times*, 18 January 1860, 9 in Wallis, *Popular Anti-Catholicism*, 225.

[12] *Bulwark*, 14, 1864-66, 300 in Wallis, *Popular Anti-Catholicism*, 226.

all liars, cannibals, and murderers; the Virgin Mary was a Protestant; convents required state inspection; and the confessional promoted immorality through priests' asking of sexually illicit questions of married women."[13]

The Oxford Movement, which reached its apex in the 1840s, was another important manifestation of a dangerous Catholic revival.[14] This movement to reassert the role of hierarchy, sacraments, and other Catholic characteristics of the state church challenged the Evangelical element that had come to dominate Anglicanism and English society in general.[15] It also inspired many prominent intellectuals, like John Henry Newman, to convert to Rome.[16] Naturally, the movement elicited vehement denouncements of popery, like this one by Victorian pundit Daniel Chapman, who blames participants of the Oxford Movement for opening the doors to Roman Catholicism in England:

[T]he very apostates from the simplicity of their own creed and worship within the pale of the National Church...are the prime movers, if not the sole authors, of the present mischief; it is by them that Popery has been enacted, and Papacy emboldened to re-assert its obsolete claims of supremacy; it is by them that the

---

[13] Wallis, *Popular Anti-Catholicism*, 232.

[14] This term generally has been restricted to the Oxford Movement itself. It is used here to characterize the larger social phenomenon described in this introduction.

[15] See Walter E. Houghton's discussion of Victorian enthusiasm and earnestness in chaps. 10 and 11 of *The Victorian Frame of Mind, 1830–1870* (New Haven: Yale University Press, 1957).

[16] As Houghton notes in *Victorian Frame of Mind*, "[b]y 1853 half of the most amiable men whom Ruskin knew at Oxford (1837–1842) were Roman Catholics" (99). Houghton goes on to provide James Froude's insightful explanation for this phenomenon: "'Pious Protestants had trusted themselves upon the Bible as their sole foundation. They found their philosophers and professors assuming that the Bible was a human composition—parts of it of doubtful authenticity, other parts bearing marks on them of the mistaken opinions of the age when these books were written; and they were flying terrified back into the Church from which they had escaped at the Reformation, like ostriches hiding their heads in a bush'" (100). From Froude's "The Oxford Counter-Reformation," in *Short Studies on Great Subjects*, 1888.

gates have been opened to the enemy of all truth and freedom, and the armies of the destroyer treacherously tempted or invited to enter, and take possession of the betrayed or corrupted citadel.[17]

"The present mischief" to which Chapman refers was an event in 1850 that brought national anti-Catholicism to a head: the re-establishment of the Roman hierarchy on English shores. Dubbed "Papal Aggression" by Parliamentary leaders and the queen herself, the movement on the part of Rome to designate Westminster as a Catholic diocese, with Nicholas Cardinal Wiseman as its head, unleashed fury in Parliament. In a *London Times* article, Prime Minister John Russell agreed with the Bishop of Durham's labeling of "the late aggression of the Pope upon our Protestantism" as "insolent and insidious"[18] and supported plans for an Ecclesiastical Titles Bill, which would outlaw papal declarations of spiritual authority in England. On the second reading of the proposed bill, Sir Robert Inglis reminded the members of the dangers revealed during the Reformation and still existing in his day: "at issue was one between light and darkness, between freedom and slavery, between the development of powers of the intellect, and the prostration of all those powers before the will of others."[19]

All the while, denunciations of Romish evils flew from the pulpits of preachers like the curate of St. Mary's Parish Church at Walthamstow, for whom "Rome is, in very truth, 'the mother'—the fruitful parent—'of harlots and abominations of the earth.'" The curate goes on to decry "the hideous pollution of the confessional; the encouragement to vice, afforded by pretended absolutions, and purchased indulgences; the crimes of the convent, and of the monastery."[20] The latter accusation, always popular in England, was made with new conviction after 1850 and

---

[17] Daniel Chapman, *The Great Principles Involved in the Present Act of Papal Aggression*, 1851, 21, as quoted in Paz, *Popular Anti-Catholicism*, 131.

[18] Lord John Russell, Letter in *Times*, 7 November 1850, in Norman, *Anti-Catholicism*, 159.

[19] Sir Robert Inglis, *Hansard* 114, 1365-75, 14 March 1851, in Norman, *Anti-Catholicism*, 182.

[20] William Bennet, *Popery as Set Forth in Scripture: Its Guilt and Its Doom*, in Norman, *Anti-Catholicism*, 171, 174.

initiated petition drives for mandatory government inspections of convents.[21]

Indeed, such anti-Catholic petition drives, as well as the public meetings at which they were produced, flourished after the Papal Aggression. An advertisement for one such public meeting promised a performance "IN ALL ITS POMP" of "THE ROMISH MASS...to demonstrate by practical illustrations the mockeries of religion, the derisions of Christianity, and the awful revilings of God, which the POPE, WISEMAN, PRIESTS, and MONKS, are doing daily, when acting the theatrical burlesque, called the ROMISH MASS, to pilfer the people of MASS MONEY."[22]

The Papal Aggression also inspired the organization of new anti-Catholic societies. The Scottish Reformation Society, the Protestant Alliance, and the British Protestant League joined ranks with early organizations like the British Reformation Society and the Protestant Association, as well as with organizations formed in reaction to the Maynooth grant, such as the Evangelical Alliance and the National Club. The societies disseminated their views on Catholicism in publications like the Scottish Reformation Society's *Bulwark*, which decried "The Blight of Popery" assailing England in 1851 by enumerating the evils evident to "an enlightened traveller" visiting Catholic countries: "dark suspicion," "degrading superstition," "servile worshippers," "grossness of creature-worship," the absence of "manly emotions," and "a corrupt and heartless system of priestcraft."[23] The article offers this grave conclusion:

With the advancement of popish power and influence there has always been a retrograde movement in virtue and civilization. The moral and social aspect of the people is more unpromising than in the days of heathenism. Intellect has become dwarfish, enterprise languishes, trade fails, poverty and rags abound, the streets swarm with beggars, filth and meanness prevail, indolence and vice are depicted in the countenance, profligates flaunt about without any apparent sense of shame.[24]

---

[21] Wallis, *Popular Anti-Catholicism*, 38.
[22] Paz, *Popular Anti-Catholicism*, 27. From an 1852 Handbill.
[23] "The Blight of Popery," *Bulwark*, 1851, 1:41-43, in Norman, 183–85.
[24] In Norman, *Anti-Catholicism*, 184.

Thus, the popular imagination of nineteenth-century British Protestants was expressed in and shaped by the abundant anti-Catholic discourse of parliamentary speeches, legislation, public meetings, petitions,
sermons, and sectarian and mainstream periodicals. With the development of the middle-class reading public, the anti-Catholic novel joined
these forms of discourse. Proliferating in the 1840s, around the years of
the Maynooth Grant and at the height of the Oxford Movement, this
novel gained force with the Papal Aggression of 1850 and continued on
through the end of the century. Writers like William Sewell, Elizabeth
Sewell, Elizabeth Harris, Benjamin Disraeli, and J. H. Shorthouse warned
against the dangers of increasing popery in the Church of England.[25]
However, the bulk of novelists concerned themselves with portraying the
evils of Romanism in general and with urging the destruction of the
Romish religion. These included the Evangelical novelists Anne Howard,
Lady Catherine Long, Charles Tayler, William Francis Wilkinson,
Stephen Jenner, and Charlotte Anley; along with Mary Sherwood, Emma
Worboise, Charlotte Elizabeth, Catherine Sinclair, Jemima Luke, and the
much-translated Eugène Sue, all of whom specialized in Jesuit villains.
Indeed, the anti-Jesuit novel became one of the preferred weapons of
writers incensed by the Papal Aggression. In the words of Margaret
Maison, who discusses the novelists mentioned above in *The Victorian
Vision: Studies in the Religious Novel,*

[i]t was the restoration of the Hierarchy in 1850 that, provoking an
extraordinary outburst of hysteria, fury and panic on the part of John
Bull, whipped Protestant novelists up into a frenzy of rage and
produced some of the most angry novels ever written, fulminating
particularly against the "snakes," "pests," "poisonous microbes", and
"emissaries of Satan," as the sons of Loyola were variously called.[26]

Because of the nature of imaginative discourse, novels had a special
role in both reflecting and shaping popular anti-Catholicism in nine-

---

[25] Joseph Ellis Baker, *The Novel and the Oxford Movement, 1932* (New York:
Russell & Russell, 1965). See especially chap. 3, "The Evangelical Onslaught."
[26] Margaret M. Maison, *The Victorian Vision: Studies in the Religious Novel*
(New York: Sheed & Ward, 1961) 171.

teenth-century Britain. As Arthur Kinney argues, while "texts, customs, and actions" are "similar cultural documents, all constitutive signs of a cultural moment," literary texts allow a "presentational imaging and metaphorizing" of that moment, "helping to constitute—and to reconstitute—it."[27] For the present study, I have chosen from the abundance of fiction vilifying Roman Catholicism eight novels that stand out, not in the sentiments they express, but in their superior "imagining and metaphorizing power," which they possess on two levels. The first is the level of basic narrative, where cultural biases are represented, along with the culture's latent fascination with popery, made evident in several phenomena: the High Anglican movement, conversions to the Roman Church, the voyeuristic desire to inspect convents, and—from the Gothic novel onward—the popular appetite for fiction that exploits monastic settings.

Jenny Franchot's thesis about Protestant Antebellum America is equally valid for Protestant nineteenth-century England: "the estranged world of Catholicism provoked a characteristically conflicted response of repulsion and longing, a fear of corruption and a hunger for communion."[28] The present study examines such a conflicted response in a number of fictional representations: the mysterious monastic settings of Scott's *The Monastery* and *The Abbot* (both 1820), the Dantean heroine of Shelley's *Valperga* (1823), the medieval atmosphere of Dickens's *Old Curiosity Shop* (1840–1841), the treacherous Jesuits of Trollope's *Father Eustace* (1847), the seductive Belgian Romanists in *Villette* (1853), the exotic Spanish officers in Kingsley's *Westward Ho!* (1855), and the Florentine mummery that comes to life in Eliot's *Romola* (1862–1863).

However, the "metaphorizing" power of these novels is more interesting on the second, or meta-plot, level. This is the field of trope, image, humor, and suggestive commentary that defies or eludes narrative control. In some ways, this field is simply where the authors more imaginatively explore the culture's "conflicted response" to Catholicism glimpsed in the narrative. Yet it reveals something more: a constructive

---

[27] Arthur Kinney, "Is Literary History Still Possible?" *Ben Johnson Journal* 2 (1995): 214.

[28] Jenny Franchot, *Roads to Rome: The Antebellum Protestant Encounter with Catholicism* (Berkley: University of California Press, 1994) xxiii.

vision explained in large part by the lives of the individual authors, for whom Catholicism has something personal to offer.

In its discussion of *The Monastery* and *The Abbot*, chapter 1 explores Walter Scott's attraction to Catholicism's playful, humorous capacities, which he finds lacking in the Calvinism of his childhood. In discussing *Valperga*, chapter 2 relates Mary Shelley's interest in Catholicism to her need for a faith that integrates rationality and imagination. Chapter 3 examines Catholic aspects of *The Old Curiosity Shop* in light of Dickens's grief over his deceased sister-in-law, Mary Hogarth. Chapter 4 connects Frances Trollope's vision of Catholicism in *Father Eustace: A Tale of the Jesuits* with her penchant for order. Chapter 5 considers Catholicism in *Villette* as Charlotte Brontë's tool for self-assertion. In a reading of *Westward Ho!*, chapter 6 examines Catholicism as the means by which Kingsley grapples with the troubling elements of sensuality and gender. Finally, chapter 7 traces in the text of *Romola* Eliot's efforts to validate pain. Of course, biographical readings of these novels cannot occur without reference to other sources. I will examine the novels in conjunction with all the texts produced by the authors, including journals, correspondence, journalism, and other creative works.

This study focuses, then, on the ways in which particular authors appropriate social discourse in their "personal" texts; however, I must underscore the cultural prominence of most of these authors and hence their potential for influencing discourse in general. Walter Scott (1771–1832) was lionized by aristocrats and royalty, becoming a baronet, receiving access to the Prince Regent's library, and hosting George IV himself during his trip to Scotland. As biographer Edgar Johnson points out, Scott's critical reputation was established very early in his writing career: "[w]ith the notes to his *Minstrelsy of the Scottish Border* Scott had already won a reputation for scholarship that ranged curiously from the Middle Ages to the sixteenth century, and the notes to his two narrative poems had enhanced that reputation...[and] his edition of Dryden established him as deeply versed in the seventeenth century as well."[29]

Scott was praised by critics as renowned as Southey—who received the laureateship only after Scott turned it down—and Goethe. As for the

---

[29] Edgar Johnson, *Sir Walter Scott: The Great Unknown*, 2 vols. (New York: Macmillan 1970) 1:292.

public, not only did they create the need for edition after edition of Scott's work, but they also mobbed the countryside settings described in it, coveting formerly scorned London neighborhoods because Scott's fiction had rendered them charming. This public fervor for Scott quickly spread abroad. In the words of John Henry Raleigh, "Scott did not cause the American Civil War, as Mark Twain claimed; nevertheless, almost every steamboat that pulled in to Hannibal bore the name of a Scott heroine. To have been alive and literate in the nineteenth century was to have been affected in some way by the Waverley novels."[30]

The astronomical sales of Scott's work, which included twenty-six major novels, allowed him both to build a country estate and to keep it, along with its furnishings, when the publishing firm in which he was a partner collapsed. His influence continued among the growing middle class of the Victorian era and especially among the novelists inspired by his historical novels, his rural settings, and his appealing depictions of "common life and common people."[31]

Given to copying passages from Scott's diary, Charles Dickens (1812–1870) was such a Scott enthusiast. Like Scott, he was an immensely popular figure, arguably the most celebrated British novelist of the nineteenth century. Already a rising star at the age of twenty-four with his popular *Sketches by Boz*, Dickens achieved fame with *Pickwick Papers.* The inexpensive serialized installments of *Pickwick*—like those of the fourteen novels following it—were mass-produced for an eager middle-class market. The sensational sales brought to the market all kinds of merchandise displaying characters from the novel and a public devotion to "Boz" that scarcely waned throughout Dickens's thirty-year career. His readers crowded the New York City docks to snatch up the last installment of the *Old Curiosity Shop*, featuring the death of the heroine Little Nell. Similarly, the death of *Dombey and Son*'s Little Dombey caused a "national mourning," according to Dickens's contemporary critic David

---

[30] John Henry Raleigh, "What Scott Meant to the Victorians," in *Critical Essays on Sir Walter Scott: The Waverley Novels*, ed. Harry E. Shaw (New York: G. K. Hall, 1996) 49.

[31] Steven Marcus, *Dickens from Pickwick to Dombey* (New York: Norton, 1965) 28. Cf. Raleigh's article, "What Scott Meant to the Victorians," for a detailed discussion of Scott's influence on the generation succeeding his own.

Masson.[32] *A Christmas Carol* and Dickens's other Christmas books became cultural treasures.

While his novels were in progress, Dickens's fans wrote him letters suggesting plot twists and revisions. The topics of his novels and journalism—the Poor Law; cheap, distant schools; Benthamism; evangelical cant; spontaneous combustion; public hangings—tapped public controversies. He was ever in demand as a fundraising speaker, and his reading tours in England, Ireland, Scotland, and the United States were greeted by enthusiastic crowds. In the United States, Dickens's fans actually mobbed him in hopes of snatching a piece of his clothing. When he died at the age of 58—having overseen three editions of his work—thousands filed by his grave at Westminster Abbey to pay him respect.

Though no match for the extraordinary celebrity of Scott and Dickens—veritable cultural icons—the popularity of Frances Trollope (1779–1863) is nevertheless noteworthy. Her *Domestic Manners of the Americans* introduced the fifty-year-old author to fame in 1832, several years before "Charles Dickens" became a household name. This travel book recorded her frequently unfavorable impressions of the United States, including a description of the controversial commune of Nashoba, Tennessee, cohabited by slaves and whites and administered by the celebrated Frances Wright, who had acquired a scandalous reputation for promoting free love. Trollope's wit and keen sense of observation, hallmarks of *Domestic Manners,* continued in the thirty-four novels and five travel books following her first volume, guaranteeing excellent sales and raising Trollope from indebtedness to prosperity. Her success won her a place among England's literati, and she was eventually joined there by her son Anthony, whose fame surpassed his mother's after her death.

Like Trollope, the Reverend Charles Kingsley (1819–1875) enjoyed his own share of popularity. Introduced to the public as Parson Lot, Kingsley contributed articles to *Politics for the People* and *The Christian Socialist.* He created a stir in ecclesiastical circles by declaring at a meeting of the Chartists, a workers organization, "I am a Church of England parson...

---

[32] David Masson, quoted in Norman Page, *A Dickens Companion* (London: Macmillan, 1984) 149.

and a Chartist!"[33] Besides *Westward Ho!*, he also wrote several other successful novels, including the popular advocates of social reform *Yeast* and *Alton Locke*, as well as tracts, lectures, and sermons. Although his political leanings temporarily damaged his status within the state church, he ultimately proved himself a defender of the established social order, receiving the positions of Canon of Chester and Westminster and Professor of Modern History at Cambridge. However, his penchant for embroiling himself in controversy continued, once again bringing him dramatically into the public eye when he criticized John Henry Newman in a review of Froude's *History of England*. A series of published debates between him and Newman ensued, calling attention mainly to Newman's brilliancy—despite Kingsley's popular support—and prompting Newman's famous spiritual autobiography *Apologia pro Vita Sua*.

The celebrity of George Eliot was of a brand different from that of any of the aforementioned novelists. Eliot, the pen name of Marian Evans (1819–1880), was a stellar intellectual who kept company with renowned thinkers like Henry Spencer and George Lewes and translated difficult works like David Strauss's *Life of Jesus*, a demythologization of the gospels; and Ludwig Feuerbach's positivist treatise *The Essence of Christianity*. Her five major novels, beginning with *Adam Bede* (1859), received critical acclaim without surrendering popular appeal and won her a reputation as England's premier novelist. She soon earned the praise of a number of revered writers, including Ivan Turgenev and Henry James. Unfortunately, for one who avoided even positive publicity, she also endured notoriety because of her unorthodox twenty-five-year cohabitation with the married George Lewes. After Lewes's death, Eliot married John Cross, whose biography of Eliot revived public interest in her during the final decades of the nineteenth century.

Though she never approached Eliot's stature in the literary world of her day, Charlotte Brontë (1816–1855) did enjoy similar success among critics and the public alike for her sophisticated fiction. Her novel *Jane Eyre* (1847), an immediate bestseller because of its realism and depth of feeling, was followed by *Shirley* (1849) and *Villette* (1853). Like Eliot,

---

[33] Thomas Hughes, Prefatory Memoir to the 1876 edition of Alton Locke, as quoted in Margaret Farrand Thorp, *Charles Kingsley 1819-1875* (New York: Octagon Books, 1961[Reprint of the Princeton edition, 1937]) 61.

Brontë also attracted public attention despite her wishes—when critics identified in her fiction emotionalism deemed inappropriate for the daughter of a parson. And, also like Eliot, she was enshrined soon after her death in a biography; the author was her friend Elizabeth Gaskell, a popular novelist of the period.

Among the novelists considered in this study, Mary Wollstonecraft Shelley alone derived little popularity from her own work during her lifetime (1797–1851). Her identity was commonly subsumed under that of her famous mother and father, Mary Wollstonecraft and William Godwin. Only her first novel, *Frankenstein* (1819), received ample attention—whether critical or popular—and even that was owed largely to her status as wife of the renowned poet Percy Bysshe Shelley, to whom many wrongly attributed authorship of *Frankenstein.* The controversial and brilliant Percy continued to overshadow his wife in the public eye even after his early death, when Mary spent much of her creative energy editing his work. I have included Shelley's novel *Valperga* in this study less for its impact on cultural discourse than for its usefulness as an index of anti-Catholicism in the cultural imagination at a critical time: long before a threatening Catholic emergence at mid-century brought polemics to fever pitch, but decades after an enervated Old Catholicism inspired in Gothic novels no more than exotic atmosphere and vague scorn for popery.[34] Mary Shelley's *Valperga* and Walter Scott's companion novels, *The Monastery* and *The Abbot,* which preceded it by three years, are testimony to social change as well as to imaginations keen enough to absorb, reflect, and ingeniously "metaphorize" it.

---

[34] For the most part, the Gothic novels of writers like Charles Maturin, Matthew Lewis, and Anne Radcliffe reveal little attraction to Catholic sensibility, a key feature of the novels examined in this study. For a discussion of the Catholic elements in the work of these and other Gothic novelists, see Mary Muriel Tarr's "Catholicism in Gothic Fiction: A Study of the Nature and Function of Catholic Materials in Gothic Fiction in England (1762–1820)," Ph.D. diss., Catholic University of America, 1946. Catholic University of America Press, 1946.

1

"UNGUARDED GAIETY":

CATHOLICISM IN WALTER SCOTT'S
THE MONASTERY AND THE ABBOT

IN 1829 SIR Walter Scott brooded over the impending revocation of England's last anti-Catholic laws. "I hold popery to be such a mean and depriving superstition," he wrote in his journal, "that I am not clear I could have found myself liberal enough for voting the repeal of them [the anti-Catholic laws] as they existed before 1780.[1] They must and would in course of time have smothered popery and I confess I should have see[n] the old Lady of Babylon's mouth stopd [*sic*] with pleasure."[2] This comment prefacing his reluctant support of the Catholic Emancipation Bill of 1829 captures perfectly the disdain Scott felt toward Roman Catholicism throughout his life. As Scott's son-in-law and first biographer, John Lockhart, attested, "no man disapproved of Romanism as a system of faith and practice more

---

[1] *The Journal of Sir Walter Scott*, ed., W. E. K. Anderson (Oxford: Clarendon, 1972) 526. Anderson supplies a footnote here: "Presumably Scott is referring to the Relief Act of 1791 which removed many of the disabilities suffered until then by Roman Catholics."

[2] *Journal of Scott*, Anderson, ed., 525–26.

sincerely than Sir Walter always did."[3] The Roman Church, with its superstitions and "ignorant bigoted priesthood," was ridiculously backwards, particularly in Ireland, where the faith of Roman Catholics had robbed them of "ambition and industrious exertion."[4]

A decade before Catholic Emancipation, Scott had found himself imagining a very different period in Scottish history, when Protestant leaders had done all in their power to suffocate Lady Babylon. The result was not one, but two novels in his Waverley series: *The Monastery* and its sequel, *The Abbot*, both published in 1820.[5] Set in the Scotland of James VI, their stories are a paean to the Protestant cause, featuring the conversion of their two heroes to the Reform doctrines, the destruction of the powerful St. Mary's monastery, and the banishment of St. Mary's abbot after Queen Mary's own banishment from Scotland. Yet Scott's creative energy is divided in these novels, for even as he casts his Catholic characters into shadows of gloom, he also transforms them and their world into arguably the most brilliant facets of these companion tales. This transformation

---

[3] John Lockhart, *Memoirs of Sir Walter Scott, 1837–1838,* 10 vols. (Edinburgh: Charles Black, 1882) 8:40, chap. 63. Chapter references have been supplied for quotations from Scott's novels and Lockhart's memoirs since the editions used here are not widely available. All references separated by a colon are to volume and page.

[4] Lockhart, *Memoirs,* 5:315–16. This statement prefaces Lockhart's explanation of Scott's support for the Emancipation Act. Lockhart goes on to elaborate: "He on all occasions expressed manfully his belief that the best thing for Ireland would have been never to relax the strictly *political* enactments of the penal laws, however harsh these might appear. Had they been kept in vigour for another half century, it was his conviction that Popery would have been all but extinguished in Ireland. But he thought that, after admitting Romanists to the elective franchise, it was a vain notion that they could be permanently or advantageously debarred from using that franchise in favour of those of their own persuasion" (8:41, chap. 63). Lockhart's explanation also provides a context for the above quote from Scott's journal.

[5] The Waverley novels, named after the first work in a series of twenty-six major novels, were published between 1814 and 1831. Scott kept his authorship formally anonymous until 1827.

cannot be explained simply by their status as underdogs or quaint relics of a bygone time. Even if fascination could be reduced to sympathy, the most sympathetic of these characters still represent an institution depicted as tyrannical in the two novels. Moreover, Scott is unwilling to examine the place of religious conviction in their inner lives, a potentially intriguing area for exploration.

As for Scott's antiquarian interests, they never brought him close to feelings of nostalgia for the Church of Rome, and Scott never explores its rituals and practices. Instead, I want to argue, the energy of these Romish characters and their world is derived from the highly mediated way in which Scott presents Catholic sensibility, a method that reflects his paradoxical attraction to it. To appreciate this indirect presentation as technique, as well as psychological strategy, we must begin by examining the anti-Catholic framework that Scott provides in *The Monastery* for his companion novels.[6]

---

[6] A summary of *The Monastery* will be helpful here: The setting for the novel is the countryside of Glendearg under the jurisdiction of the Monastery of St. Mary's. The abbot is Boniface, who is advised by a sub-prior named Father Eustace. During this tempestuous time of Border skirmishes, the widowed Lady Alice of Avenel and her daughter Mary are given shelter by Dame Elspeth Glendinning at the Tower of Glendearg. Lady Avenel secretly possesses the Bible, forbidden reading for Catholics, whose numbers include the Glendinnings and the Avenels. Lady Avenel dies, leaving Mary in the care of Dame Elspeth and her two sons, Halbert and Edward, both in love with the Avenel maiden.

Conflict is introduced with the appearance of Sir Piercie Shafton, an English renegade who seeks shelter at St. Mary's. A pretentious, foppish, Euphuuist, Sir Piercie takes a liking to Mary Avenel and insults the hot-tempered Halbert, who has claimed Mary's heart. Halbert challenges Sir Piercie to a duel and, after defeating him, flees the area, knowing that he will be prosecuted for killing someone under the monastery's protection. On the road he meets a traveling Reformed minister, Henry Warden, who takes him to Avenel Castle, now occupied by Julian of Avenel, Mary's uncle. Julian, a crude baron who plays both Protestant and Catholic sides in the local skirmishes, has promised the Earl of Murray that he will protect Henry Warden. But when Warden criticizes him for living in sin with a woman who is bearing their child, Julian casts him and Halbert into the dungeon.

THE MONASTERY AND ANTI-CATHOLICISM

Even before *The Monastery* begins, Scott confirms for his English readers their probable assumptions about his conventional Protestant bias. He describes the decline of the once-powerful monastery of St. Mary's with the ascendancy of the Reformed religion. The device that serves as the novel's preface is an exchange of letters between Scott and a colorful antiquarian by the name of Captain Clutterbuck, who has been approached by a mysterious Benedictine priest with a manuscript recounting the history of St. Mary's Monastery in Kennaquhair. Believing himself inadequate for the task of turning the manuscript into a full-fledged tale, as the Benedictine has requested him to do, the Captain turns to Scott for help. The Captain has assured Scott of the Benedictine's permission "to alter whatever seemed too favourable to the Church of Rome" so that the story would

---

Halbert, who has come to admire the outspoken, courageous Henry, escapes and seeks the Earl of Murray, whose page he becomes.

Meanwhile, Sir Piercie reappears, having been saved by the power of a mysterious spirit, the White Lady of Avenel who haunts the glen. However, the bookish Edward believes Sir Piercie has killed Halbert and therefore imprisons him. The miller's daughter, Mysie, in love with Sir Piercie, cleverly arranges his escape and, disguised as a page, accompanies him in his flight. When Julian sends his prisoner to the abbot—to avoid incurring Murray's wrath—two things are discovered: Halbert is indeed alive and the preacher is an old classmate of Father Eustace the sub-prior, who early in the story has become the true voice of authority at the monastery.

The remainder of the novel focuses on the Protestant-Catholic conflict. Several debates ensue between Eustace and Warden on their respective positions. A rather unhappy Edward enters the monastery, while hero Halbert converts to Protestantism, as does Mary Avenel. They wed and inherit Avenel when Julian dies in battle. The foppish Sir Piercie, publicly humiliated with the revelation that his grandfather was a tailor, marries Mysie. Eustace—notable for his diplomacy, courage, and conviction, and now Abbot of St. Mary's—is allowed by Murray to retain custody of the monastery at the urging of Warden, who warns Murray that to send Eustace forth as a refugee would be to win Scottish sympathy to his cause.

not be dismissed by British readers.[7] Under this condition, Scott accepts the challenge, expressing his abomination for the Church of Rome "were it but for her fasts and penances."[8]

Considering the playful tone of Scott's letter to Clutterbuck, this remark could reasonably be taken as tongue-in-cheek. However, denunciations of Catholicism abound in narrative commentary throughout *The Monastery*, despite Scott's misleading claim in his introduction to the 1830 edition of the novel that he had intended to provide in it an objective analysis of opposite religious points of view.[9] Scott attributes the zeal of Father Eustace, sub-prior of St.

---

[7] Sir Walter Scott, *The Monastery*, 1820, New Abbotsford ed., 2 vols. (Boston: Dana Estes, 1900) 1:lxxxiv.

[8] Scott, *Monastery*, 1:lxxxiv.

[9] In his 1830 introduction to *The Monastery*, Scott announced that his intention had been to "conjoin two characters in that bustling and contentious age, who, thrown into situations which gave them different views on the subject of the Reformation, should, with the same sincerity and purity of intention, dedicate themselves, the one to the support of the sinking fabric of the Catholic Church, the other to the establishment of the Reformed doctrines" (xxi). These two opposed "enthusiasts" presented themselves as "interesting subjects for narrative," in which Scott had intended to examine "the real worth of both with their passions and prejudices" (xxi). In the novel's debates between Father Eustace and Henry Warden, Scott stays true to this purpose. Each of these former classmates, mouthpieces for the chief doctrinal differences between Protestantism and Catholicism, makes his case with eloquence and feeling. Through their polemics, Scott defines with clarity and thoroughness what he sees as the fundamental issue in the battle: faithfulness to the Christianity of the early church. For Father Eustace, the Roman Church has "kept the light of Christianity alive from the times of the Apostles till now," while in the eyes of Warden, "'the primitive church differed as much from that of Rome, as did light from darkness'" (2:290, chap. 37). Scott takes pains also to be fair in representing the *ad hominem* rhetoric spewed by both sides in the battle. However, the claim in Scott's introduction is misleading. Imaginatively speaking, the debates between Warden and Eustace are peripheral to the story, which conversely is strongly shaped by Scott's anti-Catholic biases, many of which are explicitly expressed by the narrator. Considering Scott's paradoxical evenhandedness in the novel's debates and biases in the remainder of the tale, I both agree and disagree with Edgar Johnson's observations: "although Scott was sincerely assured of the

Mary's Monastery, to "his imperfect knowledge, confounding the vital interests of Christianity with the extravagant and usurped claims of the Church of Rome."[10] This Church is "a corrupted system of Christianity,"[11] Eustace's prayers for the dead are "erroneous,"[12] and young Catholic Mary Avenel's "void of mind" is due to "the narrow and bigoted ignorance in which Rome then educated the children of her church."[13] Mary's distress over the alleged death of her beloved Halbert Glendinning provides the perfect occasion for Scott to lay the blame for her disconsolate state at the door of Rome. After all, the Romish faithful found

> [t]heir whole religion was a ritual, and their prayers were the formal iteration of unknown words, which, in the hour of affliction, could yield but little consolation to those who from habit resorted to them. Unused to the practice of mental devotion, and of personal approach to the Divine Presence by prayer, she [Mary Avenel] could not help exclaiming in her distress, "There is no aid for me on earth, and I know not how to ask it from Heaven!"[14]

Scott's identification of Catholicism with primitive feelings and ignorance is most vividly seen in his image of Rome as a whale:

> In fact, that ancient system, which so well accommodated its doctrines to the wants and wishes of a barbarous age, had, since the art of printing, and the gradual diffusion of knowledge, lain floating like some huge leviathan, into which ten

---

truth of the Christian religion and was a convinced Protestant, his mind had no bent toward theology—which, like metaphysics, he might have been inclined secretly to dismiss as 'water-painting'" (748); and "emotionally neither side [of the controversy] really enlisted his sympathies" (749).

[10] Scott, *Monastery*, 1:82, chap. 8.
[11] Scott, *Monastery*, 1:91.
[12] Scott, *Monastery*, 1:92.
[13] Scott, *Monastery*, 2:183–84, chap. 30.
[14] Scott, *Monastery*, 2:184.

thousand reforming fishers were darting their harpoons. The Roman Church of Scotland, in particular, was at her last gasp, actually blowing blood and water, yet still with unremitted, though animal exertions, maintaining the conflict with the assailants, who on every side were plunging their weapons into her bulky body.[15]

It is this enervated, doomed Church that Halbert, the novel's strapping young protagonist, eventually rejects, largely thanks to the effete priests who aptly represent their weak religion. When Mary Avenel suggests that he submit to the monkish teaching of his brother Edward, Halbert explodes in indignation:

I hate the monks...with their drawling nasal tone like so many frogs, and their long black petticoats like so many women, and their reverences, and their lordships, and their lazy vassals, that do nothing but paddle in the mire with plough and harrow, from Yule to Michaelmas. I will call none lord, but him who wears a sword to make his title good; and I will call none man but he that can bear himself manlike and masterful.[16]

Although Halbert must learn to temper his impetuosity, we readers never doubt Scott's intention to present him as a model man. "[P]erfectly well made"; "possessed of grace and natural ease of manner and carriage"[17]; dressed in buckskin and armed with broadsword, arrows, and dudgeon dagger—Halbert seems the Scottish prototype of Fenimore Cooper's Leatherstocking. "Hardihood was the natural characteristic of his mind,"[18] and it expresses itself throughout the novel in courageous deeds and the desire to do good. Conversely, the novel's stubbornly Catholic young men are notable for their *lack*

---

[15] Scott, *Monastery*, 2:195; chap. 31.
[16] Scott, *Monastery*, 1:135, chap. 11.
[17] Scott, *Monastery*, 2:12, chap. 19.
[18] Scott, *Monastery*, 1:227, chap. 17.

of manliness. The introspective, bookish Edward, who envies his athletic brother enough to wish him dead, finally retires to monastic life. And the foppish Sir Piercie Shafton, spy for the Church of Rome, loses to Halbert not only a duel, but also the hand of Mary Avenel, who rejects Sir Piercie's Church along with Piercie himself.

Underlying Scott's criticism of the Roman Catholic Church in *The Monastery* is his view of a new enlightened age in which Christianity has been stripped of trappings designed to control the popular imagination and returned to some putative essentiality derived from Scripture. As Lockhart put it, Scott denounced "the extravagance of the imagination, in the province of Faith."[19] Generally speaking, Scott regarded religion contaminated by imagination as superstition, a word that riddles most of the anti-Catholic diatribes in the novel.[20] For him, monkish superstition infected Catholic worship—whose mysterious language and chants, sweet incense, glittering costumes, and ritual uses of oil, water, and wine were designed to awaken rather than dull the senses and imagination. This sensory indulgence corrupted religion, introducing into it base human passions, particularly ignorant fear, which rendered the faithful malleable in the hands of shrewd priests.

Scott did not believe that faith is simply derived from rational principles. According to Lockhart, "he shrunk from indulging the presumption of reason" as well as "the extravagance of the imagination"

---

[19] Lockhart, *Memoirs*, 10:244–45, chap. 84.

[20] The term *imagination*, which appears frequently in this study, evoked responses no less conflicting in the nineteenth century than in our own day. While Scott tended to see imagination as antithetical both to reason and to empirical and religious truths, his devoutly Christian contemporary Samuel Taylor Coleridge celebrated the imagination as a power allied to reason in its ability to transcend and transform sensory data and, in the poet, as a god-like power for creating symbols of reality, the most profound expression of truth. In their attempt to defend religion in a scientific age, other post-enlightenment philosophers tried to reconcile reason and imagination. For an illuminating discussion of these thinkers, as well as for a compelling analysis of the role of imagination in religion, see Garrett Green's *Imagining God: Theology and the Religious Imagination* (Grand Rapids: Eerdmans, 1989).

in matters of faith. Still, he measured faith in rational terms, particularly in its compatibility with those principles of the enlightenment emphasizing individual liberty and the social contract. Scott makes this clear in an 1827 journal entry: "I would if calld [*sic*] upon die a martyr for the Christian religion, so completely is (in my poor opinion) its divine origin proved by its beneficial effects on the state of society. Were we but to name the abolition of slavery and of polygamy how much has in these two words been granted to mankind by the lessons of our saviour."[21]

Because of his renunciation of the imaginative in religion, Scott must have found himself in a quandary as he planned *The Monastery* and *The Abbot*, which he envisioned as a unit.[22] In these novels the difference between Protestantism and Catholicism is an essential theme; to a degree unique in the Waverley novels, Catholic and Protestant characters represent their respective religions. It only makes sense for Scott to present Catholics as prone to imagination and primitive emotion while depicting Protestants as rational and self-controlled. But, since successful novels engage the popular audience primarily on an emotional level, how could he maintain interest in dry Protestant heroes? One way would have been to have them convert gradually to Protestantism, moving from passion to reason, which he does with his two heroes, Halbert Glendinning in *The Monastery* and Roland Graeme in *The Abbot*. But Scott as a spinner of romance lacked the inclination and ability to write a probing conversion story,[23] which, in any event, would have had to present Catholicism as

---

[21] *Journal of Scott*, Anderson, ed., 399.

[22] *The Monastery*'s introductory epistle reveals this design. The fictional Benedictine monk transmits a two-part story to Captain Clutterbuck, the first part written by his uncle and the second by him.

[23] As Walter Bagehot puts it in his 1858 analysis of Scott's fiction, "The Waverley Novels" (in *Critical Essays on Sir Walter Scott: The Waverley Novels*, ed. Harry E. Shaw [New York: G. K. Hall, 1996]), Scott "omits to give us a delineation of soul. We have mind, manners, animation, but it is the stir of this world. We miss the consecrating power; and we miss it not only in its own peculiar sphere, which, from the difficulty of introducing the deepest elements into a novel, would have been scarcely matter for a harsh criticism,

a tempting alternative to the Reformed religion. And so he simply predisposes the two converts to Protestantism and brings about their conversion by external influences. From the beginning, Halbert dislikes "womanish" priests and is led to Protestantism because of his attraction to the bold Reformed preacher Henry Warden and especially to the virile Earl of Murray. Roland Graeme clings to Catholicism out of loyalty to his grandmother and defiance of Warden, but he finally converts after instruction by Elias Hendersen at Lochleven, where Queen Mary is held prisoner. Although Halbert remains a wooden character, Roland is fairly engaging in his journey from hot-tempered, spoiled Catholic page, to conscientious Protestant heir to Avenel. This left Scott with one somewhat lively Protestant hero and a host of Catholic characters who, by definition, threatened to be interesting, even if they took only minor roles in the novels. So, Scott resorted to other methods of containing the attractiveness of Catholic characters.

CONTAINING CATHOLICISM IN THE MONASTERY

IN *THE MONASTERY* Scott deflects attention from Catholicism by creating an alternative to the superstitious ethos enveloping the Catholic inhabitants of Glendearg, who are governed by the monks of St. Mary's Monastery. His creation is based on an "ancient superstition/ Which, erring as it is, our fancy loves."[24] As the poetic epigraph of chapter 12 announces, this is a pure sort of superstition, unlike the "gross" superstition practiced by Catholic monks in "a most gross and superstitious age."[25] Scott's adjective for monkish superstition is telling. In the early nineteenth century, the word *gross* had several related meanings: "bloated with excess"; "glaring, flagrant, monstrous"; "coarse, inferior"; and "rude, uninstructed, ignorant."[26] In synthesis

---

but in the place in which a novelist might most be expected to delineate it" (44).

[24] Scott, *Monastery*, 1:140.

[25] Scott, *Monastery*, 1:1.

[26] "Gross," *The Compact Edition of the Oxford English Dictionary*, 2 vols. (Oxford: Oxford University Press, 1971) vol. 1.

these terms suggest what is base and offensively conspicuous in human nature—carnality itself—which draws us to the earth rather than to the ethereal sphere of heaven. Catholic rituals, iconography, music, and relics reduce the faithful to their animal nature by seducing the senses and inflaming the imagination. Conversely, the "ancient superstition" upon which Scott draws in creating the White Lady who haunts the vale of Glendearg frees its proponents by leading them to "something purer, more refined/And mightier than ourselves."[27]

Understanding Scott's claim requires an examination of this ancient superstition's sources. In his introduction to the 1830 edition of *The Monastery*, Scott attributes his inspiration for the White Lady to "the beautiful, though almost forgotten, theory of astral spirits, or creatures of the elements...known, to those who have studied the cabalistical philosophy, by the names of Sylphs, Gnomes, Salamanders, and Naiads, as they belong to the elements of Air, Earth, Fire, or Water."[28] As Coleman Parsons notes,[29] Scott is in fact drawing on a doctrine elaborated by Paracelsus and the Rosicrucians, though it comes to him via the German novelist Baron de la Motte Fouque. These proponents of mystery religion, like the Gnostics and cabalists before them, valued spiritual enlightenment above all things as the key to salvation. This enlightenment included an understanding of the invisible elements constituting the universe. As her name suggests, the White Lady belongs to a purely ethereal realm known not through the senses, but rather, through knowledge that mysteriously transcends them. The "ancient superstition," or Gnosticism, with which she is associated is a remedy to passion and thus—as "erring," or unorthodox, as it might be—far superior to the "gross" superstition of Catholicism.

Also superior is another source upon which Scott draws in creating his pure spirit. The White Lady, as Parsons notes, shares traits with

---

[27] Scott, *Monastery*, 1:140, chap. 12.
[28] Scott, *Monastery*, 1:xviii–xxix.
[29] Coleman Parsons, *Witchcraft and Demonology in Scott's Fiction: With Chapters on the Supernatural in Scottish Literature* (Edinburgh: Oliver and Boyd, 1964) 158–63.

the frightening water nymph and the capricious banshee found in Scottish folklore. Though these supernatural beings are greatly inferior to the noble astral spirits of mystery religion, Scott views them as part of a delightful Scottish patrimony, noble in its end—the building of community—and innocent in its disassociation from formal religion. The latter bracketing, consistent with his rational nature, was crucial to Scott, whose religion, according to Walter Bagehot,

> was of a qualified and double sort. He was a genial man of the world, and had the easy faith in the kindly *Dieu des bons gens* which is natural to such a person; and he had also a half-poetic principle of superstition in his nature, inclining him to believe in ghosts, legends, fairies, and elfs, which did not affect his daily life, or possibly his superficial belief.[30]

Yet, in his determination to drive home the point about the superiority of such a pure superstition over the profane or gross superstition of Catholicism, Scott takes a rather contradictory step with the White Lady: he has her mix with institutional religion. At first glance, she seems to be a weird advocate of Protestantism. She battles two of the monks of St. Mary's, sends Edward Glendinning to a life of monastic gloom, and most importantly, facilitates the conversion of Halbert and Mary Avenel to Reformed Christianity by conveying to them the Bible—once again, forbidden reading for lay Catholics. The illogic of associating superstition, no matter how pure, with the Reformed religion seems to escape Scott, perhaps because he believes his own motive is pure: he must enliven his depiction of Protestantism. Yet, paradoxically and perhaps inevitably, by comingling religion and fantasy in the White Lady, Scott ends up transforming this supernatural being into a fascinating tribute to the Catholic ethos he purports to denounce.

One aspect of Roman Catholicism that Scott particularly disdained was "the Catholic idea of the employment of Saints" amounting to

---

[30] Bagehot, "Waverley Novels," 43.

"Saint-worship," an "absurdity...which degrades their religion,"[31] presumably because it posits legions of beings who compete with God and each other for the loyalty of the Catholic faithful. In *The Monastery*, he places the White Lady among the ranks of such saintly rivals by appointing her guardian of the Avenel family. She is described by Tibb—the servant of Dame Elspeth, who has taken in young Mary Avenel and her mother—as a sort of patron saint for "great ancient families" who "canna be just served wi' the ordinary saunts, (praise to them!) like Saunt Anthony, Saunt Cuthbert, and the like, that come and gang at every sinner's bidding."[32] Conceding such a special patron for "your grand folk," the indignant Dame Elspeth suggests that the privileged may avail themselves of the White Lady's intercession, but that "our Lady and Saunt Paul are good eneugh saunts for me, and I'se warrant them never leave me in a bog that they can help me out o', seeing I send four waxen candles to the chapels every Candlemas...."[33] Like Elspeth, Father Eustace favors the Virgin Mary over the White Lady, but he experiences the rival's power when she descends upon him in the haunted glen and successfully takes the Bible from him, despite his invocation of the Virgin.

The White Lady's spiritual intercession is sought primarily by the Protestant hero, Halbert, in his quest for the Bible, which will win him and Mary Avenel salvation. But initially, while still a Catholic, he tests her membership in the Catholic world of supernatural beings who serve the cause of true religion. Addressing her in words that echo Father Eustace's earlier "solemn exorcism,"[34] he commands her "[i]n the name of God" to identify herself.[35] Her answer satisfies him: it is not a harmless hymn to the spring "with its thousand crystal bubbles" from whence she comes, but a dark, theological poem. In it the White Lady describes her existence in a purgatory or Dantean limbo, "[s]omething betwixt heaven and hell," where beings like her, though

---

[31] *Journal of Scott,* Anderson, ed., 33.
[32] Scott, *Monastery,* 1:43, chap. 4.
[33] Scott, *Monastery,* 1:44.
[34] Scott, *Monastery,* 1:107, chap. 9.
[35] Scott, *Monastery,* 1:141, chap. 12.

longer-lived than humans, are "[f]ar less happy, for we have/Help nor hope beyond the grave."[36] She does prove herself to be Father Eustace's patron saint, not only returning his Bible, but also miraculously healing his burned hand when he tries to retrieve the Bible from a mysterious flame.

Scott suggests the Catholic nature of the White Lady also by connecting her forest shrine with the Benedictine monastery. Early in the novel, he juxtaposes the settings in a description of Father Philip, the monastery's sacristan, who walks through the haunted valley under a full moon towards "the stately Monastery, seen far and dim amid the yellow light."[37] After an encounter with the White Lady in which she dunks him in the river and takes the Bible he is carrying, Philip cannot stop conflating her song and the music of the monastery. As he explains to the Abbot, "the tune...mingles with the psalter—the very bells of the convent seem to repeat the words, and jingle to the tune...I shall sing it at the very mass."[38] This strange conflation reinforces the identification of monastery and glen rather than suggesting that the White Lady desires to punish Catholic priests. Indeed, aside from her mischievous treatment of Father Philip, she wreaks no havoc on the monks of St. Mary's; in fact she saves Eustace from being killed by the roguish retainer of Mary's uncle, Julian Avenel. Nor does she wish to harm the Romish cause: her battle against the monks over Alice Avenel's Bible is deceptive, as a careful examination reveals.

The Bible of Alice Avenel, Mary's mother, appears to be presented in *The Monastery* as a symbol of Protestantism.[39] When Father Philip first learns that Alice has secretly possessed a Bible, he explains to Dame Elspeth why it is a "perilous volume": "it is the Holy Scripture.

---

[36] Scott, *Monastery*, 1:141.

[37] Scott, *Monastery*, 1:54, chap. 5.

[38] Scott, *Monastery*, 1:78–79, chap. 7.

[39] Judith Wilt effectively argues this point in chap. 3 of her *Secret Leaves: The Novels of Walter Scott* (Chicago: University of Chicago Press, 1985), as does Lionel Lackey in his essay on the companion novels, "*The Monastery* and *The Abbot*: Scott's Religious Dialectics," *Studies in the Novel* 19/1 (1987) 46–65.

But it is rendered into the vulgar tongue, and therefore, by the order of the Holy Catholic Church, unfit to be in the hands of any lay person."[40] The edition of Alice's Bible is not specified, but Scott undoubtedly intends one of the sixteenth-century English translations by reformers seeking to replace the authority of Rome with that of the individual conscience guided by scripture.[41] Father Philip, representative of Rome, is horrified at the thought of Scripture in the hands of the individual: "I tell thee, Elspeth, *the Word slayeth*—that is, the text alone, read with unskilled eye and unhallowed lips, is like those strong medicines which sick men take by the advice of the learned. Such patients recover and thrive; while those dealing in them at their own hand, shall perish by their own deed."[42] "The learned" are priests, of course, whose authority is challenged by such independent individuals as Alice.

The White Lady is apparently committed to instilling a spirit like Alice's in the heart of Alice's daughter, Mary Avenel. "Maiden, attend!" she cries to Mary, "beneath my foot lies hid/The Word, the Law, the Path...."[43] Following the White Lady's command, Mary retrieves the volume that Halbert has hidden beneath the floorboards. When she reads the passages marked by her mother, "her heart acquiesced in the conclusion, 'Surely this is the Word of God!'"[44] This realization marks Mary's conversion to Protestantism—the ostensible goal of the White Lady—along with Halbert's, also accomplished through the holy book. All of the White Lady's actions seem to be defined by these ends. She steals the Bible from Father Philip, roughing him up in the process; she steals it from Father Eustace; she leads Halbert to its hiding place in the center of the earth; and she reveals it to Mary Avenel. Once the White Lady has guaranteed, through the

---

[40] Scott, *Monastery*, 1:50–51, chap. 5.

[41] An excellent description of these translations as well as excerpts from some of the major ones can be found in Rollin and Baker's *The Renaissance in England: Non-Dramatic Prose and Verse of the Sixteenth Century*, ed. by Hyder Rollins and Herschel Baker (Lexington: D. C. Heath, 1954) 131–41.

[42] Scott, *Monastery*, 1:51.

[43] Scott, *Monastery*, 2:185, chap. 30.

[44] Scott, *Monastery*, 2:189.

agency of the Bible, the Protestant salvation of the Avenel family, she vanishes from the scene—and apparently, from existence itself—for the same Bible has no power to grant her eternal life. This final irony, besides the Romish qualities of the White Lady, suggests the deceptive quality of her pro-Protestant role.

Like the priests in the novel, the White Lady by and large reserves the Bible's possession for herself, even using it to manipulate others for her own amusement. This is true despite her misleading reference to the Bible as "The Word, the Law, the Path"—available to all the faithful, according to Henry Warden, who presents the Bible as the individual's answer to the ecclesiastical power of Roman Catholicism. At first she acceptably amuses herself at the expense of a Romish priest, tricking Father Philip into giving her a ride across the river on his mule, singing songs about spirits in his ear, and then shoving him into the water and stealing his Bible, which she then leaves in the open glen to be discovered by young Halbert and hidden beneath floor boards. Her game involves nursery-like rhymes about the Bible. To Father Philip the White Lady sings, "Landed—landed! the black book hath won/Else had you seen Berwick with morning sun!"[45] and to Father Eustace, "Back, back/the volume black!/I have a warrant to carry it back."[46] Then, even Protestant Halbert receives a rhyme when he requests the Bible: "Many a fathom dark and deep/I have laid the book to sleep."[47] Keeping with the Bible's function as her game piece, the White Lady casually refers to it as "the black book" or "the volume." The participants in the game make no mention of the New Testament, the Gospels, or any specific scriptural book. Only once do we hear allusions to specific passages, and even these serve as much to link Mary Avenel to her mother as to foster her reverence for the Bible.[48]

When the White Lady is not using the Bible as her game piece, she is transforming it into an object of idolatry, every bit as mystifying as the Catholic effigies and relics so repugnant to Henry Warden. In his

[45] Scott, *Monastery*, 1:61, chap. 5.
[46] Scott, *Monastery*, 1:105, chap. 9.
[47] Scott, *Monastery*, 1:144, chap. 12.
[48] Scott, *Monastery*, 2:188, chap. 30.

interview with the White Lady, Halbert demands, "I will learn the contents of that mysterious volume...What mystery is wrapt in it?"[49] The White Lady answers, "Within that awful volume lies/The mystery of mysteries!" and admits that she has hidden it "[m]any a fathom dark and deep." Her verse continues:

> Ethereal fires around it glowing—
> Ethereal music ever flowing—
> The Sacred pledge of Heav'n
> All things revere,
> Each in his sphere,
> Save man, for whom 't was giv'n.
> Lend thy hand, and thou shalt spy
> Things ne'er seen by mortal eye.[50]

This mysterious hiding place, paradoxically unavailable to most humans to whom the Bible "was giv'n," is located within the bowels of the earth, in a cavern whose splendor rivals many a Romish church, being

> composed of the most splendid spars and crystals, which returned in a thousand prismatic hues the light of a brilliant flame that glowed on an altar of alabaster. This altar, with its fire, formed the central point of the grotto, which was of a round form, and very high in the roof, resembling in some respects the dome of a cathedral. Corresponding to the four points of the compass, there went off four long galleries, or arcades, constructed of the same brilliant materials with the dome itself, and the termination of which was lost in darkness.[51]

---

[49] Scott, *Monastery*, 1:143, chap. 12.
[50] Scott, *Monastery*, 1:144.
[51] Scott, *Monastery*, 1:145.

The mysterious fire, whose radiance "[n]o human imagination can conceive," depends on "no visible fuel" and produces no "smoke or vapour of any kind."[52] Even more remarkably, within the flames rests the Bible, "not only unconsumed, but untouched in the slightest degree" though the fire "seemed to be of force sufficient to melt adamant."[53] After removing his sleeve, a tainted human product, Halbert retrieves the Bible "without feeling either heat or inconvenience of any kind."[54] The effect of this mystical experience on Halbert is appropriately monk-like. While he approached the haunted glen in a "storm of passion," "now he studiously avoided all interruption to his contemplative walk, lest the difficulty of the way should interfere with, or disturb, his own deep reflections."[55]

Ultimately, then, two apparent vehicles of Protestantism, the White Lady and the Bible, take Scott and his readers into the mystical world of Catholicism with all its idolatrous veneration of the saints, mysterious chant, ritualistic gesticulation, arcane priestcraft, and spectacular ceremony. This is the world rejected by Protestant reform in its search for a religion purified of both secrecy and ostentation, a religion that enlightens rather than mystifies and inspires self-renunciation rather than luxurious ecstasy.

THE ABBOT

Unlike *The Monastery*, its sequel, the exciting tale of Mary Stuart's defeat,[56] was acclaimed by popular audience and critics alike. The

---

[52] Scott, *Monastery*, 1:145–46.
[53] Scott, *Monastery*, 1:146.
[54] Scott, *Monastery*, 1:147.
[55] Scott, *Monastery*, 1:150.
[56] *The Abbot* can be summarized as follows. The story begins at the Castle of Avenel, home of Sir Halbert Glendinning and the Lady Mary Avenel. Halbert is frequently away on Border campaigns, leaving Lady Avenel bored and lonely. One day a local child falls into the lake surrounding Avenel Castle and is saved by Lady Avenel's dog, Wolf. Determined to adopt the boy—Roland Graeme—as her page, Lady Avenel secures the permission of his grandmother, Magdalen Graeme.

Roland is the novel's protagonist, a headstrong and impulsive youth, but good and potentially noble. Early on, we learn that he guards his Catholic identity, having been instructed by Magdalen to pose as a Protestant. He ignores the instruction of Henry Warden, who lives at Avenel, and is secretly instructed by Father Ambrose, formerly Edward Glendinning, Halbert's brother. Yet his Catholicism springs less from strong conviction than from duty towards his grandmother and a rebellious attitude toward Warden, who feels that Roland is spoiled by Lady Avenel's attention.

After Roland quarrels with Adam Woodcock, Avenel's fowler, Lady Avenel banishes him from the castle. He seeks refuge with the chaplain of the devastated St. Cuthbert's and is reunited there with his grandmother, who announces her mission to help return the Catholic Church to its rightful place by means of Roland. Roland accompanies her to a ruined convent where they find the former abbess and her niece, Catherine Seyton, with whom Roland promptly falls in love. Roland and his grandmother travel to the devastated monastery of St. Mary's where they find the monks secretly electing a new abbot after the death of Eustace. Father Ambrose is elected, a noble, brave leader of a lost and mistaken cause. During the ceremony of installation, the monastery is stormed by Protestant mummers. The new abbot upbraids them and a fray ensues, but it is quickly stifled by Sir Halbert, who takes Roland into service as his own page because of the courage he has shown in defending his brother, the Abbot.

Halbert assigns Roland to wait upon the imprisoned Queen Mary at Lockleven Castle. At Lochleven Roland discovers that Catherine Seyton is one of the Queen's attendants. He assumes a neutral position in the struggle between Queen Mary and her brother James, but he feels a strong sense of duty to protect the Queen. When the Protestant preacher at the Castle, Elias Hendersen, begins instructing Roland, who is now receptive to instruction in the Reform doctrines, he loses the trust of the Queen and of Catherine herself, who equates her political cause with Catholicism.

In the nearby village, Roland encounters for the second time a boy who looks like Catherine. He also meets his grandmother, disguised as a witch, and the abbot disguised as a nobleman's retainer. Assisted by the grandson of the Lady of Lochleven, George Douglas, who loves Mary Stuart, these three are planning to free the queen. But after Douglas is exposed, the Lady Lochleven tightens security at the castle. Having returned to the Queen's favor by defending Douglas, Roland substitutes keys he has forged for those of Lady Lochleven and assists the Queen in escaping.

In the novel's last dramatic scene, Magdalen reveals that Roland is the child of Julian of Avenel, and the Queen is taken to Dumbarton during a

novel's success was in part due to Scott's sacrificing the supernatural elements that fascinated him. As he explains to Captain Clutterbuck in his Introductory Epistle, "I have struck out...the whole machinery of the White Lady, and the poetry by which it is so ably supported, in the original manuscript. But you must allow that the public taste gives little encouragement to those legendary superstitions, which formed alternately the delight and the terror of our predecessors."[57]

Tellingly, the public also pressured Scott to avoid depicting Catholic sensibility, which—as we have seen—shaped his presentation of "those legendary superstitions." Scott explains,

> In like manner, much is omitted illustrative of the impulse of enthusiasm in favour of the ancient religion in Mother Magdalen and the Abbot [defenders of the Catholic cause in The Abbot]. But we do not feel deep sympathy at this period with what was once the most powerful and animating principle in Europe, with the exception of that of the Reformation, by which it was successfully opposed.[58]

Though Scott strives to contain Catholicism's imaginative qualities in The Monastery, the exigencies of popular taste now force him to test his creative powers even more. The result is a masterfully mediated presentation of Catholic sensibility.

---

battle between her followers and those of James. Roland goes down to mark the progress of the battle, where he sees Henry Seyton, whom he now knows to be Catherine's twin. When Seyton is mortally wounded, Roland flies back to Dumbarton, pursued by Halbert, who kills George Douglas. The forces of James are victorious. The dejected Mary agrees to banishment in England, despite the warning of Father Ambrose against trusting Queen Elizabeth. Halbert invites both Ambrose and Roland to come live at Avenel. In the final chapter we learn that he is not illegitimate, for his parents had married in secret. We also learn that after Edward goes to a monastery in France and Magdalen dies, Roland coverts to the "true Gospel" (2:307; chap. 38) of Protestantism and marries Catherine, who remains Catholic.

[57] Scott, Monastery, 1:xxix–xxx.
[58] Scott, Monastery, 1:xxx.

CONTAINING CATHOLICISM IN THE ABBOT

In *The Abbot*, Scott replaces the unacceptable supernatural world of the White Lady with the realistic but mystifying inner world of Roland's grandmother, Magdalen Graeme, who is dedicated to returning Scotland to Queen Mary and Catholicism. He distances himself and his readers from that intriguing world by presenting it as evidence of a twisted self-delusion and fanaticism:

> There were times at which she hinted, though very obscurely and distantly, that she herself was foredoomed by Heaven to perform a part in this important task; and that she had more than mere human warranty for the zeal with which she engaged in it. But on this subject she expressed herself in such general language, that it was not easy to decide whether she made any actual pretension to a direct and supernatural call, like the celebrated Elizabeth Barton, commonly called the Nun of Kent; or whether she only dwelt upon the general duty which was incumbent on all Catholics of the time, and the pressure of which she felt in an extraordinary degree.[59]

Scott underscores Magdalen's pretensions to supernatural powers by having her disguise herself as a sorceress and boast of her magic charms, "holy relics, before the touch, nay, before the bare presence of which, disease and death have so often been known to retreat."[60] She even identifies her primary agent, Roland, with spirits: "[H]ast thou never heard that there are spirits powerful to rend the walls of a castle asunder when once admitted, which yet cannot enter the house unless they are invited, nay, dragged over the threshold? Twice hath Roland

---

[59] Sir Walter Scott, *The Abbot*, 1820. New Abbotsford ed., 2 vols. (Boston: Dana Estes, 1900) 1:157, chap. 13.

[60] Scott, *Abbot*, 2:127, chap. 28.

Graeme been thus drawn into the household of Avenel by those who now hold the title. Let them look to the issue."[61]

In general, she is a sly, secretive character who inspires fear and wields uncanny power, not only over her grandson but over Mary Avenel, Henry Warden, and the Lady of Lochleven as well. She proves remarkably elusive as she executes her secret plans to rescue Queen Mary. In representing Magdalen as such a dark, witch-like character, Scott both conveys and condemns monkish superstition.

Since a novel can have only so many fanatics, Scott represents most of *The Abbot's* other Catholic characters as good, however misguided, individuals. On one hand, wishing to deflect interest in them as Catholics, he avoids directly depicting their experiences with the imaginative features of Catholic rituals or practices. On the other hand, as an artist he is determined to give them Catholic sensibilities. He mediates his contradictory goals by allowing his Catholic characters to engage in behavior that shares certain qualities with Romish rituals and practices. The results are a tremendously lively cast of characters and some finessing of the author's perspective on this liveliness.

One prominent example is Scott's treatment of masquerade. He presents it in *The Abbot* as a Romish practice, associated with the gaudy costumes of high masses, the pretense displayed in meaningless ritual, the detached voice hiding behind the confessional panel, and perhaps most of all, the false images of idolatry. Scott's official condemnation of such masquerade sounds through *The Abbot's* hero, Sir Halbert, when he condemns the carnival masqueraders for engaging in "the profane and unseemly sports introduced by the priests of Rome themselves, to mislead and to brutify the souls which fell into their net."[62] Yet, in the novel's imaginative world where Scott is released from his didactic responsibilities, he not only allows Catholic masquerade to thrive, but even presents the mummers as bold, resourceful, and imaginative.

---

[61] Scott, *Abbot,* 1:207, chap. 15.
[62] Scott, *Abbot,* 1:193, chap. 15.

Magdalen, for example, gets Roland admitted to the Castle of Avenel—and ultimately appointed as Sir Halbert's squire—by pretending to be a poor Protestant woman. She maintains access to him by pretending to be a zealous follower of Warden, who desires his education in reform doctrines. She evades being apprehended by the ridiculous Dr. Luke Lundin, chamberlain of a village fair, by appearing as the witch Mother Nicneven and instilling fear in his attendants. She convinces the Doctor himself that she is merely "one of those cursed old women...who take currently and impudently upon themselves to act as advisers and curers of the sick, on the strength of some trash of herbs, some rhyme of spells, some julap or diet, drink or cordial."[63] Then she assumes the role of a poisoner, giving the Lochleven steward, Dryfesdale, a potion she claims will kill Queen Mary. Once she is apprehended and taken to the castle, she escapes the dungeon by "assuming the mien and attitude of a Sibyl in frenzy" and offering a paean to Queen Mary, who wins her freedom.[64]

There is perhaps little danger that Magdalen's clever masquerade will inspire the reader's admiration, since her disguises reinforce Scott's depiction of her as demonic fanatic. But the novel's other mummers are undeniably sympathetic. One example is Henry Seyton, youthful member of the Catholic conspirators. Appropriately, we are first introduced to him in the midst of a performance—ironically, one directed against Catholics. One of the actors, in the role of a Pardoner, holds a phial of liquid under the noses of women in the audience, claiming that any less-than-virtuous "wife" or "maiden" will sneeze. In the garb of a maiden, the athletic Henry Seyton sneezes and assaults the clown who has taken over the Pardoner's job. Keeping up the charade, he plays along with the Pardoner, who reprimands him. He then plays with Roland, who suspects that the maiden shielding her face with a muffler is Catherine Seyton, Henry's twin sister, with whom Roland is in love. The disguised Seyton flirts with Roland and joins him in a dance on the green. Enjoying her playful repartee, Roland tries to make the maiden reveal that she is Catherine, and the

---

[63] Scott, *Abbot*, 2:103, chap. 26.
[64] Scott, *Abbot*, 2:209, chap. 32.

mummer answers, "You indeed are pleased to call me so...but I have many other names besides."[65]

Besides underscoring the humor, skill, and boldness of this masquerader, Scott associates his strength of character with popish mummery when the lovely "maiden" lectures Roland on the manliness of Catholicism. The lecture begins after Roland expresses his shock at the very unladylike curse that escapes Henry's lips when his veil slips: "You are surprised...at what you see and hear—But the times which make females men, are least of all fitted for men to become women; yet you yourself are in danger of such a change."[66] In response to Roland's indignation, Henry continues:

> Yes, you, for all the boldness of your reply...When you should hold fast your religion, because it is assailed on all sides by rebels, traitors, and heretics, you let it glide out of your breast like water grasped in the hand. If you are driven from the faith of your fathers from fear of a traitor, is not that womanish?—If you are cajoled by the cunning arguments of a trumpeter of heresy, or the praises of a puritanic old woman, is not that womanish?—if you are bribed by the hope of spoil and preferment, is not that womanish?—And when you wonder at my venting a threat or an execration, should you not wonder at yourself, who, pretending to a gentle name, and aspiring to knighthood, can be at the same time cowardly, silly, and self-interested?[67]

We might smile at this speech, considering the garb of the speaker, but throughout the novel Scott portrays Henry Seyton as a brave youth. At the end of the novel, he gloriously prepares to enter the battle of Langside. He bows to the Queen "till the white plumes on his helmet mixed with the flowing mane of his gallant war-horse, then placed himself firm in the saddle, shook his lance aloft with an air of triumph

---

[65] Scott, *Abbot*, 2:119, chap. 27.
[66] Scott, *Abbot*, 2:118, chap. 27.
[67] Scott, *Abbot*, 2:118.

and determination, and striking his horse with the spurs, made towards his father's banner, which was still advancing up the hill, and dashed his steed over every obstacle that occurred in his headlong path."[68]

When he receives a mortal blow, he bids Roland, who has come to his aid, "Hasten to save the Queen—and commend me to Catherine—she will never more be mistaken for me nor I for her—the last sword-stroke has made an eternal distinction."[69]

Abbot Ambrose, formerly Edward Glendinning, is disguised in "the ordinary dress of a nobleman's retainer."[70] Like Henry Seyton, he too is courageous, but his courage is tempered by humility and wisdom. When Roland weeps upon recognizing the Abbot, who had secretly instructed him during his stay at Avenel, Ambrose reminds him of the times:

You indeed see the Superior of the community of St. Mary's in the dress of a poor sworder, who gives his master the use of his blade and buckler, and, if needful, of his life, for a coarse livery coat, and four marks by the year. But such a garb suits the time, and, in the period of the church militant, as well becomes her prelates as staff, mitre, and crosier, in the days of the church's triumph.[71]

Dressed as a gardener, former Abbot Boniface demonstrates a similar acceptance of the time. Though his age and mental state render him an unfit solider in the church militant, he expresses his vitality through a humorous complaint. According to him, his successor has disrupted a vigorous and full life tending the eternal soil with the passing concerns of political matters:

---

[68] Scott, *Abbot,* 2:294, chap. 37.
[69] Scott, *Abbot,* 2:300.
[70] Scott, *Abbot,* 2:126, chap. 27.
[71] Scott, *Abbot,* 2:131, chap. 37.

I tell thee, Father Ambrosius...the patience of the best saint that ever said pater-noster, would be exhausted by the trials to which you have put mine—What I have been, it skills not to speak at present—no one knows better than yourself, father, what I renounced, in hopes to find ease and quiet during the remainder of my days—and no one better knows how my retreat has been invaded, my fruit-trees broken, my flower-beds trodden down, my quiet frightened away, and my very sleep driven from my bed, since ever this poor Queen, God bless her, hath been sent to Lochleven. I blame her not; being a prisoner, it is natural she should wish to get out from so vile a hold, where there is scarcely any place even for a tolerable garden, and where the water-mists, as I am told, blight all the early blossoms—I say, I cannot blame her for endeavouring for her freedom; but why I should be drawn into the scheme—why my harmless arbours, that I planted with my own hands, should become places of privy conspiracy—why my little quay, which I built for my own fishing boat, should have become a haven for secret embarkations—in short, why I should be dragged into matters where both heading and hanging are like to be the issue, I profess to you, reverend father, I am totally ignorant.[72]

Through these spirited priestly mummers, Scott playfully subverts young Halbert's words about effete monks "and their long black petticoats like so many women."[73] But he loves the disguise device for another reason: it allows him to obliterate all kinds of sacred distinctions among people and things. A case in point is the above-mentioned scene involving the crowd of masqueraders who show up at the monastery door during Father Ambrose's installation as Abbot. The group is "composed of men, women, and children, ludicrously disguised in various habits, and presenting groups equally diversified

---

[72] Scott, *Abbot*, 2:137–38, chap. 37.
[73] Scott, *Abbot*, 1:135, chap. 11.

and grotesque."[74] People are transformed into a horse, a dragon, a bear, a wolf, and "one or two other wild animals."[75] A boy becomes "the lovely Sabaea, daughter of the King of Egypt"; glorious St. George becomes a grotesque figure, "armed with a goblet for a helmet and a spit for a lance." "Men were disguised as women, and women as men—children wore the dress of aged people, and tottered with crutch-sticks in their hands, furred gowns on their little backs, and caps on their round heads—while grandsires assumed the infantine tone as well as the dress of children."[76]

Although the mummers are Protestants, they continue a tradition of the Church of Rome, which "not only connived at, but even encouraged, such saturnalian licenses as the inhabitants of Kennaquhair and the neighbourhood had now in hand," so that they might "indemnify themselves for the privations and penances imposed upon them in other seasons."[77] As we have seen, when Sir Halbert breaks in upon the mummers as they wreak havoc in the monastery they claim to be purging, he scolds them for their popish ways:

[T]hink you this mumming and masquing has not more of Popery in it than have these stone walls? Take the leprosy out of your flesh, before you speak of purifying stone walls—abate your insolent license, which leads but to idle vanity and sinful excess; and know, that what you now practise, is one of the profane and unseemly sports introduced by the priests of Rome themselves, to mislead and to brutify the souls which fell into their net.[78]

But Scott's sympathies are clearly with the dragon who, "with a draconic sullenness," answers the righteous Halbert, "[W]e had as

---

[74] Scott, *Abbot*, 1:174, chap. 13.
[75] Scott, *Abbot*, 1:175.
[76] Scott, *Abbot*, 1:175.
[77] Scott, *Abbot*, 1:176, chap. 14.
[78] Scott, *Abbot*, 1:193, chap. 15.

good have been Romans still, if we are to have no freedom in our pastimes!"[79]

We might be tempted to explain Scott's progression, or regression—from condemning to reveling in Catholic mummery—in terms of the tremendous distance separating mummery in religious ceremony from mummery in espionage. However, as the dragon suggests, Scott seems to enjoy most of all mummery that is explicitly denounced as sacrilegious by his hero. The contradiction is better explained by the inherently imaginative quality of masquerade and fiction's primary purpose of appealing to the imagination. Scott's caveats are perfunctory. They are also convenient. On one hand, they allow him to identify and condemn the insidious presence of imagination in the Catholic religion without requiring him to trace that presence in religious ceremony or spiritual fantasy. On the other hand, their perfunctory quality is still transparent enough for readers to divorce Catholic attributes from the human fun they see unfolding before their eyes. On reflection, readers may have recognized that the Catholics in *The Abbot* are much more interesting than the Protestants,[80] even as they undoubtedly resisted linking this superiority to Catholicism.

The remarkable quality of such resistance grows with each new Catholic attribute Scott introduces. Besides masquerade, a delightful secrecy is also associated with Catholicism in *The Abbot*. Naturally, the political position of the Catholic characters requires stealth, but for Scott secrecy is constitutive of the Roman religion itself. The Latin passwords used in the ruined nunnery are the same mysterious phrases used by the Roman Church at the height of her power. The covert election of Father Ambrose as Abbot is no different from the clandestine elections of abbots and popes throughout the ages. Even before they became political enemies, nuns and priests hid behind the grills or within the serpentine corridors of convents and monasteries.

---

[79] Scott, *Abbot*, 1:193.

[80] See Johnson's discussion in chap. 11 of Scott's biography, *Sir Walter Scott*. Scott's readers and reviewers praised especially his treatment of Queen Mary and Catherine Seyton.

These dark settings fascinate the antiquarian Scott, who describes the mysterious buildings in great detail. The Gothic cell of St. Cuthbert claims his special attention because of the mysterious legends associated with the saint:

> THE Cell of Saint Cuthbert, as it was called, marked, or was supposed to mark, one of those resting-places which that venerable saint was pleased to assign to his monks, when his convent, being driven from Lindisfern by the Danes, became a peripatetic society of religionists, and, bearing their patron's body on their shoulders, transported him from place to place through Scotland and the borders of England, until he was pleased at length to spare them the pain of carrying him farther, and to choose his ultimate place of rest in the lordly towers of Durham.[81]

And the monastery of St. Mary's, which figures so prominently in the first novel, is the secret convening place for the persecuted monks. It is also finally the secret burial place of Abbot Ambrose's heart, which has been laid next to his body in a dark "recess, marked by the armorial bearings."[82] The strange Benedictine's search for this relic in the prefatory section of *The Monastery* is the device by which Scott piques his audience's interest in the title character of the sequel novel.

In both novels the mysteriousness with which Scott associates Catholicism is created by an appeal to the senses and to the imagination, faculties looked upon with suspicion by the Protestant reformers in the novels. Catholicism offers its adherents expansiveness and exuberance, even a sense of humor, which they frequently carry out at the expense of stiff Protestants. Catherine Seyton, for example, is introduced as a bold and witty young woman whose "buoyancy of spirit" makes her see her awkward first encounter with Roland from "a ludicrous point of view."[83] She breaks out "into a fit of laughing"[84]

---

[81] Scott, *Abbot,* 1:96, chap. 8.
[82] Scott, *Monastery,* 1:lxii.
[83] Scott, *Abbot,* 1:132, chap. 11.

when she observes Roland shifting, at a loss for words, while "[h]is endeavours to sympathize with Catherine...could carry him no farther than a forced giggle, which had more of displeasure than mirth in it."[85] Throughout the novel, Catherine's humor reflects her firm sense of self, while Roland's lack of humor reflects his defensiveness and his indecision about political and religious matters. As we have seen, Catherine's twin brother, Henry Seyton, shares her spiritedness and confidence and enjoys playing with the confused Roland as much as his sister does. Their model in the realm of wit and mockery is the Catholic Queen herself, whose "cutting sarcasm, with which women can successfully avenge themselves, for real and substantial injuries" gives her the upper hand over her Protestant warden, Lady Lochleven.[86] The dialogue that introduces us to them begins with the Queen's ironic observation:

> We are this day fortunate—we enjoy the company of our amiable hostess at an usual hour, and during a period which have hitherto been permitted to give to our private exercise. But our good hostess knows well she has at all times access to our presence, and need not observe the useless ceremony of requiring our permission.[87]

Her remarks continue in the same vein for several pages, while the dour Lady Lochleven retorts in clipped responses reflecting her "bitter resentment."[88]

The scene containing the most prolonged mockery in either of the two novels is the one featuring the mummers who disrupt Ambrose's installation as Abbot. Despite the Protestantism of the revelers, the carnival spirit, as we have seen, is Catholic. "[W]e are in the mood of the monks when they are merriest," a mummer yells outside the

---

[84] Scott, *Abbot,* 1:132.
[85] Scott, *Abbot,* 1:133.
[86] Scott, *Abbot,* 2:5, chap. 21.
[87] Scott, *Abbot,* 2:6.
[88] Scott, *Abbot,* 2:9.

monastery door,[89] leading in a parade of revelers. The group is following in the footsteps of those who were encouraged to parody Catholic clergy by the clergy itself. When Father Ambrose addresses the mummers as "My children," the costumed Abbot of Unreason, "his burlesque counterpart," answers, "*My* children too—and happy children they are!...Many a wise child knows not its own father, and it is well they have two to choose betwixt."[90] This mimicry of the Abbot by Father Howleglas exemplifies the Roman Church's juxtaposition of sacred and profane, seen not only in the carnival, but also in the sensuousness of rituals and iconography. Such corruption of religion is decried by Reformers like Henry Warden and Elias Hendersen who have led a movement devoted to purifying Christianity of carnality, levity, and irreverence. In the carnival crowd at St. Mary's Monastery, the abhorrent contamination of religion threatens to continue in Protestantism, for the Abbot of Unreason actually corresponds to "the Calvinistic divine,"[91] not the Catholic prelate, and as such an impostor he mocks Reform leaders even as he taunts the Abbot. Hence, the somber Sir Halbert's denunciation of the "mumming and masquing" as rooted in "Popery."[92]

In the spirit of Catherine and Woodcock, Scott himself enjoys popish burlesque as he mocks the self-important Doctor Lundin, who is committed to "eschewing all superstitious ceremonies and idle anilities in these our revels."[93] This anti-papist "dignitary," Scott tells us, "had been bred to the venerable study of medicine, as those acquainted with the science very soon discovered from the aphorisms which ornamented his discourse."[94] Scott goes on to insist that, although Dr. Lundin's "success had not been equal to his pretensions," he nonetheless intimidated the villagers:

---

[89] Scott, *Abbot,* 1:173, chap. 14.
[90] Scott, *Abbot,* 1:180.
[91] Scott, *Abbot,* 1:177.
[92] Scott, *Abbot,* 1:193, chap. 15.
[93] Scott, *Abbot,* 2:95, chap. 26.
[94] Scott, *Abbot,* 2:94.

Woe betide the family of the rich boor, who presumed to depart this life without a passport from Dr. Luke Lundin! for if his representatives had aught to settle with the baron, as it seldom happened otherwise, they were sure to find a cold friend in the chamberlain. He was considerate enough, however, gratuitously to help the poor out of their ailments, and sometimes out of all their other distresses at the same time.[95]

Dr. Lundin is responsible for a village drama, "chiefly directed against the superstitious practices of the Catholic religion," as a kind of "stage artillery."[96] Scott tells us that the ingenious doctor

had not only commanded the manager of the entertainment to select one of the numerous satires which had been written against the Papists (several of which were cast in dramatic form), but like the Prince of Denmark, had even caused them to insert—or, according to his own phrase, to infuse—here and there a few pleasantries of his own penning on the same inexhaustible subject.[97]

Scott provides an example of the doctor's unoriginal verses, transmutations of ancient minstrel tales, borrowed without acknowledgment of their source. Then, as though he has not had enough fun at the expense of the pompous Lundin, he plants under his very nose the Catholic spies planning the escape of the papist Queen, a scheme owing at least some of its success to this buffoon of Kinross.

SCOTT'S ATTRACTION TO CATHOLICISM

THIS FASCINATION WITH Catholicism might explain Scott's determination to pursue a Catholic subject in *The Abbot* even after the poor

---

[95] Scott, *Abbot,* 2:94.
[96] Scott, *Abbot,* 2:107, chap. 27.
[97] Scott, *Abbot,* 2:107.

reception of it in *The Monastery*. It might also explain the sequel's more realistic depiction of a young man's struggle to relinquish the Romish religion. Outside the fiction of Scott, there is only one hint of his attraction to Catholicism, but it is an impressive one. In a letter to the Reverend George Crabbe, he notes the power of "the *Stabat Mater,* the *Dies Irae,* and some other hymns of the Catholic Church": "solemn and affecting," they possess "the gloomy dignity of a Gothic church, and remind us instantly of the worship to which it is dedicated."[98] The *Stabat Mater* seems to have been particularly "affecting" for Scott since in the final days before his death, he lapsed into singing that hymn, quintessentially Catholic in its "gross" fascination with the corporeality of Christ.

But in recognizing Christ's corporeality, Catholicism affirms pleasure as well as pain, and it is the Romish capacity for play that Scott found more appealing than any other feature of Catholicism. In the companion novels, he clearly presents this feature as the chief difference between the Roman religion and Protestantism. The passages explored above suggest this difference, but Scott's treatment of Abbot Boniface, Henry Warden, and Queen Mary drives it home.[99] In

---

[98] Lockhart, *Memoirs,* 4:33.

[99] Warden's true foil, Father Eustace, is also much more sympathetic than Warden. Eustace possesses Warden's earnestness, even his ascetic impulse, but early in the first novel he recognizes his pride in a scene involving the mysterious White Lady, which will be discussed below. Eustace even confesses his hubris to the inept Abbot Boniface. Boniface takes advantage of the sub-prior's self-humiliation by installing him as official advisor and accepting credit for his brilliant ideas. Despite his repentance, the incident does not transform Eustace into a groveling, ineffectual sycophant. For all his humility, his ego remains strong and he remains sympathetically human. We see this especially in the monastery's final stand against Protestant forces, when Eustace realizes he must assume the position of Abbot: "It could not be denied that Boniface was entirely unfit for his situation in the present crisis; and the Sub-Prior felt that he himself, acting merely as a delegate, could not well take the decisive measures which the time required; the weal of the Community therefore demanded his elevation. If, besides, there crept in a feeling of an high dignity obtained, and the native exultation of a haughty spirit called to contend with the imminent dangers attached to a post of such

The Monastery, Warden is introduced as a severe ascetic who preaches repentance. When he learns that Julian of Avenel is not married to the woman pregnant with their child, he confronts the Baron, speaking, he himself notes, "like the Holy Baptist to Herod"[100]: "Bid me bind you together for ever, and celebrate the day of your bridal, not with feasting or wassail, but with sorrow for past sin, and the resolution to commence a better life."[101] In the opening chapter of *The Abbot*, Warden makes clear that his severity, far from being limited to matters as grave as adultery, extends to all displays of human affection. As he explains, "even in the fairest and purest, and most honourable feelings of our nature, there is that original taint of sin which ought to make us pause and hesitate, ere we indulge them to excess."[102] Even the instinct of dogs—creatures "but too like the human race in their foibles"—is "less erring than the reason of poor mortal man when relying on his own unassisted powers."[103] Considering such a philosophy, the reader is not surprised to hear Warden assuring Lady Avenel, "I seldom jest...life was not lent to us to be expended in that idle mirth which resembles the crackling of thorns under the pot."[104]

By contrast, Abbot Boniface is a fallible, but endearing character, whose love for creature comforts makes him ill-prepared for his turbulent era:

> In quiet times no one could have filled the state of a mitred
> Abbot, for such was his dignity, more respectably than this
> worthy prelate. He had, no doubt, many of those habits of self-
> indulgence which men are apt to acquire who live for

---

distinction, these sentiments were so cunningly blended and amalgamated with others of a more disinterested nature, that, as the Sub-Prior himself was unconscious of their agency, we, who have a regard for him, are not solicitous to detect it" (*The Monastery*, 2:246; chap. 34).

[100] Scott, *Monastery*, 2:102, chap. 25.
[101] Scott, *Monastery*, 2: 99.
[102] Scott, *Abbot*, 1:13, chap. 1.
[103] Scott, *Abbot*, 1:12.
[104] Scott, *Abbot*, 1:12.

themselves alone. He was vain, moreover; and, when boldly confronted, had sometimes shown symptoms of timidity, not very consistent with the high claims which he preferred as an eminent member of the church, or with the punctual deference which he exacted from his religious brethren, and all who were placed under his command. But he was hospitable, charitable, and by no means of himself disposed to proceed with severity against any one. In short, he would in other times have slumbered out his term of preferment with as much credit as any other "purple Abbot," who lived easily, but at the same time decorously—slept soundly, and did not disquiet himself with dreams.[105]

Even in the present times, Boniface would slumber more frequently were it not for the hard benches that he sometimes curses in *The Monastery*, complaining "After trotting a full ten miles, a man needs a softer seat than has fallen to my hard lot."[106] His self-indulgence also takes an alimentary form. Though he preaches that "it is not beseeming our order to talk of food so earnestly, especially as we must oft have our animal powers exhausted by fasting,"[107] he sits at table, wiping his mouth and fantasizing about the haunch of venison being prepared for him in the kitchen.

It is easy to forgive Abbot Boniface his self-indulgence and his hypocrisy when the penance he assigns the contrite Father Eustace for his pride is a feast rather than a fast. His rationale is that "for those to fast who are dead and mortified to the world, as I and thou, is work of supererogation, and is but the matter of spiritual pride."[108] It is easy also because he makes us laugh, whether he is puzzling—"with great round eyes, which evinced no exact intelligence of the orator's meaning"—over the affected speech of Sir Piercie[109] or sprinkling

---

[105] Scott, *Monastery*, 1:62–63, chap. 6.
[106] Scott, *Monastery*, 1:203, chap. 16.
[107] Scott, *Monastery*, 1:206.
[108] Scott, *Monastery*, 1:125, chap. 10.
[109] Scott, *Monastery*, 1:209, chap. 16.

official-sounding Latin phrases into his speeches on the severity of novitiate days.

While the serious heroes conscientiously choose Protestantism, while Reformer Henry Warden declares, "I seldom jest," and Sir Halbert orders popish revelry to cease—in short—while Protestants in the two novels embrace austerity and earnestness, Catholics feast, joke, banter, and dissemble to their hearts' content. Imprisoned in the home of the humorless Lady Lochleven, Queen Mary sums up this difference between the ancient and the reformed religions:

> When I have been rebuked by the stern preachers of the Calvinistic heresy—when I have seen the fierce countenances of my nobles averted from me, has it not been because I mixed in the harmless pleasures of the young and gay, and rather for the sake of their happiness than my own, have mingled in the masque, the song, or the dance, with the youth of my household? Well, I repent not of it—though Knox termed it sin, and Morton degradation—I was happy, because I saw happiness around me; and woe betide the wretched jealousy that can extract guilt out of the overflowings of unguarded gaeity![110]

Scott himself was all too familiar with the sternness of Calvinism. According to Lockhart, his own father exemplified those "Presbyterian heads of families, in Scotland, [who] were used to enforce compliance with various relics of the puritanical observance."[111] One such relic was the Presbyterian Sabbath, which Scott himself noted to be "severely strict," indeed, "injudiciously so."[112] Scott and his siblings were forced to attend two somber services on Sundays and to refrain from any forms of entertainment except for the reading of moralistic literature. On Sunday evening, Scott's father would read three sermons and then proceed to drill his servants and his children on both

---

[110] Scott, *Abbot*, 2:182, chap. 31.
[111] Lockhart, *Memoirs*, 10:244, chap. 84.
[112] Lockhart, *Memoirs*, 1:361, chap. 1.

the sermons and catechism. And "in the end," Scott concluded, such a strict observance of the Sabbath, "did none of us any good."[113]

Not surprisingly, the adult Scott left the stern Presbyterian Church for the more reasonable Scottish Episcopal Church. He never changed, however, in his sober attitude toward religion, as Lockhart notes in the passage cited early in this chapter:

> The few passages in his Diaries, in which he alludes to his own religious feelings and practices, show clearly the sober, serene, and elevated frame of mind in which he habitually contemplated man's relations with his Maker; the modesty with which he shrunk from indulging either the presumption of reason, or the extravagance of imagination, in the province of Faith; his humble reliance on the wisdom and mercy of God; and his firm belief that we are placed in this state of existence, not to speculate about another, but to prepare ourselves for it by actual exertion of our intellectual faculties, and the constant cultivation of kindness and benevolence towards our fellow-men.[114]

Scott's rational approach to religion made him wary of religious enthusiasm, and he cautioned against it not only in *The Monastery* and *The Abbot*, as we have seen, but also in his other novels featuring religious zealots.[115] The same approach also made him intolerant of levity in religious matters.[116] When Sir Halbert decries the mummers

---

[113] Lockhart, *Memoirs*, 1:36, chap. 1.

[114] Lockhart, *Memoirs*, 10:244–45, chap. 84.

[115] Prominent among these are *Old Mortality*, a tale of the religious rebellion of the Coventanters, and *The Heart of Midlothian*, which describes the suffering caused by fanaticism.

[116] The same might be said for traditions Scott observed religiously. When the Scottish regalia, lost for a century, were rediscovered in Scott's presence, he exploded in anger when a commissioner joked about them. Lockhart gives this account: "His daughter tells me that her father's conversation [about the regalia] had worked her feelings up to such a pitch, that when the lid was again removed, she nearly fainted, and drew back from the circle. As she was

for their profane games, he expresses the "sober, serene, and elevated frame of mind" of Scott himself. And so, he reserves such antics for characters who are Catholic, characters tainted by Catholicism, or characters like Lundin, who satirizes Catholics.

The perimeters delineating the profane fun of Scott are simply one more example of the many contradictions in his fiction noted by critics and even by Scott himself ever since his novels appeared.[117]

---

retiring, she was startled by his voice exclaiming, in a tone of the deepest emotion, 'something between anger and despair,' as she expresses it, 'By G—, No!' One of the Commissioners, not quite entering into the solemnity with which Scott regarded this business, had, it seems, made a sort of motion as if he meant to put the crown on the head of one of the young ladies near him, but the voice and aspect of the Poet were more than sufficient to make the worthy gentleman understand his error; and, respecting the enthusiasm with which he had not been taught to sympathize, he laid down the ancient diadem with an air of painful embarrassment. Scott whispered, 'Pray forgive me;' and turning round at the moment, observed his daughter deadly pale, and leaning by the door" (*Memoirs* 5:283; chap. 40).

[117] The contradictions within Scott's novels were noted early on. Samuel Coleridge identified two chief sources of tension in Scott's novels—one thematic, the other narratorial. The thematic tension resulted from Scott's conflicting attractions to a romantic Scottish past and to a realistic Scottish future (see David Brown's chapter on "Scott's Outlook on History" in *Walter Scott and the Historical Imagination* [London: Routledge and Kegan Paul, 1979]). The narratorial tension, or competing narrative voices, resulted from a similar conflict between Scott's fecund imagination and his empiricism. For a discussion of Coleridge's remarks on Scott's treatment of superstition, see Fiona Robertson's *Legitimate Histories: Scott, Gothic, and the Authorities of Fiction* (Oxford: Clarendon, 1994) 13. Critics since Coleridge have continued to explore these two kinds of tension in Scott's novels. An important example earlier in this century was Georg Luckacs, who noted in Scott a "divided psychology," according to Robertson, "a creative life and social self ideologically opposed" (12). Robertson herself is a contemporary example, seeing in Scott's work "different forms of narratorial and historical authority" (3). As Robertson goes on to explain, even Scott himself was aware of the "competing voices" in his fiction: "Scott...was attracted to the metaphor of the joint-stock company as a way of representing the sources of his work...and it usefully emphasizes the competing voices and authorities in his fiction" (12).

Scott was a man with a sense of keenly felt moral responsibility. His earnestness is summarized by biographer Edgar Johnson:

> By nature strongly emotional, even obstinately willful, Scott molded himself into a man of reason amenable to logical judgment and control. Ultimately he proved able to say of himself, and with truth, "My feelings are rather guided by reflection than impulse...*Agere atque pati Romanum est.*" Amid the crash of his fortunes [in 1826] he wrote in his *Journal*: "I am rightful monarch and, God to aid, I will not be dethroned by any rebellious passion that may raise its standard against me." And, in another entry: "Something of the black dog still hanging about me, but I will shake him off. I generally affect good spirits in the company of my family, whether I am enjoying them or not. It is too severe to sadden the harmless mirth of others by suffering your causeless melancholy to be seen; and this species of exertion is...its own reward; for the good spirits which are at first simulated become real."[118]

In his fiction, he expressed this moral earnestness by promoting what he believed to be best for Scotland: commercial progress, rationalism, a class system, British patriotism, and of course, Protestantism. He did this by means of his plots, his conventionally intrusive narrators, and especially his heroes, who—though dallying with revolutionary causes—always in the end support his ideals.[119]

---

[118] Johnson, *Sir Walter Scott*, 1251–52.

[119] Their symbolic roles explain the frequent stiffness in Scott's heroes, according to Daiches ("Scott's Achievement As a Novelist," 1951. In *Walter Scott: Modern Judgements*, ed. by D. D. Devlin [London: Macmillan, 1968]). In an essay contributing to the rebirth of critical interest in Scott, Daiches writes, "The high-ranking characters in the novels are often the most symbolical, and they cannot therefore easily step out of their symbolic role in order to act freely and provide that sense of abundant life which is so essential to a good novel" (43). The ideals I have noted in Scott have often been

Yet, having provided these didactic elements, Scott allowed his vivid imagination to roam freely in the morally neutral margins of his fiction.[120] This is where he explored both supernatural phenomena and Catholicism. Explaining Scott's strong attraction to the supernatural, Coleman Parsons concludes, "As long as reason could be suspended, deflected, disciplined to function separately from the imagination, ghosts and gooseflesh could have their temporary way."[121] The same can be said of Scott's fictional Catholics, with all their mummery and irreverent fun and games. He distanced himself from their religion by explicitly condemning it in the narrative and by refraining, by and large, from directly representing its rituals and practices. He then explored the Catholic ethos in a highly mediated fashion—through an astral spirit of Scottish lore and through the wonderful disguises,

---

underscored by critics rejecting popular views of Scott as a Romantic. See, for example, Brown and Johnson.

[120] Scott's minor characters also inhabit this zone and consequently are often livelier than his heroes and heroines, as Daiches notes in the essay cited above. This is certainly the case with Adam Woodstock, the falconer who becomes Roland Graeme's faithful retainer. An exception to the abstemious Protestants in *The Abbot*, he is a staunchly Protestant character whom Scott allows to indulge in revelry, drinking, and even popish mummery as Howleglas, the Abbot of Unreason. Scott is free to indulge his own imagination by means of Woodcock because he has provided the novel with an earnest Protestant hero, whose nobility is attested to by Woodcock himself in the novel's final battle scene: "And it was Master Roland himself...And to see how gay he is! But these light lads are as sure to be uppermost as the froth to be on the top of the quart-pot—Your man of solid parts remains ever a falconer" (2:305; chap. 17).

Ferris notes the "decentering" that must have occurred for Scott and his readers in light of the double zones of his novels. For these readers, the ostensible plot of the novel, "moving easily within the naturalized assumptions of time, seemed so transparent as to be hardly a plot at all, and it was the reassurance provided by this invisible plot that allowed Scott and his readers to surrender themselves to the dispersiveness that simultaneously challenged that reassurance. With his passive hero Scott effectively empties out the conventional center as the focus of narrative interest and blocks the centripetal drive of conventional novel reading" (101).

[121] Parsons, *Witchcraft*, 14.

secrecy, and revelry of Catholic characters, antics that he ostensibly condemned. *The Monastery* and *The Abbot* allowed Scott to imagine a religion that includes pleasure, without offending his Protestant audience and without betraying his own Protestant con science.

2

"THE LESSONS OF TRUE RELIGION":

MARY SHELLEY'S TRIBUTE TO CATHOLICISM IN *VALPERGA*

LIKE MANY OF her English contemporaries during the century of Catholic Emancipation, Mary Wollstonecraft Shelley openly scorned Roman Catholicism. Admittedly, she and her enlightened circle had little use for Christianity in general, but at least Protestantism was born of a fight for liberty while Catholicism was the oppressor. During her 1842 travels through Luther's Germany, she wrote,

> There is something pleasing in the mere outward aspect of these Protestant German towns: they look clean, orderly, and well-built. Hail to the good fight, the heart says everywhere; hail to the soil whence intellectual liberty gained, with toil and suffering, the victory—not complete yet—but which, thanks to the men of those time [*sic*], can never suffer entire defeat! In time, it will spread to those countries which are still subject to Papacy.[1]

---

[1] Mary Wollstonecraft Shelley, *Rambles in Germany and Italy in 1840, 1842, and 1843* (London: Edward Moxon, 1844) 1:209. References separated by a colon are to volume and page.

One country still darkened by papal control, her beloved Italy, inspired her most venomous attacks on centuries of power-hungry popes "who teach him [man] to fast and tell his beads—to bend the neck to the yoke—to obey the church, not God."[2] Although she was concerned with political as well as intellectual liberty, apparently the latter cause especially kindled Shelley's idealism. It was by nourishing ignorance, superstition, and dependency on the clergy[3] that the Catholic hierarchy dehumanized the faithful, both robbing them of their freedom to reason and instilling in them vices associated with unenlightened thinking. In her 1824 short story "The Bride of Modern Italy," the protagonist's inconstancy and lack of dignity are ascribed to the "Catholic religion, which crushes the innate conscience by giving a false one in its room; the system of artifice and heartlessness that subsists in a convent; the widely spread maxim in Italy, that dishonour attaches itself to the discovered not the concealed fault."[4] Several of her short stories echo such a sentiment.[5]

Not surprisingly, Shelley populates *Valperga*, her only novel set completely in Italy, with superstitious peasants and corrupt and cruel priests. But a careful inspection of this novel reveals another picture of Catholicism, one so remarkably attractive that a reader unfamiliar with the views of the author might find it hard to believe she ever found serious fault with the Roman Church.

---

[2] Shelley, *Rambles*, 2:186.

[3] Shelley especially condemned the Roman Church for encouraging superstition during the plague of 1837, leading the population to remain in Rome in expectation of miraculous delivery. See *Rambles*, 2:236–37. She denounces dependency on the Church a few pages later: "From the Pope to the lowest priestly magistrate, all live on the public revenues, whence springs a system of clients, which existing principally in Rome, yet extends over the whole of the papal dominions, and creates a crowd of dependants [*sic*] devoted to the clergy" (246).

[4] Mary Wollstonecraft Shelley, *Collected Tales and Stories*, ed. Charles E. Robinson (London: Johns Hopkins University Press, 1976) 34.

[5] See the treatment of superstition in "The Dream," and of oppressive convents in "The Brother and the Sister" and "The Heir of Mondolfo," all in *Collected Tales*.

A prefatory word about Shelley's literary achievements will be helpful since they are still generally unknown, none but *Frankenstein* winning enough popularity to remain in print since it was published. Between 1818, when the twenty-year-old author's famous novel appeared, and her death in 1851, Shelley published four more novels, three volumes of biographies for Lardner's *Cabinet Cyclopaedia*, two travel books, and a number of short stories.[6] She also published two editions with invaluable commentary on the poetry of her husband, Percy Bysshe Shelley, contributing in no small way to his place among the great Romantic poets.

Until the 1950s, critical and biographical interest in Shelley was confined to aspects of her life and work that shed light on her husband's genius. Biographies considering Shelley in her own right finally started appearing in the middle of this century and have continued appearing ever since.[7] In the 1970s, however, *Frankenstein* began receiving substantial critical attention by psychoanalytic and feminist critics, who revealed this novel to be "an essential text for

---

[6] The novels Shelley published after *Frankenstein* were *Valperga* (1823), *The Last Man* (1826), *Perkin Warbeck* (1830), and *Lodore* (1835). Shelley's novella, *Mathilda*, was not published until 1959. Her travel book describing France, Switzerland, Germany, and Holland was published in 1817; the book describing Germany and Italy in 1844. Most of her short fiction appeared in magazines like *The Keepsake* between 1824 and 1839. Her two volumes on the *Lives of the Most Eminent Literary and Scientific Men of Italy, Spain, and Portugal* appeared in 1835 and 1837; the volume on men of France between 1838 and 1839. Of her novels besides *Frankenstein*, only *The Last Man* was reprinted in this century (1965) until the 1996 reprinting of *Valperga* by Woodstock Books. Her collected stories were published in an edition by Robinson in 1976. *The Novels and Selected Works of Mary Shelley* (8 vols., ed. Crook) appeared in 1996. Recent editions of Shelley's journals and letters are cited in this chapter.

[7] Early examples are Spark's *Child of Light: A Reassessment of Mary Wollstonecraft Shelley* (1951) and the first biography to use Shelley's newly released original papers, Nitchie's *Mary Shelley, Author of Frankenstein* (1953). More recent examples are Mellor's *Mary Shelley: Her Life, Her Fiction, Her Monsters* (1988) and Sunstein's *Romance and Reality* (1989).

our exploration of female consciousness and literary technique."[8]
Studies of Shelley as a critic of patriarchy have continued to flourish,
alongside studies focusing on her critique of Romantic ideology.[9] Such
perspectives have begun to lead scholars beyond *Frankenstein* to the
rest of her work, including *Valperga*.[10]

VALPERGA'S REPRESENTATION OF CATHOLICISM

SET IN THE Italian city states of the early fourteenth century, *Valperga*
(1823) was inspired by the historical figure Castruccio Antelminelli, a
Ghibelline who returned to Italy from exile to crush his Guelph
enemies and ruthlessly tyrannize Tuscany with the support of the
invading German Emperor.[11] But, as it progresses, the three-volume

---

[8] Anne K. Mellor, *Mary Shelley: Her Life, Her Fiction, Her Monsters*
(New Brunswick: Rutgers University Press, 1988) xi. An important study
affirming the critical status of the ever popular *Frankenstein* is *The
Endurance of Frankenstein* (1979), edited by Levine and Knoepflmacher.
Perhaps the most well-known feminist treatment of *Frankenstein* is that of
Gilbert and Gubar in *The Madwoman in the Attic* (1979). Another is
Poovey's *The Proper Lady and the Woman Writer: Ideology as Style in the
Works of Mary Wollstonecraft, Mary Shelley, and Jane Austen* (1984).

[9] Mellor's work examines both dimensions of Shelley. See also the essays in
part 1 of *The Other Mary Shelley: Beyond Frankenstein* (1993), ed. by Fisch,
Mellor, and Schor; and Clemit's *The Godwinian Novel: The Rational Fictions
of Godwin, Brockden Brown, Mary Shelley* (1993).

[10] Jane Blumberg's 1993 study of *Mary Shelley's Early Novels: This Child
of Imagination and Misery* (Iowa City: University of Iowa Press,
1993)—including *Valperga*—is a recent example cited in this essay. *The Other
Mary Shelley: Beyond Frankenstein* also includes two essays on *Valperga*.

[11] Shelley's husband, Percy Bysshe Shelley, described the events of *Valperga*
in a letter to a prospective publisher: "[Castruccio] was a little Napoleon, and,
with a dukedom instead of an empire for his theatre, brought upon the same
all the passions and errors of his antitype. The chief interest of his romance
rests upon Euthanasia, his betrothed bride, whose love for him is only
equalled by her enthusiasm for the liberty of the republic of Florence which is
in some sort her country, and for that of Italy, to which Castruccio is a
devoted enemy, being an ally of the party of the Emperor. Euthanasia, the last
survivor of a noble house, is a feudal countess, and her castle is the scene of

novel shifts its focus from political strife to the personal turmoil of two women who love Castruccio: the prophetess Beatrice and the Countess of Valperga, Euthanasia.[12]

One might be tempted to see the character of Beatrice as the embodiment of Mary Shelley's anti-Catholicism.[13] Beatrice is the child of heretic Wilhelmina of Bohemia, who professes to be "the Holy Ghost incarnate upon earth for the salvation of the female sex."[14] Though she is rescued from the sect, she grows up to claim for herself extraordinary spiritual powers. For her blasphemy, she is persecuted by Dominican Inquisitors eager for her death and saved only by Castruccio's intervention. Later in the novel she is imprisoned and sexually abused by the fiendish priest Tripalda, who exemplifies many priests in the tale, corrupting even "the lessons of our divine master... to satisfy the most groveling desires."[15]

---

knightly manners of the time" (as quot. in Blumberg, *Shelley's Early Novels*, 83).

Despite her love for Castruccio, Euthanasia refuses to marry a tyrant and reluctantly agrees to join forces against him. Her benevolent sovereignty over her peasant subjects is answered by their loyalty. Many of them die as they unsuccessfully resist the invading Castruccio, who strips his former love of her power and destroys her castle, Valperga, where he used to court her. At the end of the novel, she dies at sea on her way to exile. During his campaigns, Castruccio has also managed to ruin the emotionally unstable prophetess, Beatrice. Abandoned after his seduction of her, Beatrice flees to Rome, where she is imprisoned and sexually abused by a priest. Returning to Florence, she finds a protector in Euthanasia, who, learning that Castruccio has played a part in her distraught condition, tries to teach Beatrice to conquer her wild imagination and emotions with reason. Ultimately, however, Beatrice cannot resist her feelings for Castruccio. They lead her into the hands of a sorceress, who vows to help her win him back. Using Beatrice for her own ends, the sorceress finally murders her with poison.

[12] Euthanasia's central role led Shelley to change the original title of the novel from *Castruccio: Prince of Lucca,* to *Valperga: The Life and Adventures of Castruccio, Prince of Lucca.*

[13] Such a conclusion is reached by William Walling, in *Mary Shelley* (New York: Twayne, 1972) 60.

[14] Shelley, *Valperga,* 2:26.

[15] Shelley, *Valperga,* 1:194.

Yet, Tripalda is the only Church representative to play a central role in the ruin of Beatrice, inquisitors and other priests having little effect on her or on the story in general. And, as a counterexample to this monstrous member of the clergy, Shelley provides a character even more closely identified with the Church's power: the kind Bishop of Ferrara. In book 2, chapter 11, the Bishop relates to Castruccio the events leading to his adoption of Beatrice as a young child. At the time, Wilhelmina has recently died, and the heretic's disciple Manfreda is under arrest by the Inquisition. Despite his fears about involving himself with the misguided sect, the Bishop, then a young priest, takes pity on the suffering Manfreda, promising to protect Beatrice, now her ward. Risking contagion, he enters the dwelling of a leper hiding the girl and takes her into his care. "[N]eed I say," the Bishop asks Castruccio, "how much I have ever loved this hapless girl, and cherished her, and tried to save her from the fate to which her destiny has hurried her?"[16] He confides in Castruccio, whom he mistakenly deems "humane and generous," in order "to secure another protector for my poor Beatrice, if I were to die, and she fell into any misfortune or disgrace."[17]

Thus, it seems that for all her condemnation of clerics who inflict misery on Beatrice, Shelley declines to cast the Church in general as villain in her tale. Included among those who deceive and abuse the naive prophetess are Castruccio, who seduces and abandons Beatrice, and the witch, who precipitates her death after playing upon her desperation, by drugging her. Yet, by far the worst culprit in the emotional and spiritual destruction of Beatrice, according to Shelley, is her own undisciplined imagination.

The dangers of her fantasies are first perceived by the Bishop. As a child, Beatrice would sit in contemplation for hours at a time, only to weep hysterically when the Bishop questioned her about her thoughts. Then, he confesses to Castruccio, "[a]s she grew older, her imagination developed," and her meditations on God and Nature "[yielded] a sentiment that overwhelmed and oppressed her, so that she could only

---

[16] Shelley, *Valperga*, 2:40.
[17] Shelley, *Valperga*, 2:44.

weep and sigh."[18] She begs him to teach her the truths of the Catholic faith, but "the more she heard, and the more she read, the more she gave herself up to contemplation and solitude, and to what I cannot help considering the wild dreams of her imagination."[19] The Bishop blames these wild dreams for Beatrice's heresy and arrest, but they also contribute to her seduction. In her prayer to the Blessed Virgin, Beatrice—"burning with passion" for Castruccio—"wove a subtle web, whose materials she believed heavenly, but which were indeed stolen from the glowing wings of love."[20] "[A]las!" the narrator laments, "to her they [her dreams] were realities."[21]

Beatrice herself recognizes her wild imagination as the source of her agony, and in a speech to Euthanasia she curses God for creating it:

Did not the power you worship create the passions of man; his desires which outleap possibility, and bring ruin on his head?...And the imagination, that masterpiece of his malice; that spreads honey on the cup that you may drink poison; that strews roses over thorns, thorns sharp and big as spears; that semblance of beauty which beckons you to the desart [sic]...He, the damned and triumphant one, sat meditating many thousand years for the conclusion, the consummation, the final crown, the seal of all misery, which he might set on man's brain and heart to doom him to endless torment; and he created the Imagination.[22]

When she turns to Euthanasia for solace, the Countess explains that the soul, like a cave, contains dark recesses where a "madman" dwells. Only those whose shadowy corners are exposed to an "inborn light" should explore them; otherwise, the madman "makes darkling,

---

[18] Shelley, *Valperga*, 2:41.
[19] Shelley, *Valperga*, 2:42.
[20] Shelley, *Valperga*, 2:79.
[21] Shelley, *Valperga*, 2:80.
[22] Shelley, *Valperga*, 3:46–47.

fantastic combinations" and leads the soul to destruction.[23] Most people, she suggests, should avoid those recesses and linger in others where "Content of Mind" rules over noble passions, including an apparently positive form of Imagination.[24] Euthanasia's allegory of the soul is meant to teach Beatrice "to regulate its various powers."[25] But Beatrice responds in anguish: "No content of mind exists for me, no beauty of thought, or poetry; and, if imagination live, it is as a tyrant, armed with fire, and venomed darts, to drive me to despair."[26]

While Beatrice represents a critique of irrationality rather than Catholicism, Euthanasia does voice some of Shelley's negative views of the Roman Church. When Castruccio suggests that Beatrice be entrusted to a convent after her abuse in Rome, Euthanasia rejects his advice as "chilling councils."[27] She sees the piety of Florence's "noblest citizens" as little more than "faith in astrology and portents."[28] She denounces the "treacherous and unprincipled" Tripalda[29] and corrupt priests who "make a revenue" from "the absolution" they confer in the confessional.[30] She is loathe to align herself with the oppressive papacy against the German Emperor and does so only because "[s]he is attached to the cause of the freedom of Florence," as Count Fondi reports, "and not to the power of her Popes."[31]

The anti-Church sentiments she places on the lips of her heroine are unquestionably vituperative. However, in many ways Shelley portrays Euthanasia as a model Catholic. The Countess piously invokes the Virgin Mary's assistance in defending Castruccio from the deceitful Tripalda and his forces[32] and in prison prays to her, repeating "the Catholic ejaculation, '*Stella, alma, benigna, ora pro*

---

[23] Shelley, *Valperga*, 3:101–102.
[24] Shelley, *Valperga*, 3:102.
[25] Shelley, *Valperga*, 3:99.
[26] Shelley, *Valperga*, 3:102.
[27] Shelley, *Valperga*, 3:103.
[28] Shelley, *Valperga*, 2:3.
[29] Shelley, *Valperga*, 3:199.
[30] Shelley, *Valperga*, 1:195.
[31] Shelley, *Valperga*, 1:177.
[32] Shelley, *Valperga*, 3:209.

nobis!' then, crossing herself, she lay[s] down to rest, and quickly...
[sleeps], as peacefully and happily, as a babe rocked in its mother's
arms."[33]

Her devout Catholic life has prepared her for this final crisis. Early
in the novel, she obeys the *Ave Maria* bell summoning all to worship,
leading her guests to Valperga's chapel and joining "in the devotions of
the priest."[34] She admires a "procession of monks...chaunting in a
sweet and solemn tone, in that language which once awoke the pauses
of this Roman air with words of fire."[35] Consoling the downcast Beatrice on her way to Rome, she offers to be her confessor, assigning her
"light penances of cheerfulness and hope."[36] This metaphoric function
becomes literal after Beatrice's return: kneeling before Euthanasia, the
heretical Beatrice exclaims, "Trust me, you shall make me a Catholic
again, if you will love me unceasingly for one whole year."[37] Euthanasia promises to bring her back into the true fold, thereby "in part
fulfilling my task on the earth."[38]

Indeed, in her role as "ministering angel"[39] to her subjects, to
Beatrice, and to Castruccio (who bestows her with this title), Euthanasia is identified with the most revered saint of the Roman Church:
the Virgin Mary. Granted, much literature of the nineteenth century
portrays women as angelic beings, often in language evoking the
Virgin[40]; even *Valperga*'s heterodox Beatrice is described in this way at
times. But Euthanasia's identification with the Blessed Virgin is

[33] Shelley, *Valperga*, 3:243.
[34] Shelley, *Valperga*, 1:288.
[35] Shelley, *Valperga*, 1:203.
[36] Shelley, *Valperga*, 2:184.
[37] Shelley, *Valperga*, 3:52.
[38] Shelley, *Valperga*, 3:54.
[39] Shelley, *Valperga*, 3:37.
[40] Coventry Patmore's *Angel in the House* (London: George Bell and Son,
1885) captures prevalent Victorian thinking about the spiritual role of
women. For an illuminating discussion of this ideal, see chapter 11 of
Alexander Welsh's *City of Dickens* (Cambridge: Harvard University Press,
1971).

striking, particularly in light of her role as teacher of the faith and her own devotion to the Virgin.

In her first appearance in the novel, Euthanasia is presented with the traditional features of Marian iconography: "a veil that was wreathed round her head"; blue eyes whose orbs seem "to reflect...the pure and unfathomable brilliance, which strikes the sight as darkness, of a Roman heaven"; a brow upon which "Charity dwelt"; an expression of "wisdom exalted by enthusiasm"; a gown "rather plain, being neither ornamented with gold nor jewels"; and "a silk vest of blue [that] reached from her neck to her feet, girded at the waist by a small embroidered band."[41] Later, the narrator refers to Euthanasia's "Madonna face,"[42] and when Tripalda furnishes a letter claiming that Euthanasia has joined his conspiracy against Castruccio, his ally Vanni indignantly exclaims, "I expect next to hear that some of the saints or martyrs, or perhaps the Virgin herself has come down to aid you."[43]

EUTHANASIA'S SCHOLASTIC TENDENCIES

For all her piety, it is her great nobility that makes Euthanasia the heroine of *Valperga*. But, like her piety, this nobility is of a Catholic nature—that is, it is achieved through the harmonization of faith and reason.

From her scholarly father, Euthanasia has learned "to fathom my sensations, and discipline my mind; to understand what my feelings were, and whether they arose from a good or evil source."[44] Her lessons in rationality sustain her in the agony she endures when Castruccio chooses power over love for her, preventing both her despair and her surrender to him at the price of her ideals. But for Euthanasia, rationality cannot be separated from faith, as we see in the passage following Beatrice's "anathema against the creation"[45]:

---

[41] Shelley, *Valperga*, 1:185–86.
[42] Shelley, *Valperga*, 3:230–31.
[43] Shelley, *Valperga*, 3:224.
[44] Shelley, *Valperga*, 1:194.
[45] Shelley, *Valperga*, 3:51.

[Euthanasia] thought over her wild denunciations; and, strange to say, she felt doubly warmed with admiration of the creation, and gratitude towards God, at the moment that Beatrice had painted its defects. She thought of the beauty of the world and the wondrous nature of man, until her mind was raised to an enthusiastic sentiment of happiness and praise. "And you also shall curb your wild thoughts," whispered Euthanasia, as she looked at the sleeping girl; "I will endeavour to teach you the lessons of true religion...."[46]

The "true religion" promised by Euthanasia requires replacing Beatrice's "wild," "wandering thoughts"[47] with sound judgments about the goodness of creation, what the Church's Scholastic Fathers in the century before *Valperga*'s events called "right reason." This faculty apprehends order in the world and God as the source of this order. In fact, according to Thomas Aquinas, the Church's greatest Scholastic, God as the source of all existence can be determined by reason. Reason's starting point is the senses, as Aquinas explains in his *Summa Contra Gentiles*:

For, according to its manner of knowing in the present life, the intellect depends on the sense for the origin of knowledge; and so those things that do not fall under the senses cannot be grasped by the human intellect except in so far as the knowledge of them is gathered from sensible things. Now, sensible things cannot lead the human intellect to the point of seeing in them the nature of the divine substance; for sensible things are effects that fall short of the power of their cause. Yet, beginning with sensible things, our intellect is led to the point

---

[46] Shelley, *Valperga*, 3:54.
[47] Shelley, *Valperga*, 3:54.

of knowing about God that He exists, and other such characteristics that must be attributed to the First Principle.[48]

Euthanasia's frequent meditations on the world apprehended by her senses yield such defining characteristics of the Deity. She grasps in imperfect, created beings a reflection of the three most fundamental aspects of Perfect Being: unity, goodness, and truth. The following passage shows such an insight raised to the level of mystical experience:

> To look on the hues of the sunset, to see the softened tints of the olive woods, the purple tinge of the distant mountains, whose outline was softly, yet distinctly marked in the orange sky; to feel the western breeze steal across her cheek, like words of love from one most dear; to see the first star of evening penetrate from out the glowing western firmament, and whisper the secret of distant worlds to us in our narrow prison; to behold the heaven-pointing cypress with unbent spire sleep in the stirless air; these were sights and feelings which softened and exalted her thoughts; she felt as if she were a part of the great whole; she felt bound in amity to all; doubly, immeasurably loving those dear to her, feeling an humanizing charity even to the evil.[49]

In this paean to "the great whole," to the "secret of distant worlds" revealed in it, and to the "amity" and "charity" inspired by it; Euthanasia exalts the unity, truth, and goodness underlying creation. In the next paragraph, she explicitly acknowledges the divine source of the created world and suggests that in loving even its evil elements—like Castruccio—she fulfills the design of the creator: "Oh! sooner shall

---

[48] Thomas Aquinas, *On the Truth of the Catholic Faith: Summa Contra Gentile*, trans. Anton Pegis (Garden City: Doubleday, 1955) bk. 1, chap. 3, p. 63.

[49] Shelley, *Valperga*, 2:164–65.

that [sun] forget its path which it hath ever traced, since God first marked it out, than I forget to love!"[50]

According to Aquinas, though God's existence and essential attributes are discovered by human reason, the truths of revelation—in other words, Christian dogmas—"absolutely surpass its power."[51] But even such specific teachings, he argues, are not *contrary* to reason, for "it is impossible that the truth of faith should be opposed to those principles that the human reason knows naturally."[52] In her frequent discrimination between superstition and true Catholic piety, Euthanasia exhibits the Thomistic view of faith's reasonability. No wonder she offers this rational counsel to the crazed Beatrice: "Why will you not recal [*sic*] the creeds of your childhood, as your adoptive parents taught them you? I cannot school you better than they."[53]

Why argue that Shelley takes her transcendentalism from Aquinas rather than from Coleridge, another Christian metaphysician? After all, the philosophy of Coleridge influenced all the Romantics, including Mary and her husband; in fact, Coleridge himself, friend and student of William Godwin, was a frequent visitor in Mary's childhood home. The answer is that when it came to heavenly matters, Shelley found her greatest inspiration not in Coleridge, but in Dante, whose *Paradiso* she exalted in her fiction, correspondence, and journals.[54] And Dante found his inspiration in Aquinas, his "greatest teacher,"[55] who "more than any other summed up for Dante the Christian

---

[50] Shelley, *Valperga*, 2:166.

[51] Aquinas, *On the Truth*, bk. 1, chap. 3, p. 63.

[52] Aquinas, *On the Truth*, bk. 1, chap. 7, p. 74.

[53] Shelley, *Valperga*, 3:55.

[54] In *Rambles*, for example, Shelley notes that "the soul is elevated and rapt by the sublime hymns to heavenly love, contained in the *Paradiso*. Nothing can be more beautiful than the closing lines...which speak of his return to earth, his mind still penetrated by the ecstasy he had lately felt" (1:96).

[55] This observation appears in John Sinclair's commentary on canto xi in Dante Alighieri, *The Divine Comedy of Dante Alighieri*, 3 vols. Translated with commentary by John D. Sinclair (New York: Oxford University Press, 1939) 3:173.

doctrine of God."[56] In his *Paradiso*, Dante places Aquinas in the glorious sphere of the Sun, where he instructs the earthly visitor at great length on a truth that frequently elevates the spirit of *Valperga*'s heroine: "the splendor of that Idea" which "shines through more and less" all creation.[57]

Unlike the philosophical views of Coleridge, those of Aquinas were well-suited to Shelley's sensibilities. In his epistemology, Aquinas was a realist in the tradition of Aristotle, while Coleridge was an idealist influenced by Kant. These two approaches yield distinct implications about human knowledge and indeed about human nature itself. Whereas realism emphasizes the dependency of human knowledge on being, idealism gives priority to the power of intellect itself as a creative force. According to Kant, we know only that which is presented to our minds by *a priori* categories of reason. Coleridge echoes this conclusion in poems like "Dejection: An Ode," in which Nature is depicted as lifeless apart from our imagination. Like his Romantic contemporaries, Coleridge exalts the individual genius, the brilliance of poetic imagination. It is a "repetition in the finite mind of the eternal act of creation in the infinite 'I AM'" that "dissolves, diffuses, dissipates, in order to recreate...It is essentially *vital*, even as all objects (*as* objects) are dead."[58]

Such exaltation of human creativity at the expense of a universe external to the imagination would be abhorrent to Aquinas, who understood knowledge as representing the world to the mind. As Aquinas argues in the *Summa Contra Gentiles*, humans are drawn by reality, as it were, and ultimately by God as the final end of intellect:

And since operations of this kind [understanding] take their species from their objects, by which also they are known, it follows that the more perfect the object of any such operation,

---

[56] This characterization is Sinclair's in Alighieri, *Divine Comedy*, 160.
[57] Alighieri, *Divine Comedy*, 191–93.
[58] Samuel Coleridge, *From Biblographia Literaria*, in *Norton Anthology of English Literature*, ed. M. H. Abrams, 5th ed. (New York: Norton, 1986) chap. 13, 2:396–97.

the more perfect is the operation. Consequently to understand the most perfect intelligible, namely God, is the most perfect in the genus of the operation which consists in understanding. Therefore to know God by an act of understanding is the last end of every intellectual substance.[59]

As a student of Aquinas via Dante, Shelley rejected Coleridge's glorification of human imagination. We see this illustrated in *Valperga* not only in Euthanasia's warnings to Beatrice, but also in the emphasis Euthanasia places on worship as the end of the ecstatic moments she experiences in contemplating nature. Her response to Beatrice's "anathema against creation" bears this out, as we have seen: "she felt doubly warmed with admiration of the creation and gratitude towards God" and "an enthusiastic sentiment of happiness and praise"—attitudes that immediately precede her promise to teach Beatrice "the lessons of true religion."[60]

In her essay "Why Women Didn't Like Romanticism," Anne Mellor explains the abhorrence Shelley felt for romantic ideology in terms of the destruction it caused in her own lifetime. On a large scale, "a romantic idealization of radical political change"[61] had produced fifteen years of horror in France after the French Revolution. Poets like Percy Bysshe Shelley, whose verse acted as "a clarion call to revolutionary political action,"[62] celebrated the creative process and ignored "the creative product." According to Mellor, Shelley critiques such irresponsibility in her character Victor Frankenstein, who forgets the product of his creation. Shelley believed that at the root of this irresponsibility was an inflated sense of self, as Mellor explains:

---

[59] Thomas Aquinas, *Introduction to St. Thomas Aquinas*, ed. Anton Pegis (New York: Random House, 1945) bk. 3, chap. 25, p. 443.

[60] Shelley, *Valperga*, 3:54.

[61] Anne Mellor, "Why Women Didn't Like Romanticism," in *The Romantics and Us: Essays on Literature and Culture*, ed. Gene W. Ruoff (New Brunswick: Rutgers University Press, 1990) 283.

[62] Mellor, "Why Women," 283.

Mary Shelley was profoundly disturbed by what she saw to be a powerful egotism at the core of the romantic ideology: an affirmation of the human imagination as divine defined the mission of the poet as not only the destroyer of "mind-forged manacles" and political tyranny but also as the savior of mankind, the "unacknowledged legislators of the world." She had seen at first hand how self-indulgent this self-image of the poet-savior could be.[63]

Her "first hand" experience had shown Shelley that romantic ideology wreaks destruction in the home as well as in society. Mellor goes on to list the "poet-savior[s]" in Shelley's life who had brought misery to their families: her father, William Godwin; Coleridge; Byron; Leigh Hunt; and even her husband, Percy Bysshe Shelley. In concluding her essay, Mellor suggests that women of the Romantic period, like Austen and Shelley, promoted an alternative ideology that "celebrated the education of the rational woman and an ethic of care that required one to take full responsibility for the predictable consequences of one's thoughts and actions, for all the children of one's mind and body."[64] This brand of romanticism—"equally revolutionary"[65]—is what Shelley's mother, Mary Wollstonecraft, had called "a REVOLUTION in female manners."[66] Certainly, in *Valperga* we see that Euthanasia, a victim of male romanticism, exalts reason over emotion and urges the abused Beatrice to do the same.

Shelley creates in Euthanasia a thinking moral agent who not only must resist her own feelings for Castruccio, but also must suffer the painful consequences—for herself and the people under her care—of adhering to principles of liberty, responsibility, and patriotism. By giving her such a role, Shelley challenges contemporary conceptualizations of the feminine ideal as a secularized Virgin Mary, passive

---

[63] Mellor, "Why Women," 284.

[64] Mellor, "Why Women," 285.

[65] Mellor, "Why Women," 285.

[66] Mary Wollstonecraft, *A Vindication of the Rights of Woman*, quot. by Mellor, "Why Women," 285.

and ineffectual, free "from any need for internal moral struggle" because of her otherworldly innocence.[67] Euthanasia's association with the Virgin drives home Shelley's determination to subvert such a conceptualization, thereby following in her mother's footsteps. In *A Vindication of the Rights of Woman*, Mary Wollstonecraft insisted on full humanity for women as rational beings, held to the same moral standards as men and capable of the same moral achievements.[68] For Euthanasia, these achievements include a "humanizing charity even to the evil,"[69] inspired by her deeply held conviction that even morally repugnant persons like Castruccio are creatures of God.

Dante, whose vision of hell includes the worst sinners in history, is the model of such compassion—at least, toward souls condemned for weakness rather than malice, like Ciacco, the glutton; and Francesca and Paolo, guilty of unlawful love. In the *Inferno*'s circles of punishment, he recognizes the gradations of divergence from humanity's inherent orientation toward goodness, a concept elucidated in Aquinas's explanation in canto 13 of the *Paradiso*: "beneath the stamp

---

[67] Tricia Looten, *Lost Saints: Silence, Gender, and Victorian Literary Canonization* (Charlottesville: University of Virginia Press, 1996) 53. In chapter 2 of *Lost Saints*, Looten discusses at length the Marian conceptualization formulated in nineteenth-century England, exploring the ways in which it essentially silenced women authors by annihilating their authority as participants in the flesh-and-blood world of sexual, social, and political realities.

[68] Wollstonecraft actually saw herself in a better position than that of men for asserting moral authority. As Stuart Curran notes in his essay "Women Readers, Women writers," in *The Cambridge Companion to British Romanticism*, ed. Stuart Curran (Cambridge: Cambridge University Press, 1993), Wollstonecraft and Helen Maria Williams both saw themselves as "citizens of the world" who, although unable to vote or participate in political decisions affecting the fates of countries, could speak with the disinterest necessary about the need for representative government after the events of the Reign of Terror in France. Curran concludes, "Their dual assumptions—that the sole power women can claim comes from the pen, and that only the disinterested can wield moral authority...have informed the polemical stance of women well into the modern age" (186).

[69] Shelley, *Valperga*, 2:165.

of the [divine] idea the light then shines through more and less; hence it comes that trees of one and the same species bear better and worse fruit and you are born with different talents.[70] For Aquinas, this comment applies also to degrees of moral perfection, as he explains in question 5 of the *Summa Theologica*.[71]

THE FUNCTION OF CATHOLICISM FOR SHELLEY

SHELLEY'S HEROINE BESPEAKS more than a mere desire to balance criticism of Catholicism with examples of individuals who excel despite their Roman faith (a desire she suggests a few times in her travel writing).[72] Indeed, as we have seen, Euthanasia's nobility largely *depends* on her Catholic faith, understood in a way that appeals to an intellectual with deeply religious sensibilities.

Despite the influence of freethinkers and of her husband, an avowed atheist, Mary Shelley stubbornly clung to a belief in God throughout her whole life. Her journals, correspondence, and even travel writing record passionate prayers of praise and surrender to the Divine Will, as well as professions of faith in life beyond the grave.[73] Like many from her enlightened circle, she rejected Christianity, as she asserted to Lord Byron when he teased her about her religious sensibilities[74]; however, she was reared by her father to admire the

---

[70] Alighieri, *Divine Comedy*, 193.

[71] Aquinas, *Introduction*, 34–45.

[72] One person who, according to Shelley, embodied the charity of the Catholic Church was Pascal. Cf. *Rambles* 3:234–35.

[73] An example of Shelley's fervor is this prayer written in her journal [*The Journals of Mary Shelley, 1814–1844*, ed. Paula R. Feldman and Diana Scott-Kilvert, 2 vols. (Oxford: Clarendon, 1987)]: "Oh You supreme Power—you who may reign here—who may watch over here—to whom I bow—if it is your will that I may die during this year—behold me ready to obey your commands that will call me from this prison to the shining atmosphere that you inhabit" (31 December 1827).

[74] Mary Shelley, *The Letters of Mary Wollstonecraft Shelley*, ed. Betty T. Bennett, 3 vols. (London: Johns Hopkins University Press, 1980–1988). In Shelley's letter to Jane Williams (22 April 1823), she refers to a conversation in which Byron, noting an increase in her piety, asked whether she was

teachings of Jesus, and occasionally she attended church services to reflect on them. More importantly, her view of God, made particularly evident in the visions she gives to Euthanasia, corresponds to Dante's Thomistic version of it in his *Paradiso*. Above a hierarchy of spirits, Dante's God is "Eternal Light," and the soul's greatest joy is to contemplate that light, indeed to merge with it, as Dante exclaims: "Thus my mind, all rapt, was gazing, fixed, still and intent, and ever enkindled with gazing. At that light one becomes such that it is impossible for him ever to consent that he should turn from it to another sight...."[75]

It is not surprising that Shelley, whose parents exalted reason, admires a heaven of eternal enlightenment, the absolute fulfillment of the mind. The God of light and beauty infinitely surpasses the anthropomorphic, frequently vindictive God she descries in her early essay, "A History of the Jews."[76] Still, Dante's God remains a personal Divinity, not simply a philosophical ideal. This God is a Being like Dante himself, who, according to Shelley, "regards the objects of the visible creation with...sympathy,"[77] offering solace in contemplation and guaranteeing the eternal survival of souls.

Such a God was crucial to a woman like Mary Shelley, tragically bereft of three children and her young husband, wounded to the point of emotional collapse by the betrayal of her friend Jane Williams, and

---

turning Christian. She answered that she was not, but if she were, she would not be "religious."

[75] The original of John Sinclair's translation reads:
  Così la mente mia, tutta sospesa,
  mirava fissa, immobile e attenta,
  e sempre di mirar faciesi accesa.
  A quella luce cotal si diventa,
  che volgersi da lei per altro aspetto
  è impossibil che mai si consenta. (canto 33, 97–102, 482)

[76] This manuscript essay can be found in appendix A of Blumberg's *Mary Shelley's Early Novels*. Blumberg offers a singularly enlightening discussion of it in chapter 2.

[77] Shelley, *Rambles*, 1:96.

denounced by others in her mature years.[78] These hardships, along
with her final illness, would have disheartened even the most unflagging optimist; they nearly devastated the pessimistic, depression-prone
Shelley. Muriel Spark expresses the views of many scholars in noting
that there seemed to be "some force within her [Shelley] that repelled
happiness or even an equitable state of well-being."[79] Indeed, Shelley's
correspondence is filled with lamentations like the one she utters to
Jane Williams in the letter referring to her increasing religiosity:
"vain wishes & dispair [sic] are my dayly [sic] occupations. I look
with inconceivable horror on the future...."[80] But she found strength
in her religious convictions, especially her belief in an afterlife with
her husband, as this emotional passage from her journal illustrates:

> Sorrow—Sorrow—Why am I here?—but that I am destined to
> be wiser, better & happier than I am—if it be not so—oh my
> God! quickly extinguish this spark of life, the tormented atom,
> this u [sic] wretched thing of aspiration & despair—but I have
> faith—a firm & true knowledge that I go to him, & so, not
> tearless, not alas! uncomplain[in]g—yet resigned, I nerve
> myself for the future.[81]

---

[78] Muriel Spark describes Shelley's love for Jane Williams as "obsessional"
(99) in *Child of Light: A Reassessment of Mary Wollstonecraft Shelley*
(Hadleigh, Essex: Tower Bridge, 1951). Mary had an emotional breakdown
when she learned that her friend had spread rumors that, just before his death,
Percy Shelley lavished attention on Jane because of the depressed Mary's cold
treatment of him. Later, friends like John Trelawny and Leigh Hunt accused
her of betraying her liberal husband when she edited possibly scandalous
portions of his works and made other publishing decisions to avoid public
shame. A social outcast during her unconventional life with her husband,
Mary longed for acceptance in her later years, both for her own sake and for
that of her only surviving child, Percy.

[79] Spark, *Child*, 120.

[80] Shelley, *Letters of Mary Wollstonecraft Shelley*, 23 April 1823.

[81] Shelley, *Letters of Mary Wollstonecraft Shelley*, 19 December 1822.

The complementarity of reason and faith brought to Shelley's life a wholeness in the midst of frequent losses. Like her heroine Euthanasia, she found spiritual nourishment in both study[82] and contemplation. As much as she prized the "intellectual liberty" Protestantism represented for her, in her philosophical sensibilities she resembled Medieval mystics or theologians more than the radical Protestants of her own day.[83] For Evangelicals in the Church of England and Dissenters, like the Methodists, who gave birth to the Evangelical spirit, scholarly pursuits had little relevance to a mission of awakening a simple but profound faith in Christ among the working and middle classes.[84]

---

[82] According to Emily Sunstein, *Mary Shelley: Romance and Reality* (Boston: Little, 1989), Shelley's impressive scholarship began in her early years under her father's tutelage. She read history, the Latin and Greek classics, Shakespeare, Milton, and the major European poets. In her description of these early studies, Sunstein notes that "Mary probably had at least as fine an education as any girl in England" (40). Her voracious appetite for reading only grew during her years with Shelley. Her reading list of 1815 alone includes among its thirty-three entries Gibbon's *History of the Decline and Fall of the Roman Empire*, Ovid's *Metamorphoses* in the original Latin, and Rousseau's *Confessions*. Cf. vol. 1:88–89 of *The Journals*.

[83] The same might be said for members of the Broad Church movement, indebted to intellectuals like Coleridge.

[84] Walter E. Houghton, *The Victorian Frame of Mind, 1830–1870* (New Haven: Yale University Press, 1957).

As Houghton notes in defining Evangelicalism in England, "There is no satisfactory term to apply to this movement. To call it Evangelical is to introduce a confusion between the movement as a whole and the Evangelical party in the English Church. Puritan is better, but the spirit of piety, reflected in the common designation of 'the religion of the heart,' marks a clear differentiation from Calvinism...Either the Wesleyan Movement or the Christian Revival would, I think, be better terms,...but Evangelical and Puritan have...long been used, and by the Victorians themselves" (228 note). Houghton goes on to comment that while eighteenth-century evangelicals like Isaac Milner, Thomas Scott, and John Newton were interested in theology, the "pietistic core of the Wesleyan movement soon came to the front" (125). For a discussion of the pervasiveness and influence of this movement—within secular life as well as in institutional Protestantism—see Houghton, chapter 5 (on anti-intellectualism) and chapter 10 (on earnestness). Cf. Richard Altick's excellent discussion of Evangelicalism in chapter 5 of *Victorian People and*

True, forebears of the reform movement inspired by Milton's *On Education* had established outstanding and progressive schools known as Dissenting Academies, which endured through 1796.[85] Moreover, John Wesley, John Wilberforce, Hannah More, and other early reform leaders were scholars who promoted education for the working class. Still, what characterized the reform movement during Mary Shelley's early life were missionary fervor, works of charity (including the establishment of charity schools), and campaigns against the slave trade. Needless to say, in the zealous dedication to practical Christianity— many elements of which would have won Shelley's support—there was little place for speculative theology.

Later in the century, as Walter Houghton notes, critics of Evangelicalism even accused the movement of anti-intellectualism. Mark Pattison, elected rector of Oxford's Lincoln College in 1861, was one such critic:

> Pattison traced "the professed contempt of all learned inquiry, which was a principle with the Evangelical school" to its protest against the intellectual, if too dry and rational, character of eighteenth-century apologetics: "Evangelism, in its origin, was a reaction against the High-Church 'evidences'; the insurrection of the heart and conscience of man against an arid orthodoxy. It insisted on a 'vital Christianity,' as against the Christianity of books. Its instinct was from the first against intelligence. No text found more favour with it than 'Not many wise, not many learned.'"[86]

No doubt Pattison's assessment needs to be considered in light of his High-Church biases. Moreover, it is a somewhat anachronistic interpretation of "the Evangelical school['s]" past attitudes in terms of

---

Ideas: A Companion for Modern Readers of Victorian Literature (New York: Norton, 1973).

[85] Anthony Armstrong, *The Church of England, the Methodists, and Society, 1700–1850* (Totowa NJ: Rowan and Littlefield, 1973) 41–42.

[86] Houghton, *Victorian Frame*, 125.

its mid-century disdain for the erudition of John Henry Newman and the Oxford Movement's tracts. As Houghton explains, the 1830s and 1840s were years of anxiety, when "the foundations of religious and political life were being shaken by new ideas, and Church and State seemed often in peril."[87] The remedy offered by Evangelicals was the Bible. Deemed infallible on "all questions," it eliminated the need to seek truth from any other written source.[88] Pattison's assessment also fails to take into account intelligent women in the early Evangelical movement who interpreted Scripture in a radically new way. In *The Reader's Repentance*, Christine Krueger demonstrates that in their writing, reformers like Hannah More and Charlotte Elizabeth Tonna were "revising and subverting the dominant Christian ideology" about the subordinate role of women in society in order to "re-envision women's lives and represent them authoritatively."[89] Many such reformers, like Shelley herself, emphasized rationality as the means to authority for women, since emotionalism left them vulnerable to manipulation and abuse.

Still, if "anti-intellectual" is too severe a label for Protestant reformers of the early nineteenth century, we might venture to say that even intellectuals like John Wesley and Hannah More (after her conversion) would consider self-indulgent—if not altogether wasted— a life devoted to the intellect, as Mary Shelley's was, nourished by the work of Homer, Virgil, Dante, enlightenment philosophers, and the atheist-radical Percy Bysshe Shelley. The Evangelical mission was a

---

[87] Houghton, *Victorian Frame*, 127.

[88] Houghton, *Victorian Frame*, 126.

[89] Christine L. Krueger, *The Reader's Repentance: Women Preachers, Women Writers, and Nineteenth-Century Social Discourse* (Chicago: Chicago University Press, 1992) 9. Krueger emphasizes that in their writing, women reformers challenged patriarchy by means of the very Bible that was evoked in justifying its authority, thereby "calling on male readers to repent" (6). A similar claim can be made for Mary Wollstonecraft, who appealed to reason to justify attributing it to women. The same sort of rationale explains Shelley's appropriation of Catholicism's discourse on faith and intellect, discussed below, even as she attacks the oppressive patriarchy of the Roman Church.

practical one that relied on confessional faith, dedication, and
organizational strategies—all in the service of charitable works and
the winning of souls. Purely intellectual pursuits were, at best,
irrelevant and, at worst, misguided substitutions for Christian service
and the reading of Scripture.[90]

Conversely, the Roman Church had a long tradition of encouraging
study of the humanities and had canonized mystics and scholars, as
well as theologians like Aquinas, who expanded the Christian faith
into volumes of esoteric discourse rather than attempting to condense
it to a simple profession. The Church had championed the life of the
mind, which brings to faith definition while probing its sublimity, as
Dante's *Paradiso* demonstrates. In direct opposition to anti-intellectualism, the Church formalized its traditional teaching in *Dei Filius*,
a document of the First Vatican Council (1870):

> Not only can there be no conflict between faith and reason,
> they also support each other since right reason demonstrates
> the foundations of faith and, illumined by its light, pursues the
> science of divine things, while faith frees and protects reason
> from errors and provides it with manifold insights. It is
> therefore far remote from the truth to say that the Church
> opposes the study of human arts and sciences; on the contrary,
> she supports and promotes them in many ways.[91]

Besides this harmonization of faith and reason, Catholicism offered
another kind of integration, which also must have inspired Shelley as
she planned *Valperga*. Her husband describes it well in his

---

[90] The reading of Scripture was seen as an activity requiring no formal
training. As Krueger notes in *Reader's Repentance*, "Evangelicals believed
scripture to be radically accessible. Attacking the mystification of scripture
that demanded of 'legitimate' readers expertise available to a select few, they
maintained that God would reveal to babes what he concealed from the wise"
(8).

[91] *The Christian Faith*, in *The Doctrinal Documents of the Catholic
Church*, ed. by S. J. Dupuis and J. Neuner (Dublin: The Mercier Press, 1976)
49.

introduction to *The Cenci*, a play written just before Shelley started her novel on Castruccio and based upon a historical document she had transcribed for him.[92] As an apology for what may seem "to a Protestant apprehension" an "unnatural" intimacy the Catholic characters, even the evil ones, seem to share with God, the author explains that

[R]eligion in Italy is not, as in Protestant countries, a cloak to be worn on particular days; or a passport which those who do not wish to be railed at carry with them to exhibit; or a gloomy passion for penetrating the impenetrable mysteries of our being...Religion coexists, as it were, in the mind of an Italian Catholic with a faith in that of which all men have the most certain knowledge. It is interwoven with the whole fabric of life. It is adoration, faith, submission, penitence, blind admiration; not a rule of moral conduct. It has no necessary connexion with any one virtue. The most atrocious villain may be rigidly devout, and without any shock to established faith, confess himself to be so. Religion pervades intensely the whole frame of society, and is according to the temper of the mind which it inhabits, a passion, a persuasion, an excuse, a refuge; never a check.[93]

In the language of Catholic theology, we might understand such a phenomenon as the union of grace and nature, regardless of how corrupted nature has become in specific individuals. Shelley's own acceptance of such a complexity might very well explain why the heroine of *Valperga* refuses to surrender her faith in the face of hypocrisy and cruelty on the part of Christian leaders and priests—

[92] Percy Bysshe Shelley used Mary's transcription of a history of Beatrice Cenci, which she found in the archives of Palazzo Cenci in Rome. As Mary notes in her 1839 preface to the play in *The Poetical Works of Percy Bysshe Shelley*, *The Cenci*—whose fifth act she praised—was the only one of her husband's works she discussed with him during composition.
[93] Percy Bysshe Shelley, *Shelley's Prose and Poetry*, ed. by Donald H. Reiman and Sharon B.Powers (New York: Norton, 1977) 241–42.

why, perceiving God even in the most corrupted natures, she gravitates toward those who are fallen.

In the tragedies she endured, in the magnitude of her depression, Mary Shelley knew the despair experienced by Beatrice the prophetess and Beatrice's "analogue" in *The Cenci*.[94] In her persistent faith, however, she clung to the example she created in her heroine Euthanasia, a character who might have filled a role missing in *The Cenci*, according to its preface: "Revenge, retaliation, atonement, are pernicious mistakes," while "the fit return to make to the most enormous injuries is kindness and forbearance, and a resolution to convert the injurer from his dark passions by peace and love."[95]

Of course, the idealistic Euthanasia is doomed from the beginning, since Shelley remains faithful to the facts of history about the ruthless Castruccio. Like the liberty of Florence, Euthanasia is the victim of a cruel tyrant. However, as William Walling correctly argues, Shelley intends *Valperga* as a critique of the traditional understanding of success and heroism. Like some of her Romantic contemporaries disillusioned by Napoleon's exploits, she rejected the Machiavellianism embodied in him and tyrants before him, like the Caesars and Alexander the Great. The purpose of *Valperga*, Walling contends, is to show the "essential emptiness" of Castruccio's life and the superiority of "liberty and of the domestic virtues and of the absence of personal ambition"—all embodied in Euthanasia, who tells Castruccio to "love obscurity."[96] Walling argues that even though Euthanasia is "reduced to a captured member of the utterly defeated republican party, she can still assert to the victorious Castruccio the moral point of his ostensibly successful career: that his life is 'miserable' and 'unworthy'— while Castruccio, driven for the moment into the clarity of genuine insight, can do nothing more than agree."[97] Thus, the novel ends with

---

[94] James Rieger, "Shelley's Paterin Beatrice," *Studies in Romanticism* 4 (1965): 178. In this essay, Rieger identifies Sismondi's *Histoire des Republiques Italiennes du Moyen Age* as a source common to *The Cenci* (1819) and *Valperga*.

[95] "The Cenci," *Shelley's Prose and Poetry*, 240.

[96] Walling, *Mary Shelley*, 70.

[97] Walling, *Mary Shelley*, 70.

the death of the Countess since, "when the moral standard of *Valperga* vanishes in the person of Euthanasia, Castruccio's career becomes meaningless."[98]

The story of Euthanasia, like the history of tyranny, is certainly tragic. However, Euthanasia, though finally imprisoned and drowned at sea, is morally victorious because she never ceases to live by her principles. Instead of being borne to Ghibelline Sicily, she is borne to her death, and in her death—as her name suggests—she possesses forever the peace she has promoted throughout her life. Like Dante's beautiful guide to Paradise (the namesake of whom the Paterin Beatrice falls short), Euthanasia expresses Shelley's own idealism. [99] No wonder in describing Titian's "Assumption of the Virgin" Shelley declares, "Such a picture, and the 'Paradiso' of Dante as a commentary, is the sublimest achievement of Catholicism."

---

[98] Walling, *Mary Shelley*, 60.

[99] Conversely, Blumberg argues that Mary Shelley presents in Euthanasia a critique of inflexible idealism, that the Countess of Valperga is as obsessed with principles as Castruccio is with power and both kinds of obsession are destructive. Blumberg bases this conclusion on Euthanasia's resemblance to Mary's husband whose own inflexible idealism Mary could not accept. However, I find no evidence in *Valperga* itself or in any remarks made by Shelley about her novel that Euthanasia is intended to be seen as anything but heroic. And, as Emily Sunstein asserts—though she also claims that Euthanasia idolizes principles—"Mary Shelley never discarded the Godwininian assumption that to be conquered by emotion is to have failed" (190).

3

LITTLE NELL, CATHOLICISM, AND DICKENS'S INVESTIGATION OF DEATH

LITTLE NELL, THE heroine of Dickens's 1840–1841 novel, *The Old Curiosity Shop*, is an angelic girl who becomes ill after leading her gambling grandfather to a rural refuge, far away from the temptations of the city.[1] The prospect of her death terrified her middle

---

[1] This chapter concerns only the movements of Little Nell, which form a fairly simple plot. In London, Little Nell and her Grandfather Trent, run a shop full of junk and old curiosities. When Trent's compulsive gambling makes him indebted to Daniel Quilp, a grotesque and lecherous shipbreaker, Little Nell convinces her grandfather to flee to the countryside, far away from the city's dangers. Keeping one step ahead of Quilp, the pair encounter a number of people—both kind and threatening—along their desperate journey. These characters include a helpful schoolmaster, who introduces Nell to a dying boy, and Codlin and Short, puppeteers who plan to cheat Nell and her grandfather out of the lone gold coin in their possession. Nell fears her grandfather's mental instability as much as she does those who might exploit the two of them, and her anxiety persists throughout their stay with Mrs. Jarley, who employs Nell to give tours of her waxworks show. When Nell overhears her grandfather plotting with two thieves to steal from Mrs. Jarley, Nell drags him away through a filthy factory town, where they must resort to begging. Nell's health begins declining when another kind schoolmaster takes the pair to his village, where they set up house in a ruined monastery. Her health worsening, Nell gives tours of the church in Tong, befriends a sexton and an old bachelor, and spends her time contentedly ruminating over ruins

nineteenth-century fans. William Macready, who begged his friend
Dickens to spare the child, dreaded reading the installment of *The Old
Curiosity Shop* containing the tragic scene. Anxious crowds on a New
York City dock called to the ship bearing that fateful number, "Is
Little Nell Dead?" Dickens appears to appease his sentimental
audience—despite his admitted "Nellicide"—for although the young
heroine dies, "the physical realities of death," as Malcolm Andrews
notes in his introduction to the novel, "seem to disappear for Nell."[2]
On closer inspection, however, one discovers that grim reminders of
mortality encompass Dickens's spiritualized protagonist throughout
The Old Curiosity Shop to such an extent that she becomes identified
with them. Moreover, these solemn, overwhelmingly medieval vestiges
suggest that Dickens explores not only mortality by means of his
heroine, but a vision of mortality that is surprisingly Roman Catholic
as well.

Typically, Dickens expressed vehement disdain for the
unenlightened and oppressive "Romish" religion. Perhaps the first
published evidence of such an attitude is found in his novel *Barnaby
Rudge*, which appeared in 1841. Although this novel descries the
fanatical Protestantism behind the Gordon riots and sympathetically
depicts the Catholic underdog Haredale, it ends with a description of
Haredale in a monastery, where, after a life of "merciless penitence,"

---

and the graves she has taken to tending. Growing to love Nell, the whole
village hopes her health will return. But Dickens has destined her to die and be
apotheosized in the poetry of chapter 71. Grandfather Trent's death follows
close upon Nell's.

Aside from the colorful characters encountered by Nell on her journey, the
most enchanting aspects of *The Old Curiosity Shop* for many of today's
readers are found in the subplot, in which a fascinating cast of comic
characters either assist or oppose Quilp. These include Quilp's associates
Sampson and Sally Brass, their abused servant, the Marchioness (originally
intended by Dickens to be Quilp and Sally's illegitimate daughter), and the
loveable ne'er-do-well Dick Swiveller, who eventually marries the
Marchioness.

[2] Malcolm Andrews, "Introduction," in *The Old Curiosity Shop*, by
Charles Dickens (London: Penguin, 1972) 29.

he takes the vows that "shut him out from nature and its kind until the day of his burial in the gloomy cloisters."[3] Then, when Newman's Tract 90 brought the Tractarians under official ban later that year by arguing for the compatibility of the 39 Articles and Roman Catholicism, Dickens apparently forgot even his qualified sympathy for victims of extremist Protestant bigotry as he became swept up in a wave of national indignation. In an 1843 letter to Douglas Jerrold, he announced his intention to write a "little history of England for my boy" that would steer him from "any conservative or High Church notions."[4] In the *Examiner*, a month after his letter to Jerrold, Dickens launched his celebrated lampoon, "Report to the Commissioners Appointed to Inquire into the Condition of the Persons Variously Engaged in the University of Oxford." In this article, he scoffed at those who would identify "Religion and Salvation" with "Lighted Candles."[5]

Pictures from Italy, which records the impressions from Dickens's tour of the Catholic country from 1844 to 1845, is perhaps his most comprehensive condemnation of Roman Catholicism's evils. They include meddlesome and manipulative clerics, full of "sloth, deceit, and intellectual torpor";[6] the superstitious veneration of statues and "sprawling effigies of maudlin monks";[7] and the "unmeaning degrad-

---

[3] Charles Dickens, *Barnaby Rudge*, 1841, in *The Oxford Illustrated Dickens* (Oxford: Oxford University Press, 1954) 628.

[4] Charles Dickens, *The Letters of Charles Dickens*, 1841-1865, vols. 1-2, Madeline House, et.al. The Pilgrim Edition (Oxford: Clarendon, 1965-1999) 482. Indeed, *A Child's History of England*, which did not actually take shape until 1851 when it began appearing in *Household Words*, condemns monasteries for their manipulation of believers with questionable and gruesome relics, popes for their subversion of English autonomy, and the misguided William Laud, Archbishop of Canterbury, for bringing in "an immensity of bowing and candle-snuffing" (*Letters*, 3:457).

[5] Charles Dickens, *Miscellaneous Papers, Plays, and Poems*, ed. B. W. Matz, Centenary, 36 vols. (London: Chapman and Hall, 1911) 35:105.

[6] Charles Dickens, *Pictures from Italy*, 1846, ed. David Paroissien (New York: Coward, McCann, and Geoghegan, 1974) 79.

[7] Dickens, *Pictures*, 85.

ation" imposed upon the faithful by many religious rituals.[8] Predicta-
bly, the *Dublin Review* denounced *Pictures* for such negative charac-
terizations of Catholicism. As David Paroissien convincingly argues,
Clarkson Stanfield, who had agreed to illustrate the travel book,
declined to do so after reading the increasingly anti-Catholic descriptions—probably because of his own Catholicism as well as his
association with Catholic Bishop Wiseman, who advocated restoring
the Catholic hierarchy to England. Dickens's anti-Catholic sentiments
find further expression in his 1849 and 1851 letters to Angela Burdett
Coutts, condemning the "pernicious and unnatural" nature of Puseyite Sisterhoods[9]—which he mocked in *Bleak House*[10]—and characterizing Catholicism as "that curse upon the world."[11] The latter condemnation was inspired by the Papal Bull of 1850, which reestablished Catholic dioceses in England. Dickens's formal response to
this move was an article that same year in *Household Words*: "A
Crisis in the Affairs of Mr. John Bull." In it he declares that "the Bulls
of Rome are not only the enemies of our family [England] but of the
whole human race."[12]

In view of such extensive evidence, the suggestion that Dickens
actually admired anything or anyone Catholic might seem absurd.
Indeed, on the basis of some of the above documents, Humphry House
concludes that "[s]uspicion of the moral, social, and political work of
Catholicism was not compensated in [Dickens's] mind by any sympathy for sacramental ideas or any understanding of the need for
spiritual authority."[13] Edgar Johnson, John Butt, and Kathleen
Tillotson echo such a judgment, and more recently, Andrew Sanders
argues in *Charles Dickens Resurrectionist* that the Catholic revival

---

[8] Dickens, *Pictures*, 208.

[9] Dickens, *Letters*, 5:541–42.

[10] Susan Shatto, *The Companion to Bleak House* (London: Unwin
Hyman, 1988) 85.

[11] Charles Dickens, *Letters from Charles Dickens to Angela Burdett-
Coutts, 1841–1865*, ed. Edgar Johnson (London: Jonathan Cape, 1953) 186.

[12] Dickens, *Miscellaneous*, 35:274–80.

[13] Humphrey House, *The Dickens World* (London: Oxford University
Press, 1941) 128.

seems to have "enraged [Dickens] rather than to have engaged his mind."[14] Yet, despite Dickens's anti-Catholicism, which grew with increasing threats from Oxford and Rome, the crusader against ignorance saw himself as a critic not of the Roman Catholic faith, but only of a blind acceptance of its frequently oppressive practices and ministers.[15] Dickens explains his position in the preface to *Pictures*:

I hope I am not likely to be misunderstood by Professors of the Roman Catholic faith, on account of anything contained in these pages. I have done my best, in one of my former productions, to do justice to them; and I trust, in this, they will do justice to me. When I mention any exhibition that impressed me as absurd or disagreeable, I do not seek to connect it, or recognize it as necessarily connected with, any essentials of their creed. When I treat of the ceremonies of Holy Week, I merely treat of their effect, and do not challenge the good and learned Dr. Wiseman's interpretation of their meaning. When I hint a dislike of nunneries for young girls who abjure the world before they have ever proved or known it; or doubt the *ex officio* sanctity of all Priests and Friars; I do no more than many conscientious Catholics both abroad and at home.[16]

Dickens praised conscientious Catholics like St. Charles Borromeo—"[a] charitable doctor to the sick, a munificent friend to the poor" who acted "not in any spirit of blind bigotry, but as the bold opponent of enormous abuses in the Roman church"[17]—and the

---

[14] Andrew Sanders, *Charles Dickens Resurrectionist* (New York: St. Martin's, 1982) xi.

[15] Jane R. Cohen makes a similar point in *Charles Dickens and His Original Illustrators* (Columbus: Ohio State University Press, 1980) 182.

[16] Dickens, *Pictures*, 36–37.

[17] Dickens, *Pictures*, 137–38.

martyrs of the early church who lived in the dark catacombs "for years together, ministering to the rest, and preaching truth, and hope, and comfort, from the rude altars, that bear witness to their fortitude at this hour...."[18] While in Italy, he even dreamed that his beloved sister-in-law Mary Hogarth, who had died in his arms in 1837, appeared to him from the grave solely to urge his conversion to Catholicism. When he asks her whether Catholicism is the best religion— "perhaps it makes one think of God oftener, and believe in him more steadily?"—Mary, "full of such heavenly tenderness for me, that I felt as if my heart would break," answers, "[F]or *you* it is the best!"[19]

Like this dream, several passages of *Pictures* attest to Dickens's attraction to the Catholic expressions of faith that make "one think of God oftener." Consider, for instance, his elaborate description of San Marco:

> A grand and dreamy structure, of immense proportions; golden with old mosaics; redolent of perfumes; dim with the smoke of incense; costly in treasure of precious stones and metals, glittering through iron bars; holy with the bodies of deceased saints; rainbow-hued with windows of stained glass; dark with carved woods and coloured marbles; obscure in its vast heights, and lengthened distances; shining with silver lamps and winking lights; unreal, fantastic, solemn inconceivable throughout.[20]

Without question, the somberness of the cathedral fascinates rather than repels him, the building sanctified—rather than degraded—by those entombed within it, by the antiquity of the art and the darkness of the atmosphere. This church and others like it in Venice intrigue Dickens especially because they hauntingly juxtapose life and death: "Pictures were there, replete with such enduring beauty and expres-

---

[18] Dickens, *Pictures,* 187.
[19] Dickens, *Letters,* 4:196.
[20] Dickens, *Pictures,* 122.

sion: with such passion, truth, and power: that they seemed so many young and fresh realities among a host of spectres."[21]

Dickens allows himself to explore such rich Catholic sensibility in much greater depth in *The Old Curiosity Shop*, completed four years before his trip to Italy and several months before "the waves of Oxford" were felt in England.[22] If this novel contained no other allusions to Catholicism, George Cattermole's illustrations—which Dickens helped plan and to which he gave final approval[23]—would in themselves suggest his intent to evoke the somber spirit of the Roman religion. In the very first illustration, two nuns surrounded by dismembered suits of mail, battle axes, and grisly masks attend the sleeping Nell. On her pillow Nell inclines her head toward the nuns, and they kneel in prayer while fixing their eyes on her, as though praying for her soul. A crucifix, perched against Nell's makeshift nightstand, completes the pious triangle. All of the illustrations of the curiosity shop duplicate this Catholic atmosphere. They not only exhibit specifically Catholic religious articles like the crucifix, which reappears in the second chapter's plate, but they also display the medieval suits of armor and weaponry Dickens associates with Catholic surroundings, as he demonstrates later in the novel when he places them in the cloister of the Gothic church at Tong. The illustrations also explicitly link Nell to the Virgin Mary. In the plate titled "At Rest," the deceased Nell is laid out on a bed whose headboard prominently displays the Madonna. And the final illustration of cloud-sheathed angels bearing the dead Nell to heaven appropriately resembles traditional portrayals of the Virgin's Assumption.

Of course, the text itself inspires Cattermole's plates. In the beginning of the novel we read of "the old dark murky rooms" of the shop and their "gaunt suits of mail with their ghostly silent air."[24] As

---

[21] Dickens, *Pictures*, 125.

[22] John Butt and Kathleen Tillotson, *Dickens at Work* (London: Methuen, 1957) 84.

[23] Cohen, *Charles Dickens*, 75:125–34.

[24] Charles Dickens, *The Old Curiosity Shop*, 1840–1841, in *The Oxford Illustrated Dickens* (Oxford: Oxford University Press, 1951) 14.

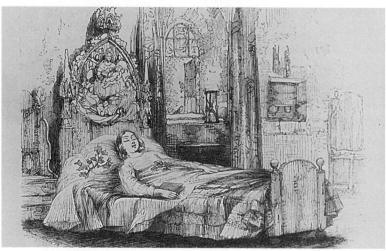

George Cattermole's illustrations. Above, "The Child in her Gentle Slumber;" below, "At Rest."

the tale advances, Nell gravitates toward grotesque settings that either suggest or explicitly refer to Catholic influences. Mrs. Jarley's waxworks, which include a nun "telling her beads," anticipate the religious statuary and "bodies of deceased saints" in the Roman churches that will later fascinate Dickens during his travels in Italy. More significantly, Nell achieves her final peace in "a church [that] had been built many hundreds of years ago, and had once had a convent or monastery attached."[25] "It is a very beautiful place!" Nell declares of this medieval haven, whose oak furnishings display the "rich carving from old monkish stalls."[26] The scene describing Nell's tour of the premises, especially of the ancient crypt, vividly conveys the spirit of Nell's refuge and her sense of belonging there:

[The bachelor] took her down into the old crypt, now a mere dull vault, and showed her how it had been lighted up in the time of the monks, and how, amid lamps depending from the roof, and swinging censers exhaling scented odours, and habits glittering with gold and silver, and pictures, and precious stuffs, and jewels all flashing and glistening through the low arches, the chaunt of aged voices had been many a time heard there, at midnight, in old days, while hooded figures knelt and prayed around, and told their rosaries of beads. Thence, he took her above-ground again, and showed her, high up in the old walls, small galleries, where the nuns had been wont to glide along—dimly seen in their dark dresses so far off—or to pause like gloomy shadows, listening to the prayers. He showed her too, how the warriors, whose figures rested on the tombs, had worn those rotting scraps of armour up above—how this had been a helmet, and that a shield, and that a gauntlet...All that he told the child she treasured in her mind; and sometimes, when she awoke at night from dreams of those old times, and rising from her bed looked out at the dark church,

---

[25] Dickens, *Old Curiosity*, 348.
[26] Dickens, *Old Curiosity*, 386.

she almost hoped to see the windows lighted up, and hear the organ's swell, and sound of voices, on the rushing wind.[27]

It is in this place of "gloomy shadows" and "rotting scraps of armour" that Nell becomes, like the Virgin Mary engraved on her bed, finally elevated to the level of legendary. Just as the Virgin lives on in the popular Marian cult that celebrates her Assumption, so Nell gains immortality in the great death-bed description in which she is preserved exactly as she was in life:

And still her former self lay there, unaltered in this change. Yes. The old fireside had smiled upon that same sweet face; it had passed, like a dream, through haunts of misery and care; at the door of the poor schoolmaster on the summer evening, before the furnace fire upon the old wet night, at the still bedside of the dying boy [an acquaintance], there had been the same mild lovely look. So shall we know the angels in their majesty, after death.[28]

What is it about the somber Catholic sensibility that captivates Dickens, and what exactly does his wonder have to do with introducing the transcendental Nell to mortality? In large part the answer to this question lies in Catholicism's understanding of suffering, derived in turn from its incarnational theology. The Catholic revival, or Oxford Movement, which began in 1833 with John Keble's Assize Sermon on National Apostasy, was in full swing by the time Dickens started writing *The Old Curiosity Shop* in 1840. In reaction to the Evangelicals who deemphasized the historical aspects of Christian faith (specifically, Christ's incarnation and continual sacramental communion with believers in an historical institution), the Oxford Movement promoted the "incarnational theology of

---

[27] Dickens, *Old Curiosity*, 401–402.
[28] Dickens, *Old Curiosity*, 539.

Church and the sacraments," according to Eugene Fairweather.[29] In his study of the Oxford Movement, Fairweather explains this characterization of its mission:

It was, [the Tractarians] insisted, supremely fitting that the life-giving flesh and blood of God's Eternal Son who was made man should be communicated through fleshly signs wrought by human hands. Indeed they were prepared to argue that the failure to recognize the "extensions of the Incarnation" stemmed from a feeble apprehension of the twofold truth of the Incarnation itself—on the one hand, that man's salvation comes from God alone; on the other, that God's saving action really penetrates and transforms man's world and man's life.[30]

In short, God works only through and in the material world. Christ's incarnation validated human flesh in one historical moment, and his sacramental presence continues to validate it (for example, communicants eat and drink, those confirmed are touched by the bishop, recipients of extreme unction have the five senses anointed). In his passion and death, Christ also validated human suffering through which, according to Catholic theology, believers participate mystically in the act of redemption. The sacraments ritualize such a salvific mystical union.

As he wrote about the angelic Nell, Dickens remembered his young sister-in-law, Mary Hogarth, with whom he had formed a strangely intimate bond. The devastating grief he endured after her death revived. Catholicism's validation of suffering promised him relief, perhaps once and for all. It is not altogether astonishing, then—even considering his criticism of the Roman religion—that when he meditates on mortality, he evokes Catholicism, particularly when it figured so prominently in the religious discourse of his time and, as this study demonstrates, influenced literary discourse as well. How-

---

[29] Eugene R. Fairweather, ed., *The Oxford Movement* (New York: Oxford University Press, 1964) 11.

[30] Fairweather, ed., *Oxford Movement,* 11.

ever, as much as Dickens explores Catholic allusion, he cannot in the final analysis accept the Catholic understanding of suffering as the means to redemption. This becomes clear upon comparing the Virgin Mary and Nell in their roles as feminine figures of sorrow.

The sorrowful Virgin—often depicted in paintings and sculpture with her "breasts stuck full of swords, arranged in a half-circle like a modern fan,"[31] as Dickens himself notes—exemplifies mystical union with Christ through suffering. That the Virgin shares her son's destiny to suffer is announced in the Gospel of Luke by the prophet Simeon. After foretelling her infant's passion and death, he predicts that "a sword will pierce through your own soul also." Popular piety has dwelt on her agony at the foot of the cross since the medieval composition of the *Stabat Mater*, which crystallized the Virgin's role as a *Mater Dolorosa* par excellence. The following excerpt is from one of the many variations of this lyric:

> "Stond wel, Moder, under rode,
> Bihold thy child wyth gladde mood;
> Blithe, Moder, myghtestow be."
> "Sone, how may I blithe stonde?
> I see thy feet, I see thyne honde
> Nayled to the harde tree."

> "Moder, do wey thy wepyng,
> I thole this deeth for mannes thyng;
> For my gilt ne thole I non."
> "Sone, I fele the dethese stounde;
> That swerd is at myn hertes grounde,
> That me bihete Simeon."

> "Moder, rewe upon thy bern;
> Though wassh awey the blody teren:
> It doth me worse thanne my deeth."
> "Sone, how myghte I teres werne?

---

[31] Dickens, *Pictures*, 188.

I see the blody woundes erne
From thyn herte to my feet."[32]

In this dialogue with the spirit of her dead son, the Virgin absorbs the graphic details of his death: his feet and hands nailed to the wood, blood running from his wounds to her feet, even his pierced heart. The Virgin's healthy sense of sorrow and anger indicates that she confronts the horrible scene before her and struggles to make sense of it. She even scoffs at her son's irrational suggestion that she stand "wyth gladde mood" under the tortured body of her child, protesting that she herself feels death because of the sword in her own heart, that her child's death "doth me worse thanne my deeth" since she cannot wash her bloody tears away.

Yet, for all her reluctance to be "gladde" at the death of her son and her own participation in it—even though suffering redeems—the lyric's final verses, summarized in the phrase "Blessed be thou, quene of hevene!," acclaim the sanctity of the Virgin. Such a benediction suggests that, despite her son's wish to alleviate her hurt, she had done well to *feel* her misery, to face rather than romanticize the sorrow accompanying her suffering. After all, it is through experiencing the limits of the human condition that one attains final bliss.[33] In shaping Nell, the introspective girl reared in a gloomy curiosity shop who leads tours of waxworks and graveyards, Dickens evokes the sorrowful spirit of the Virgin. We often find that Nell's "courage [has] drooped," that she is "fearful," "alarmed," "frightened and repelled," and filled with "uneasiness" because of the dangers threatening her beloved grandfather. Yet Nell's frequent meditations on death reveal just how strongly she departs from her Marian prototype. Consider her inability to face the thought of her grandfather's death:

---

[32] *One Hundred Middle English Lyrics*, ed. Robert D. Stevick (Indianapolis: Bobbs-Merrill, 1964) 29–30.

[33] Several Tractarians also noted the Virgin's association with redemptive suffering, particularly as it is commemorated in the mysteries of the rosary. See, for example, the selection from William George Ward's "Ideal of a Christian Church Considered in Comparison with Existing Practice," in chapter 3 of Fairweather.

[L]ooking out into the street again, [she] would perhaps see a man passing with a coffin on his back, and two or three others silently following him to a house where somebody lay dead; which made her shudder...If [her grandfather] were to die—if sudden illness had happened to him, and he were never to come again, alive—if, one night, ...he should kill himself and his blood come creeping, creeping, on the ground to her own bedroom door! These thoughts were too horrible to dwell upon, and again she would have recourse to the street.[34]

Just as the graphic details of death begin to overwhelm her, Nell flees from them. Admittedly, a fourteen-year-old has less capacity for facing the thoughts of death than does an adult, but without hesitating, Dickens gives Nell a woman's responsibilities, suggests her identification with the Virgin, and surrounds her with constant reminders of death (in the curiosity shop, the waxworks, the medieval church). It is as though he is challenging her to confront her agony. In light of this, we are left to wonder why he cannot also give her some of the Virgin's maturity so she might confront the unpleasant inevitability of her grandfather's death.

When Nell is not trying to prevent herself from having thoughts of death altogether, she romanticizes them, as she does after the death of the sick boy whom she has befriended. Just as she begins to face her loss, Nell's thoughts transcend the grim details of his death: "[T]he sad scene she had witnessed, was not without its lesson of content and gratitude; of content with the lot which left her health and freedom...[and] [h]er dreams were of the little scholar: not coffined and covered up, but mingling with angels, and smiling happily. The sun darting his cheerful rays into the room, awoke her."[35]

The incongruity of feeling "content and gratitude" at the death of a friend is remarkable, as is the unwillingness to contemplate the details of a funeral for one who has never lived away from funereal

---

[34] Dickens, *Old Curiosity*, 69–70.
[35] Dickens, *Old Curiosity*, 194.

surroundings. In fact, when Nell sets out to contemplate the signifi-
cance of the church's tombs (after Dickens's repeated intimations that
she herself will soon die), she resorts to the same escapism. "[F]inding
herself alone in that solemn building," she decides the air—though
"redolent of earth and mould" and "laden with decay"—had been
"purified by time of all its grosser particles" and stops at the tombs:

> The child sat down, in this old, silent place, among the stark
> figures on the tombs—they made it more quiet here, than
> elsewhere, to her fancy—and gazing round with a feeling of
> awe, tempered with a calm delight, felt that now she was
> happy, and at rest....What if the spot awakened thoughts of
> death! Die who would, it would still remain the same; these
> sights and sounds would still go on, as happily as ever. It would
> be no pain to sleep amidst them.[36]

This representative passage highlights the discrepancy between
Nell's emphatically Catholic context and her conspicuously un-
Catholic response to suffering and death, her unwillingness to
contemplate their gory details, to admit her own fears, to investigate
the *implications* of death for her grandfather or for herself. Such a
discrepancy, I would argue, reveals Dickens's own inner conflict: he
wants to confront mortality as Catholicism does, but not under the
conditions of Catholicism—that suffering is the means to redemption.
Perhaps, if Dickens could acknowledge the possibility of mystical
union with Christ (or even the promise of heaven) in suffering, he
could glorify it, but such a doctrine is egregiously absent from *The Old
Curiosity Shop*. As several critics have noted, Nell's references to
"Good Spirits" guarding the earth and to her sense of "drawing near
to heaven" are mere gestures toward the existence of the supernatural.[37] Reading this novel, one finds an afterlife only in the memory of the living, where one comes to dwell not through suffering, but

---

[36] Dickens, *Old Curiosity*, 397–98.
[37] One example of such critics is Steven Marcus. See chapter 4 of his
Dickens from Pickwick to Dombey (New York: Norton, 1965).

through good actions. "Do you think there are no deeds, far from here, in which these dead may be best remembered?" the schoolmaster says to reassure Nell, adding, "[T]here may be people busy in the world, at this instant, in whose good actions and good thoughts these very graves...are the chief instruments."[38] He concludes his sermon by characterizing such deeds as "the redeeming actions of the world."

If the Catholic context for suffering cannot ultimately serve Dickens as a philosophical approach, it has at least provided him with abundant imaginative material. Taken as he was with the spirit of Catholicism in *The Old Curiosity Shop*, he turned once again to a somber Catholic subject in *Barnaby Rudge*, his next novel, and within a few years documented his fascination with Italian religiosity in *Pictures from Italy*, in which he provides the vivid description (quoted above) of San Marco: "a grand and dreamy structure...glittering through iron bars; holy with the bodies of deceased saints." Perhaps descriptions like this one allowed Dickens to exorcise Catholicism from his imagination before the efforts of Oxford and Rome grew to such audacious proportions that his liberal English spirit could no longer tolerate such fantasies.

---

[38] Dickens, *Old Curiosity*, 406.

4

"THE SHELTER OF AUTHORITY": FRANCES TROLLOPE'S CONCESSION TO ROME IN *FATHER EUSTACE*

FOR SEVERAL YEARS after 1845, when John Henry Newman scandalized his Anglican compatriots by converting to Roman Catholicism, a cadre of novelists made it their mission to warn readers of Babylon's seductive glitter.[1] One of these novelists was Frances Milton Trollope, probably now best known for her stinging travel book of 1827, *Domestic Manners of the Americans*, but popular in the 1830s, -40s, and -50s for over thirty novels produced at a prodigious pace, all after her fiftieth birthday. Her contribution to the anti-Catholic crusade was *Father Eustace: A Tale of the Jesuits*, published in 1847. This was not Trollope's first anti-Catholic novel, being preceded by *The Abbess* more than a decade earlier, but it was the first in which she took Catholicism seriously. *The Abbess* was a Gothic romance whose formulaic melodrama—complete with pregnant nun, live burial, and monkish villain—simply exploited exotic elements in a religion nationally despised. Though not completely above such tactics, *Father Eustace* carefully examines the

---

[1] See Margaret M. Maison's discussion of "Cautionary Tales for Higher Anglicans," in *The Victorian Vision: Studies in the Religious Novel* (New York: Sheed and Ward, 1961) chap. 3, pp. 55–77.

Catholic sensibilities of the Protestant heroine and the sympathetic Catholic antagonist whom she loves. In this novel, I propose to show, Trollope identifies with both heroine and antagonist and creates a fictional model for reconciling their sensibilities with the Protestant independence she cherished.

As the full title of *Father Eustace* indicates, the novel's Catholic representatives are Jesuits, strongly identified in the English imagination with the Church of Rome itself—and with good reason. The Society of Jesus, founded by Ignatius of Loyola in 1534, quickly made its mission the defeat of the newly emerging Protestant movement.[2] As champions of Catholicism, the Jesuits formally vowed obedience to the Pope, distinguishing themselves from other religious orders who vowed obedience only to their own superiors. The Jesuits came to England in 1580, some twenty years after the country declared itself a Protestant nation in the Acts of Uniformity and Supremacy and ten years after the Catholic John Felton nailed a Bull of Excommunication on the door of the Bishop of London. They were immediately suspected as political insurgents and then outlawed altogether in 1585, when they continued working undercover at the risk of execution for high treason.[3] The image of Jesuit as spy crystallized in the public imagination when Catholic Spain, supported by the Pope, plotted against England, finally sending the Armada to attack its shores in 1588. From this time onward, spurious propaganda linked the Jesuits to acts against the state. The most famous of these alleged acts was the famous Gunpowder Plot of 1605.[4] The hatred inspired by anti-Jesuit propaganda was especially exploited

---

[2] Francis Edwards, *The Jesuits in England from 1580 to the Present Day.* Tumbridge Wells, Kent, England: Burns and Oates, 1985). See Edwards's intro.

[3] Edwards, *The Jesuits,* chap. 1. This occurred despite the Jesuit *Explanation* of the Bull, which assured Catholics that they could in good conscience remain loyal to the Queen in all policies not related to faith, also despite the absence of any evidence that the Jesuits helped plan or even desired a political revolution or, later, a Spanish victory over England.

[4] In the case of the Gunpowder Plot, the source of propaganda was the government itself. Edwards, *The Jesuits,* 42.

during the nineteenth century, when Catholic emancipation became a reality—despite the cries of "No Popery"—and the move to reestablish the Roman hierarchy in England was successful. In the decades surrounding these events, the anti-Jesuit novel flourished.[5]

THE JESUITS AND THE ROMAN CHURCH IN FATHER EUSTACE

Trollope draws from a well-stocked store of metaphors for the villainous Jesuits in Father Eustace. The members of the Society of Jesus "have, each and every of them, more eyes than are fabled in the head of a spider, and...weave webs of more delicate and wide-spreading texture, and of threads more nicely vibrative, than all the spiders in the world."[6] In their treacherous cunning, they are as "Wise as serpents."[7] If they do possess any "human feeling," which is doubt-ful in Trollope's estimation, it is hidden beneath a "mask of marble."[8] And if they do resemble any human creatures, it is an unmentionable "class of our metropolitan population...brought to such perfection in the management of their fingers, that their movements are made as imperceptible to feeling as to sight."[9] This is an allusion to the well-trained pickpockets depicted by Dickens in Oliver Twist, written a decade before Father Eustace.

But the true danger of the Jesuits cannot be captured by metaphors comparing them to creatures of instinct—no matter how deadly—or to destitute urchins. Tale of the Jesuits is about the calculation, cunning, and masterful manipulation perfected over the centuries by an organization intent on winning psychological power over others to feed ego and pocketbook. The novel begins with the death of Richard

---

[5] As Maison notes in her chapter "The Wicked Jesuit and Company," "Few modern horror comics could equal in crudity, sadism, hysteria, and blood-curdling violence the story of Jesuits in popular Victorian fiction" (169).

[6] Frances Milton Trollope, Father Eustace: A Tale of the Jesuits, London: Henry Colburn, 1847 (New York: Garland Publishing, 1975) 1:71. All references separated by colons are to volume and page.

[7] Trollope, Father Eustace, 1:246.

[8] Trollope, Father Eustace, 1:160.

[9] Trollope, Father Eustace, 1:234.

de Morley of Cuthbert Castle, who—under the influence of his Jesuit
confessor, Father Ambrose—bequeaths all his un-entailed property to
the Society. Father Ambrose has played upon De Morley's sense of
guilt for his marriage to a Protestant "heretic" and suggests the
bequeathal as restitution for this sin. Ambrose reports back to the
Jesuit General in Rome, Scaviatoli, suggesting the means to the rest of
De Morley's wealth: De Morely's daughter and heir, Juliana. Her
innocence and contemplative sensibilities make Juliana an excellent
candidate for conversion to the true faith and admission to a
convent—*after* signing over her property to the Society, of course. The
only obstacle is the girl's mother, Lady Sarah, a staunch Protestant.
Encouraged by Ambrose's report, Scaviatoli decides to send young
Father Eustace, a handsome and naive young Jesuit, to gain Juliana's
trust.

Disguised as Edward Stormont, the pious Eustace gladly embarks
upon his mission to convert Juliana. He even succeeds in interesting
her in his faith, but not before inadvertently winning her heart and
losing his own to her. When she accurately senses that her feelings are
returned and begins thinking of marriage to Stormont, she determines
to convert to Catholicism to avoid the kind of estrangement experienced by her parents because of their different faiths. Meanwhile,
Stormont—resisting his love for Juliana—sends for assistance from
England's highest-ranking Jesuit, Father Edgar, who arrives with his
cousin, a nun. (Having anticipated the young priest's infatuation,
Scaviatoli has supplied Eustace with a letter to Father Edgar.)
Assuming the identities of Mr. Mills and Mrs. Vavasar, the interlopers
successfully finagle their way into the lives of the families of Cuthbert
until "there was scarcely a decided opinion, or a decided feeling,
extant in any bosom (among the ladies and gentlemen) at Cuthbert, of
which Mr. Mills and Mrs. Vavasar did not hold the string which could
bring them into play."[10]

However, only Stormont and Juliana suffer gravely under the
Jesuit scheme. Stormont is pushed into painful intimacy with Juliana,
even after he realizes that she has misinterpreted his confidences. Torn

---

[10] Trollope, *Father Eustace*, 3:134.

between his vow of obedience and his anguish at deceiving her, he nearly collapses. When Father Edgar coaxes him to seduce the young heiress for the greater glory of God, Stormont finally runs away, leaving a letter for Juliana in which he confesses his identity and the Jesuit plot. Already having converted to Catholicism, the devastated Juliana returns to the Anglican faith and renounces marriage—both because Stormont's deceit has left her disillusioned and because she continues to love him. As for Father Eustace, he abandons the Jesuits to embrace a simple faith and finally returns years later to Cuthbert, much aged and ill, only to die in Juliana's arms after receiving her forgiveness.

In the ruin of Eustace, we behold the ironic subversion of rationality by an organization that never stops thinking. This is Trollope's major position on the Jesuits. They have "cultivated" Eustace's "admirable talents...into the greatest possible perfection; all, save the power of reasoning... For no sooner was a youth suspected of thinking, than he was marked out as the lame one amidst the herd, and doomed to destruction, of some sort or other, at the very earliest opportunity."[11] If the Jesuits play God—without God's benign purposes—they do so because of a blasphemous sense of their own importance. Preparing Eustace for his mission, Scaviatoli asks, "Why have all other earth-born constitutions rusted, withered, dwindled, and worn themselves away, even as the organized clay of which our mortal bodies are composed, and this alone—this thrice holy COMPANY OF JESUS endured?"[12] Then, true to form, he supplies the answer himself:

[I]t is only because He [God] has ordained, expressly ordained, from age to age, that such men as you are should be born; it is only because of and by means of this, that the Holy Company of Jesus still exists!...Read the varied pages of this world's history...What will you find there? Records of principalities

---

[11] Trollope, *Father Eustace,* 2:222–23.
[12] Trollope, *Father Eustace,* 1:247.

and powers; records of dynasties, lasting and powerful as the
wit of man could make them. Where are they now![13]

In claiming such outrageous authority, the Jesuits in *Father
Eustace* represent the Roman Catholic Church, whose doctrines they
champion. The identification is seen in Trollope's commentary on the
suffering Eustace endures because of his obedience:

> There are many scoffers at the Jesuit practice, and the Romish
> faith, who may feel inclined to smile at this statement of the
> young monk's sufferings. But they know not what they laugh
> at.
>   Such a predicament as that of Father Eustace *has* existed.
> And it was no laughing matter.[14]

It is also suggested in Trollope's remark on "popish altars, wherein
the suspension rather than the employment of the mental faculties
appears to constitute the service offered."[15] The reader can assume
that this form of "mummery," as Trollope calls it, allows the Pope to
control his herd, as it does the Jesuit General his.

Of course, the Jesuit scheme to exploit Juliana depends upon her
conversion to the Roman faith, possible because of the Catholic
sensibilities she possesses. On reporting to Scaviatoli, Father Ambrose
lists Juliana's qualities that suggest her receptiveness to "the power of
truth"—that is, Catholicism:

> Her imagination is impressionable, her feelings easily excited,
> her temper tender and gentle, and her memory of her departed
> father strongly mingled with a feeling of self-reproach for not
> having honoured him sufficiently during his life. She is fond
> of reading, and her taste leads her to poetry. She is fond of
> music, but the airs she oftenest repeats are rather tender and

---

[13] Trollope, *Father Eustace*, 2:249–51.
[14] Trollope, *Father Eustace*, 3:162.
[15] Trollope, *Father Eustace*, 2:77.

plaintive, than sprightly and gay. She is kind-hearted and open-handed; and my belief is, that if once brought to believe that her father's soul is in danger of perdition from his heretic marriage, and that his punishment may be lessened were she to sacrifice her estate to propitiate the prayers of the Church, every acre might easily be obtained for the purpose.[16]

Father Ambrose is clearly more impressed by Juliana's vulnerability than by any incipient attraction to Catholicism she might have demonstrated. But, unlike Juliana's sensitive and exploited counterpart Fanny in Trollope's earlier novel, *The Vicar of Wrexhill,* Juliana is intelligent and contemplative, a woman of substance who gravitates toward mysticism.[17] When the Catholic housekeeper presents her with a silver crucifix once possessed by her father, she is "affected by the disclosure of this Papist symbol" as those in "many an English house" would not have been.[18] Moments later she demonstrates such "reverential affection" for the portrait of a Cardinal that she "brought tears to those [eyes] of her old servant."[19] The portrait and a statue of the Virgin Mary, she discovers, conceal "a small Catholic chapel, the altar of which was carefully and elegantly decorated."[20] Some time before Father Eustace exerts any influence on her, she frequently comes here to pray. Part of Catholicism's charm for Juliana lies in its association with her father, estranged from her during his life because of her Protestantism. Her attraction is brought into relief by her mother's disdain for any reminder of the faith that drove her apart from her husband. When Father Eustace, as Edward Stormont, does finally arrive at Cuthberth and accepts Juliana's invitation to see

---

[16] Trollope, *Father Eustace,* 1:178–79.

[17] Published in 1837, this novel decries the evangelical movement's emotionalism, which facilitated the manipulation of infatuated girls by cunning ministers. Tellingly, Trollope does not sympathize with the evangelical Fanny as she does with the mystically-inclined Juliana.

[18] Trollope, *Father Eustace,* 1:321.

[19] Trollope, *Father Eustace,* 1:332.

[20] Trollope, *Father Eustace,* 1:343.

the chapel, the heiress responds to his sign of the cross as her staunchly Protestant mother would never do:

> If, instead of the heiress of Cuthbert, it had been her mother who thus unexpectedly found herself the spectator of this popish ceremony, the effect of it would have been very different. Lady Sarah would probably have turned away and left the chapel, without attempting to disguise the disagreeable impression which everything that recalled "the ancient faith" was sure to produce on her. But no feeling of this sort was either expressed or felt by Juliana. On the contrary, no one could have looked at her at that moment, without perceiving that this unexpected action impressed her with as much solemnity, and reverence, as surprise. Her whole aspect was immediately changed by it. She suddenly drew back, as if to avoid the danger of interfering in any way with an act of devotion; her hands seemed spontaneously to cross themselves on her bosom, and she bowed her head and fixed her eyes upon the ground.[21]

Given such devotion, the reader is not surprised to find Juliana enraptured by the requiem Stormont later plays on the organ, nor to find her offering a Catholic prayer for the soul of her father and then repeating it in "very deep and true devotion...once more upon the steps of that Roman-Catholic altar" herself chanting "those striking words of the requiem, which implores rest for the departed spirit."[22] Trollope blames these Romish sensibilities for Juliana's eventual misguided conversion to Catholicism. The heiress has an inordinate love of solitude, which makes her "shrink from association" in the cloister of her castle.[23] The "reverence" and "tenderness" she exhibits before the Cardinal's portrait—and indeed before the crucifix and in

---

[21] Trollope, *Father Eustace,* 2:168–69.
[22] Trollope, *Father Eustace,* 2:204–205.
[23] Trollope, *Father Eustace,* 1:278.

the Catholic chapel—are mixed with "a strange thrilling of superstitious fear."[24]

TROLLOPE'S PARADOXICAL ATTRACTION TO CATHOLICISM

IN A PERIOD marked by increasing conversions to Catholicism and novels admonishing those tempted by the mystique of the Roman Church, Trollope presents Juliana's temperament as a breeding ground for insidious popish superstition.[25] Yet, in general, she presents Juliana sympathetically, as a woman of depth, a truth-seeker who has profited by the very sensibilities that render her vulnerable to Catholic machinations. The very solitude that has proven dangerous has also proven priceless: "That such cultivation as her faculties had received [from solitude] is an advantage beyond all price cannot be doubted."[26] Juliana conscientiously debates the question of conversion, acknowledging to herself that love for Stormont no doubt plays a role in her inclinations, but reasonably concluding that the difference in their religions is one of "a mere form!"[27] Moreover, her experience has shown her that stubbornly clinging to form destroys families. Besides her sincerity in seeking the truth, Juliana possesses admirable gentleness—a "gentleness rather of strength than of weakness"—and remarkable unselfishness, being "prepared to sacrifice her own taste, and her own inclination, rather than endure [a struggle]."[28] Of all her qualities, that most highly regarded by the independent Trollope appears to be resoluteness: "It was but another symptom of this same

---

[24] Trollope, *Father Eustace*, 1:332.

[25] The Oxford Movement encouraged conversions to Roman Catholicism. Many converts, like Newman, described their often painful experiences in novels of the period. See "Gain and Loss: Conversions and Reouncements," chapter 7 of Maison's study, *Victorian Vision*. According to Houghton, another reason for conversion to Roman Catholicism was the voice of "external authority" it offered in a time of religious turmoil (99). See his discussion of the "Recoil to Authority" in *The Victorian Frame of Mind, 1830–1870* (New Haven: Yale University Press, 1957) 99-102.

[26] Trollope, *Father Eustace*, 1:279.

[27] Trollope, *Father Eustace*, 2:207.

[28] Trollope, *Father Eustace*, 2:210.

peaceful temperament which led her, upon any point which she felt it important to maintain, to declare her purpose distinctly, and to abide by it firmly" even as "the most tyrannical autocrat could have done."[29]

Trollope seems to share her sensitive heroine's appreciation for the beauty of Roman Catholic ritual, as the opening of *Father Eustace* suggests:

> There are few spectacles more impressive than the death-bed of a Roman Catholic, when attended by all the forms appointed by his picturesque and hieroglyphic faith, and accompanied by enough of ecclesiastical splendour to atone to the imagination, or rather to the senses of the spectator, for superseding the tragedy of nature, by the pomp and solemnity of ceremonious rites.[30]

As puzzled as readers familiar with Trollope's anti-Catholic views might be by this paean, they would find no evidence of irony in the narrative as it proceeds. The "Romish chapel" adjacent to De Morley's room is "highly decorated," and its altar, "resplendent with gems, was illuminated by a multitude of tapers."[31] Even a reference to Protestant "heretics" who would be moved by the midnight masses at Cuthbert Castle is a fair representation of papal views:

> Some collateral affinity to a long departed Pope had furnished a plea for the privilege [of such masses], which, perhaps, had been the more readily granted to the English branch of the De Morley race, from the hope that a ceremony so every way impressive might produce the happiest effects, by inducing the surrounding heretics to be present from curiosity at a

---

[29] Trollope, *Father Eustace*, 2:210–11.
[30] Trollope, *Father Eustace*, 1:1.
[31] Trollope, *Father Eustace*, 1:2.

solemnity but rarely within the reach of any, and which was a nature to be contemplated with indifference by none.[32]

The staunchly Protestant Lady Sarah attests to the impossibility of indifference as she observes a mass being said in her dying husband's chapel. Of those present, she is "the most awake to the picturesque character of the circumstances by which it was attended."[33] "Picturesque" is also the word Trollope uses later in the novel to describe Stormont's chapel as it basks in moonlight, its "gorgeous crucifix" prominent above the "richly carpeted steps" to the altar.[34]

Trollope's similarity to Juliana does not end with her appreciation of Catholic aesthetics. She also expresses appreciation for its theological views in commentary more explicit and probing than Juliana's own insights on the essential orthodoxy of Catholicism. The Church's view of obedience is a case in point. Although Trollope confines discussion of this duty to the vow of obedience taken by Jesuits, she alludes to its requirement of all the Catholic faithful. Chapter 12 of the first book begins as an apology for this duty: "It certainly cannot doubted that, to some natures, the doctrine of passive obedience is repugnant; but there are many others to which it is greatly the reverse. Nor should these latter be rashly classed as imbecile and worthless."[35] Obedience, she goes on to explain, has two legitimate purposes. For those of "ardent and very noble natures," whose overly active imaginations lead them to torture "heart and head to decide upon questions greatly beyond the reach of ordinary understandings,"[36] obedience provides "the shelter of authority."[37] Secondly, for those of such strong imagination who are inclined toward fanaticism—whether they be disciples "of the Church of Rome or of John

---

[32] Trollope, *Father Eustace*, 1:3.

[33] Trollope, *Father Eustace*, 1:4.

[34] Trollope, *Father Eustace*, 2:74–75.

[35] Trollope, *Father Eustace*, 1:261.

[36] Trollope, *Father Eustace*, 1:262.

[37] Trollope, *Father Eustace*, 1:261.

Wesley"[38]—obedience supplies what their own flawed judgment cannot.

Closely linked to obedience is another virtue prized by the Jesuits and defended by Trollope: self-denial. This virtue explains Stormont's admirable desire to please his neighbors, a desire that "would be more frequently possessed if individual self-gratification did not interfere to prevent it."[39] Although Trollope admits that "self-abnegation" has won for Stormont influence in the parish, she defends his sincerity. This virtue "never, perhaps, reaches to that degree of systematic perfection in which Mr. Stormont possessed it, save where the acquirement has been both motived and assisted by a strong purpose and a steadfast will."[40]

For all their intrigue, the Jesuits, like their progenitor the Church of Rome, embody just such an unflagging sense of purpose. Each individual member pledges absolute obedience to the General, frequently compared to his military counterpart plotting his campaign. *Father Eustace* certainly exposes the deceit and cruelty produced by such religious fascism, as well as the egotism of its leaders. Still, the authoritarian basis of the Society wins Trollope's respect, as this description of the Jesuit General Scaviatoli suggests:

> He might have seen rather more than fifty winters; but endowed with a constitution and a frame of iron, and inured to temperance, constant and well regulated, but unmixed with any strength-exhausting ascetic severity; with vigour of mind and body, unbroken by penance, and unshaken by any terrors of discipline, either of this world or the next; recognising no authority that could make his spirit quail, or paralyse the native energy of his character; no man of any age, or of any perfection of comeliness, could have been found to excel him in impressive majesty of appearance.[41]

---

[38] Trollope, *Father Eustace*, 1:262.
[39] Trollope, *Father Eustace*, 2:97.
[40] Trollope, *Father Eustace*, 2:97.
[41] Trollope, *Father Eustace*, 1:162.

In Eustace's first interview with the General, Scaviatoli relentlessly drills the young soldier on the code of the society:

Is it your conviction, brother, that, as a priest and a Jesuit, you are bound, as you value the safety of your immortal soul, to advance and maintain the interest of the holy Company of Jesus under all circumstances, in defiance of every obstacle?...to abdicate all individual will, all individual judgment, and to live, think, speak, and act, wholly, solely, and without reservation, according to the judgment and the commands of your superiors?[42]

Eustace's affirmative response to this and all the other re-phrasings of the General's single question is uttered with "undoubting conviction and unshrinking zeal."[43] This attitude cannot be explained completely by Eustace's poor judgment of the commander's character, for in Scaviatoli's words, "[t]here were none of the ordinary symptoms of self-seeking authority, or of presumptuous cant. It was as if a voice from Heaven made itself heard through his lips, for the express purpose of preparing the young Jesuit brother for some enterprise upon which the fate of millions hung."[44] Moreover, Trollope never identifies anything but the glory of God and winning of souls as the General's ostensible goals, despite her insinuations that beneath such idealism lurks sheer lust for power—however blind to it Scaviatoli might be. Throughout her military analogies, Trollope suggests that were it not for the ambition of Jesuit superiors, the impressive sense of duty subjecting all members of the Society to the iron will of their leader would render the order a shining example of dedication, unity, and strength.

Trollope's presentation of Catholicism, in short, reveals her strong admiration for a conceptualization of the self as profoundly

---

[42] Trollope, *Father Eustace,* 1:240–41.

[43] Trollope, *Father Eustace,* 1:242.

[44] Trollope, *Father Eustace,* 1:244–45.

subordinate to a higher good. Duty, in a word, is for Trollope perhaps the best means to human nobility. Duty means obedience to those in authority, at least in the case of sensitive souls who cannot trust their own inclinations because they spring from confused emotions. Hierarchical structures guide the development of individuals and create order and unity, which, if directed toward noble ends, lead to communal perfection. Catholic rituals, art, and music appeal to Trollope because they express a reality that transcends and unites individuals.

Trollope's attractions are surprising not only because of her views of Jesuit mind-control, but because they belie the relentless dedication to individualism and self-reliance she evinced throughout her life.[45] Trollope first dramatically demonstrated her independence in 1827 when, leaving behind her husband and braving scandal, she embarked with two of her children and the artist Auguste Hervieu for frontier America. Her plan was to join reformer Frances Wright at her experimental commune of Nashoba, Tennessee—near Memphis— where freed slaves and white settlers lived and worked together. Besides her admiration for the idealistic Wright, what motivated this excursion according to Heineman was Trollope's desire to escape her morose husband and seek a livelihood for her son Henry. When she found appalling conditions at Nashoba, she whisked her children away from the commune, setting out for Cincinnati, where she set up a household and conceived the idea for the Cincinnati Bazaar, an impressive Moorish structure that would house commercial and cultural enterprises. The ultimate failure of the Bazaar, according to Heineman, was owed to Trollope's independence and progressive ideas about the role of women in society, which offended the citizens of Cincinnati:

---

[45] Biographer Helen Heineman has brought to light these qualities in her *Life of Trollope*, as well as her critical study of Trollope's novels, *Mrs. Trollope: The Triumphant Feminine in the Nineteenth Century* (Athens: Ohio University Press, 1979).

In personal and business affairs Frances Trollope found the rigid proprieties of life in America for women very trying. Here, women did not usually enter the business world. Even in social activities like balls and dinners, women remained in separate groupings, eating with and talking primarily to other women. In her domestic habits Mrs. Trollope had often seemed bold and unfeminine to her Cincinnati neighbors—walking alone, engaging in business, living alone although married.... Americans saw her bazaar as a dangerous and subversive attempt to change the entrenched patterns of American life. Activities scheduled for the bazaar were designed to mingle men and women in social and economic life. Even advertisements for auctions, for example, seemed directed at bringing women out into the public sphere...It was this dangerous proselytizing attitude regarding the social habits of American womanhood that was most provocative to the Cincinnati audience she hoped to attract.[46]

Trollope was especially outspoken about the virtue of female independence in her condemnation of evangelical revivals, described in the travel book resulting from her sojourn in the United States, *Domestic Manners of the Americans*. At these revivals, hysterical women, "uttering howlings and groans, so terrible that I shall never cease to shudder when I recall them,"[47] fell under the charms of preachers who "moved about among them, at once exciting and soothing their agonies. I heard the muttered 'Sister! dear sister!' I saw the insidious lips approach the cheeks of the unhappy girls; I heard the murmured confessions of the poor victims, and I watched their tormentors, breathing into their ears consolations that tinged the pale cheek with red."[48]

Such sights inspired Trollope to write her 1837 novel, *The Vicar of Wrexhill*, in which an emotional widow and her daughter succumb to

---

[46] Heineman, *Frances Trollope*, 9–10.
[47] Frances Milton Trollope, *Domestic Manners of the Americans*, 1832 (Dover NH: Alan Sutton, 1984) 122.
[48] *Domestic Manners*, 123.

the machinations of the Reverend Cartwright, forfeiting their financial independence and their happiness. In the spirit of Frances Wright and Mary Wollstonecraft before her, Trollope urged women to cultivate reason—particularly in religious matters—and to resist the socially encouraged passive roles that led to their victimization. Strong, independent women are featured in the best of Trollope's novels, beginning with *The Widow Barnaby*. Indeed, the Widow Barnaby was a reflection of Trollope herself, who rescued her family from her husband's financial ineptitude through her own enterprise as an author of novels and travel books. Even before her husband's early death she became the family's true head and sole provider and afterwards went on to achieve prosperity and preside over her own business and domestic affairs until her final decline and death.

We might be surprised that such a woman praises the abnegation of self, especially in a novel in which she condemns Jesuit tyranny, but we are glimpsing here Trollope's complexity at least as much as her inconsistency. The self-sufficient advocate of women's rights valued social order above individualism. She believed it was achieved through authoritarian government and state religion[49] and expressed through

---

[49] Heineman explains Trollope's "praise for the authoritarian style of monarchy" (*Frances Trollope*, 45) in Germany as, in part, a reaction to the Belgian revolution and, also in part, an expression of her disdain for the reform movement in England. In *Belgium and Western Germany*, Trollope remarks, "At home, I had of late been accustomed to hear every voice from the class, emphatically styled *the people*, whether heard through the medium of the press, or in listening to their conversation, expressive of contempt and dislike for their own country, its institutions, and its laws...Far different is the state of public feeling in Germany. Ask a Prussian...his opinion of his country...and you will be answered by such a hymn of love and praise, as might teach those who have ears to hear, that passing a reform bill is not the most successful manner of securing the affection and applause of *the multitude*."

Trollope also expresses her strong support of a state church in *Domestic Manners*: "Where there is a church-government so constituted as to deserve human respect, I believe it will always be found to receive it, even from those who may not assent to the dogma of its creed; and where such respect exists, it

refined manners, as well as architectural and cultural accomplishments inspired by classical standards. This explains in large part her disdain for America, where, in the name of freedom for all, "a false and futile axiom,"[50] there thrived "an endless variety of religious factions,"[51] a "want of refinement" in manners,[52] and a horrifying "familiarity of address...universal throughout all ranks in the United States."[53] In short, "All the freedom enjoyed in America, beyond what is enjoyed in England, is enjoyed solely by the disorderly at the expense of orderly; and were I a stout knight, either of the sword or of the pen, I would fearlessly throw down my gauntlet, and challenge the whole Republic to prove the contrary..."[54] Indeed even Trollope's lamentation over the status of women in America is related to her aristocratic sensibilities. If women, "guarded by a seven-fold shield of habitual insignificance,"[55] were freed from domestic drudgery and allowed to mingle with men in elegant social gatherings, the manners of both sexes would improve, for social "court...is the glass wherein the higher orders dress themselves, and which again reflected from them to the classes below, goes far towards polishing, in some degree, a great majority of the population."[56]

Trollope inherited her conservatism from her own family, according to her daughter-in-law Frances Eleanor, who had access to early letters of young Frances Milton in which she described herself as "shocked at the seditious tone" of her liberal fiancé.[57] Frances Eleanor believed that this conservative tendency crystallized when her mother-

---

produces a decorum in manners and language often found wanting where it does not" (78).

[50] *Domestic Manners of the Americans*, 49.
[51] Trollope, *Domestic Manners*, 76.
[52] Trollope, *Domestic Manners*, 33.
[53] Trollope, *Domestic Manners*, 71.
[54] Trollope, *Domestic Manners*, 75.
[55] Trollope, *Domestic Manners*, 48.
[56] Trollope, *Domestic Manners*, 109.
[57] As quoted in Frances Eleanor Trollope, *Frances Trollope: Her Life and Literary Work* (London: Richard Bentley, 1895) 63.

in-law discovered the horrors of "republican America."[58] While
Frances Eleanor's husband Thomas preferred to attribute his mother's
conservatism to the later "intellectual influence" of Prince Metternich
of Austria,[59] we do find Trollope first expressing her Tory convictions
in *Domestic Manners.*

Not coincidentally, the same book records favorable remarks about
the autocratic Roman Catholic Church. The decorum of the Roman
Church in America distinguishes it from the evangelical sects whose
"unseemly vagaries" have "the melancholy effect of exposing *all*
religious ceremonies to contempt."[60] Trollope suggests that such
decorum, so appealing to her sensibilities, proceeds from the firm hand
of centralized government: "The Catholics alone appear exempt from
the fury of division and sub-division that has seized every other
persuasion. Having the Pope for their common head, regulates, I
presume, their movements, and prevents the outrageous display of
individual whim which every other sect is permitted."[61] She goes on to
praise the Catholic bishop of Cincinnati, claiming to "have never
known in any country a priest of a character and bearing more truly
apostolic...His manners were highly polished; his piety active and
sincere, and infinitely more mild and tolerant than that of the
factious Sectarians who form the great majority of the American
priesthood."[62] She then offers this conclusion to her diatribe: "I believe
I am sufficiently tolerant; but this does not prevent my seeing that the
object of all religious observances is better obtained, when the
government of the church is confided to the wisdom and experience of
the most venerated among the people."[63] Given her admiration for
ecclesiastical ritual and hierarchy and her vehemence for democracy
and the demise of culture engendered by it, one might conclude that
Frances Trollope's liberalism is limited to her views on women.

---

[58] Trollope, *Frances Trollope,* 64.
[59] Thomas Adolphus Trollope, *What I Remember* (New York: Harper,
1888) 492.
[60] Francis Milton Trollope, *Domestic Manners,* 77.
[61] Trollope, *Domestic Manners,* 77.
[62] Trollope, *Domestic Manners,* 77.
[63] Trollope, *Domestic Manners,* 77.

Indeed, she resembles her contemporary, Mary Shelley, who in her mature years relished social propriety although she never believed this to preclude a life of intelligence and independence for women. *The Vindication of the Rights of Woman* by Shelley's mother, Mary Wollstonecraft, expressed an ideal espoused by Shelley and Frances Trollope, namely that women be held to the same moral standard binding for men, reason. With an education that cultivates reason, women, like men, would demonstrate independence of thought and action without threatening the traditional social order. Yet Trollope's liberal views—like those of Shelley—extend beyond the rights of women to a fundamental abhorrence for tyranny of any kind, be it in the realm of gender, government, or thought. For this reason, despite her attraction to the autocracy of Catholicism, she supported the Republican cause in Italy, where she lived in the final decades of her life. As Frances Eleanor notes in her memoir,

> Her strongly conservative principles and sentiments made it sad for her to witness the sapping of all authority, which was going on around her. On the other hand, her benevolence and her common sense caused her to sympathize keenly with the victims of tyranny and oppression, who were very numerous throughout the States of the Church, the kingdom of Naples, and the Austrian-ruled provinces of Lombardy and Venetia. And then the consequences of autocratic misgovernment are immediate, palpable, comprehensible by every one; while the consequences of democratic misgovernment require a wider view to perceive them thoroughly, being—unless in the case of rampant *sans-culottism*—more subtle, and disguised in a rosy mirage of hope. "If it were but possible to find the just medium between the two, for Italy!" said Mrs. Trollope.[64]

Should such a middle ground be absent, Trollope clearly preferred a people to err on the side of democracy, probably even the kind she had beheld in the United States. And if the unschooled masses horrified

---

[64] Francis Eleanor Trollope, *Frances Trollope*, 105–106.

her, her inclination was to reform social ills rather than to rule with an iron fist. As Helen Heineman observes, Trollope "was an early explorer of controversial social problems across a whole range of subjects," producing an antislavery novel, a novel exposing the evils of child labor and life in the slums, and a novel anticipating Dickens in its attack on cruelties of the New Poor Law."[65]

More despicable to her than tyranny in the realm of government was tyranny in the realm of ideas. When her cherished friend Frances Wright set out to publish her radical thoughts on religion, the Nashoba venture, and the sexual rights of women, Trollope feared the reception such a controversial work would receive in England but refused to advise censorship:

> I dare no more venture to give breath to my opinions, than I would set fire to the castle at Windsor—all this makes society very flat stale and unprofitable—Heaven knows I do not want to be talking...radicalism—nor infidelity—but I should like to live among human beings who would not look upon reason as crime, nor on free discussion, as treason and blasphemy.[66]

Her "zest for Poetry and Art,"[67] in the words of Francis Eleanor, required nourishment by a range of ideas. Hence, her love for both the orthodox Dante and the outrageous George Sand, whose "politics...ethics...and religion were all alike abhorrent to the Englishwoman," though these did "not prevent the latter from personally admiring and openly extolling the exquisite style, the wonderful power of description, and the poetic imagination of the great Frenchwoman."[68]

---

[65] Heineman, *Frances Trollope*, 137–38.

[66] Quoted in Helen Heineman, *Mrs. Trollope: The Triumphant Feminie in the Nineteenth Century* (Athens: Ohio University Press, 1979) 43.

[67] Heineman, *Mrs. Trollope*, 57.

[68] Frances Eleanor Trollope, *Frances Trollope*, 642.

TROLLOPE'S PROJECT IN FATHER EUSTACE

TROLLOPE'S PROLIFIC WRITING provided the perfect means for expressing both her conservatism and liberalism. The records of her travels in coarse America, rebellious France, and orderly Prussia were especially good vehicles for her conservative views—her horror of democracy and revolution and her admiration of state religion, authoritarian kings, and absolutism, in general. These views lent her "a strong and coherent authorial voice" that made these works highly popular.[69] In her fiction, conversely, the progressive strain in her character seems predominant—the novels abounding with independent female protagonists and damning portrayals of slavery, factory and workhouse conditions, and religious piety. Perhaps the license of fiction allowed her to express her contradictory sentiments as travel books could not. *Father Eustace* shows signs of both tendencies, as we have seen, while ultimately remaining true to the pattern of Trollope's other novels. However, this novel transcends the formulaic move suggested in the triumph of the independent heroine and the punishment of religious tyrants. In *Father Eustace* Trollope honestly probes the traditional principles that she herself shares with her Jesuit villains and makes a conscientious effort to reconcile them with the freedom and independence also vital to her.

The title character provides the focus for Trollope's interrogation. Reared as a Roman Catholic to renounce his own inclinations and obey patriarchal authorities, he is perfectly prepared to enter the Society of Jesus, which demands obedience above every other virtue. His qualities make him even more exemplary than Juliana is: he matches her in beauty, goodness, intelligence, and sensitivity, but surpasses her in a noble quest for perfection that takes him to the very limits of self-abnegation. Trollope's superlatives in her description of Eustace are sincere. What, then, brings his ruin? The obvious answer is the evil superiors who have exploited his natural goodness for their own selfish and cruel ends, but this answer is incomplete. In addition to her extensive commentary on Jesuit villainy, Trollope devotes pages

---

[69] Heineman, *Frances Trollope*, 44.

to diagnosing a more profound evil: "an abstract principle of duty" which, though it contains "something very essentially sublime," has the power to wreak moral destruction.[70]

For Trollope, true duty is natural, proceeding from a noble heart. "Nature," we learn in *Father Eustace*,

> had been bountiful to him [Eustace], most bountiful in all her choicest gifts—for he was born not only with the organization which leads to a brilliant development of all the finer faculties of our nature, but, if it could philosophically be said of any man that he was born good, it might have been said of Father Eustace. To the extent that an action conforms to the inclinations of such a one as Eustace it will truly be a duty, leading "to reverential devotion to the God of the universe."[71]

However, when a naturally good person replaces these inclinations as the basis of moral authority with the commands of other people, "a *diseased* idea of duty results."[72] This "slavery of the soul" makes the good person "recoil from the acts" he is commanded to perform but which his own heart rejects.[73] Thus the first sense of abstraction we glean from the novel is the removal of morality from its proper foundation in the individual conscience.

This kind of self-alienation yields inevitable ironies. To ignore the heart's natural impulses requires rigorous self-discipline, the hallmark of Jesuit training: "the mind of a Jesuit is schooled into having such 'sovereign sway and masterdom' over itself and the body it belongs to, that none may guess from any outward sign *what* either mind or body feels."[74] Father Ambrose, a case in point, is sardonically described by Trollope:

---

[70] Trollope, *Father Eustace*, 3:26.
[71] Trollope, *Father Eustace*, 2:100.
[72] Trollope, *Father Eustace*, 2:101.
[73] Trollope, *Father Eustace*, 2:101.
[74] Trollope, *Father Eustace*, 1:153.

There was a solemn, quiet, impenetrable expression in his features, which gave the idea of such complete abstraction of spirit, that none could suspect him of being conscious of *any* external influence.

Neither was he.

The sun shone; but he saw it not. The birds sung; but he heard it not. Neither did he feel the soft fresh breath of early morning, though it came upon a brow fevered by unwonted fatigue, and furrowed by many years of mental toil.[75]

Ambrose has so perfectly internalized "external influences" in the moral realm that the spiritually nurturing influences of nature cannot reach his heart. As for Eustace, whose strong passions make his "abstraction of spirit" anything but complete, we find this pitiful Jesuit in the absurd position of praying "not to do right, not to be guided by the holy voice of conscience, to eschew evil and do good—but that he might speedily be sustained by the imperious voice of command, uttered by one on whom the Company of Jesus had conferred power to utter it!"[76] This prayer suggests a second sense in which duty has become an abstraction for Eustace and his Jesuit brothers. In it, he begs for the grace of entrusting to his Jesuit superiors "not his own destiny only, but that of Juliana, the lovely, innocent, confiding Juliana."[77] Obedience requires Eustace to deceive Juliana about his identity, to win her implicit trust, and to maintain his charade even when she falls in love with him and aspires to become his wife. The goal of this pretense is Juliana's conversion to Catholicism and admission to a convent—a worthy project in Eustace's eyes since it means the salvation of his beloved and the procurement of her wealth for the Society whose mission is the winning of souls and the glory of God. But, knowing how much Juliana loves him, he knows, too, "all the misery which the DUTY upon which he was engaged must

---

[75] Trollope, *Father Eustace*, 1:153.
[76] Trollope, *Father Eustace*, 2:231.
[77] Trollope, *Father Eustace*, 2:230.

bring upon *her*."[78] Eustace's superior, Father Edgar, observes the struggle which such a duty causes in the breast of the young priest and fears Eustace's resolve in "sacrificing her [Juliana] in the manner in which...a thoroughly good Jesuit ought to do, if the interests of the Company demand it."[79] Father Edgar's fears are well founded since the battle being waged in Eustace's soul between his love for Juliana and his vow of obedience to Jesuit superiors has every chance of ending in the victory of his affections. At first glance, Trollope's support for such a victory may lead us to misinterpret what she means by "abstract principles of duty." True, Eustace's good impulses spring from a very real love for a very real person, while his vows correspond to an intellectual ideal. Trollope's point, however, is not to replace principles of duty with affections, but to insist that principles of duty have persons and not concepts as their foundation. In this approach, she resembles Kant, whose categorical imperative—or principle of duty—requires that persons be treated as ends in themselves and not merely as means to satisfy our own ends.[80] To treat someone as an end always involves respect for that individual's freedom. Therefore, even a mission to win salvation for Juliana—an earnest quest for Eustace, if not for his superiors—must not involve deception, manipulation, or coercion. Eustace's understanding of this proscription comes slowly. Despite his reluctance to deceive or manipulate Juliana, he carries out the initial schemes of his superiors. It is only when these schemes call for coercive measures—Juliana's seduction—that he rebels and flees to Scaviatoli, only to find that the General approves of Father Edgar's plan to send a ruined Juliana to the convent. In the end, his love for Juliana teaches Eustace that love defines duty. This is the message of the "Gospel," which he finally discovers to be "the book

---

[78] Trollope, *Father Eustace*, 3:25.

[79] Trollope, *Father Eustace*, 3:95.

[80] One formulation of the categorical imperative in Immanuel Kant's *Foundations of the Metaphysics of Morals* (1785, trans. Lewis White Beck, Indianapolis: Bobbs-Merrill, 1959) is: "Act so that you treat humanity, whether in your own person or in that of another, always as an end and never as a means only" (47).

of life to the Christian, and not *that* containing the laws of the Company of Jesus."[81]

Catholicism, in Trollope's view, provides the perfect foil for demonstrating the true nature of duty. In exalting obedience, the Romish Church fosters self-division and exploitation, antitheses of the integrity and respect for freedom constitutive of true duty. This is certainly true, Trollope suggests, when obedience becomes the highest of all virtues—as it does in the Company of Jesus as she depicts it—an extreme manifestation of the Roman Church. The Jesuits in the novel are identified with blind obedience, which, in turn, is identified with oppression. This view of Catholicism, and the Jesuits in particular, was readily shared by Trollope's audience, as the popularity of *Father Eustace* and other Victorian anti-Jesuit novels attests. Yet in her careful examination of obedience's positive and destructive elements, Trollope transcends the popular genre. In *Father Eustace*, the Jesuits fully engage her imagination because they provide the perfect symbol for an issue close to her heart but controversial. How better explore her abhorrence for the kind of constraints that affected her personally as an independent woman, especially in America but also in her own society,[82] than by illustrating them in extreme form in a hated institution. It is no accident that the intended victim of the Jesuits is a naive young woman who recovers from an attack on her dignity and freedom because of her strong will, intelligence, and independence—both financial and emotional.

Unquestionably, however, the novel's more pitiable victim is Father Eustace himself. To a certain degree, this fact supports the above argument: the beautiful, sensitive, artistic, priest who, tellingly, attracts no woman in the parish except for Juliana, joins her as one whose feminine sensibilities renders him vulnerable. But, as her

---

[81] Trollope, *Father Eustace*, 3:318.

[82] In *Frances Trollope* Heineman discusses the stifling conventions that women authors were expected to uphold and which'Trollope was accused of violating, "daring," as she did, "to treat subjects reserved for male authors and for venturing to create new characters and styles inappropriate to the current mode" (140).

counterpart, he throws into relief their differences, allowing Trollope to explain why of these two souls marked by Catholic sensibilities only Juliana achieves happiness.

First of all, Juliana learns to temper her contemplative inclinations without abandoning them. Early in the novel, we learn that "the hours which she passed alone were the only portion of her life that she really enjoyed."[83] This love of quiet and solitude, along with her strong emotions, explain the mystical bent of her spirituality, which finds expression in the solemn elements of Catholic ritual and music. As we have seen, Trollope indicates the dangers of such sensibilities: "That such cultivation as her faculties had received is an advantage beyond all price cannot be doubted, but it now led her to be too much alone."[84] After the painful episode with Eustace, her continued preference for her own counsel is dramatized when her former lover returns to Cuthbert many years later and dies in her presence: "What Juliana de Morley felt at seeing the man she had loved so truly, expire at her feet, no human being can know; for never throughout the course of a long life was she heard to allude in any way either to the life, or death of Edward Stormont."[85] But solitude is not an escape from her feelings. Her passion for Eustace, never expressed in words during her lifetime, manifests itself after her death in the chain found around her neck that holds Eustace's last message to her, "ingeniously protected by a black silken cover, which permitted its being opened for perusal with great facility."[86] Her love is also manifested in the tablet bearing his name, installed in the chapel, "exactly opposite" her seat from which she gazed on it during the service, and in her directions for a joint burial vault for her and Eustace in which both coffins be covered in a "black velvet pall."[87]

---

[83] Trollope, *Father Eustace*, 1:281.
[84] Trollope, *Father Eustace*, 1:279.
[85] Trollope, *Father Eustace*, 3:319.
[86] Trollope, *Father Eustace*, 3:320.
[87] Trollope, *Father Eustace*, 3:323.

This mystical marriage is especially accentuated by the celibacy Juliana embraces for the rest of her life.[88] As a kind of secular nun, she fulfills, ironically, Eustace's plans to lead her to the convent. Indeed, she becomes the Mother Superior of Cuthbert Castle, quietly managing the affairs of the estate and supervising her mother's new family, confining herself to the library, and instituting daily prayer services in the chapel. But her nun-like inclinations foster community, not self-absorption. Her meditations are transformed into "family morning prayer," her chants into "the singing, by the whole congregation, herself included, of the daily hymn."[89] She insists that her family reside with her at Cuthbert, and their welfare—not morbid longings—becomes the focus of her life. "[T]he crowning joy of all" for her is the marriage of her half-brother Julian and the daughter of her friend Fanny.[90]

Indeed, Juliana's sense of duty is never in danger of turning into an abstract principle. She devotes her life to her mother and stepfather and to their children—especially their son, Julian, to whom she bequeaths all her wealth. She invites her friend Fanny and her new husband to live at Cuthbert, anticipating Fanny's expulsion from her own home by her jealous cousin. She extends her largesse to all in the parish and ministers to the poor beggar who turns out to be Stormont, forgiving him for all the pain he has inflicted upon her.

While Juliana lives a life of quiet joy, Eustace deteriorates, body and soul. Despite his contrition for the pain he has caused Juliana, he continues to struggle, "rigorously confined within the walls of his own convent"[91]—and within his own mind. After many years of weighing

---

[88] Juliana's vehemence about remaining unmarried is noted in the penultimate chapter of the novel. When Lady Sarah broaches the subject of marriage to her daughter, the "conversation was abruptly brought to a chose by Juliana's rising, and leaving the room. She was as pale as death, but on reaching the door, she turned round, and said distinctly, but in a voice that could never have been recognized for her own, 'Never again! Mother! Father! Never say these words again.'"

[89] Trollope, *Father Eustace*, 3:323–34.

[90] Trollope, *Father Eustace*, 3:324.

[91] Trollope, *Father Eustace*, 3:318.

abstract principles, he rejects them for the principles of the Gospel, only to die before he can transform these abstractions into love of neighbor. Eustace's religious formation in a "bigotted faith" and the inculcation of a "slavish obedience" at an early age largely explain this failure.[92] But he also lacks Juliana's strength of character, which, as we have seen, "led her, upon any point which she felt it important to maintain, to declare her purpose distinctly, and to abide by it firmly."[93] Ironically, she first demonstrates such firmness of purpose in her decision to convert to Roman Catholicism against the wishes of her mother. Autonomy is the key to her happiness and, as far as she and Trollope are concerned, it is also in accordance with the will of God, to whom alone she owes "[s]ubmission of the spirit."[94]

Autonomy mattered dearly to Trollope. She was head of her household even before her husband's death. She lived apart from him in America—despite public disapproval—first in a radical commune then as an entrepreneur. She traveled alone through Europe and supported herself and her children through the industry of her writing. And in that writing she challenged the conventional role of women and justice of certain social institutions, incurring the censure of reviewers. As we would expect then, *Father Eustace* closes with the triumph not only of the individual conscience, but of the independent woman. Yet, Juliana's independence, like that of the nuns she resembles and that of the widowed Trollope herself, is contingent upon the related conditions of celibacy and vicarious living—in Juliana's case through Julian, the half-brother who calls her "Mother" and the woman who marries him, her namesake Juliana. These conditions require "self-abnegation" and discipline. What better model of such qualities than the Romish Church's Society of Jesus—despite their dangerous errors.

---

[92] Trollope, *Father Eustace*, 2:217.
[93] Trollope, *Father Eustace*, 2:211.
[94] Trollope, *Father Eustace*, 3:305.

5

A CATHOLIC BAPTISM FOR
VILLETTE'S LUCY SNOWE

IF ANY NOVEL has earned the epithet *quintessentially anti-Catholic*, it is
Charlotte Brontë's *Villette*.[1] In it, the author refuses to confine her

---

[1] Charlotte Brontë, *Villette*, 1853 (London: Penguin, 1979). *Villette* recounts
the trials and eventual triumph of the unassuming, impoverished, and sensitive
Lucy Snowe, who finds employment as a girls' boarding school teacher in a
fictional version of Brussels. Lucy manages to win the respect of her unruly
students and of the calculating headmistress, Madame Beck. She painfully stands
by as the man she loves—Graham Bretton, or Dr. John, the school's English
physician—becomes infatuated with the shallow Ginevra Fanshawe before
falling in love with Pauline Home, a friend from his youth. Graham's
affectionate letters ignite Lucy's hopes, but when she finally realizes he cannot
return her feelings for him, she falls into despair. At the nadir of her dejection
and sense of isolation, she visits a Roman Catholic Church and pours out her
anguish in the confessional.

Eventually, Lucy turns her attention to Madame Beck's cousin—the exacting,
tyrannical professor M. Paul Emmanuel—whose kind and generous heart, she
discovers, belies his unpleasant demeanor. After initial conflicts, the two fall in
love. M. Paul provides Lucy with the financial resources necessary to start her
own school when he goes to the West Indies to manage his family's financial
affairs. Brontë supplies an inconclusive ending in which she vaguely describes
shipwrecks in the stormy Atlantic—without explicitly stating that M. Paul has
died.

verdicts to the historical realm, as do Scott and Shelley, or to the Society of Jesus, as does Trollope. She excoriates contemporary Catholicism in its multiple manifestations, even raising her rebuke to the level of mission for the protagonist. Such a move suits the climate of the early 1850s, the period of *Villette*'s composition, when the recent reestablishment of the Roman Church in England fomented national indignation. In her condemnation of "priestcraft," heroine Lucy Snowe speaks with the vituperation of John Calvin in his refutation of Cardinal Sadolet. Under the machinations and equivocations of the clergy, like those of Père Silas in his determination to control M. Paul, the pitiful faithful are reduced to servitude:

> Poverty was fed and clothed, and sheltered, to bind it by obligation to "the Church"; orphanage was reared and educated that it might grow up in the fold of "the Church"; sickness was tended that it might die after the formula and in the ordinance of "the Church"; and men were overwrought, and women most murderously sacrificed, and all laid down a world God made pleasant for his creatures' good, and took up a cross, monstrous in its galling weight, that they might serve Rome, prove her

---

Two incidents alluded to in this chapter should be mentioned. One is the recurring appearance of a ghostly nun at the school, which makes the already overwrought Lucy doubt her own sanity. The nun, however, turns out to be the disguised suitor (successor to Graham) of Ginevra Fanshawe. The other incident concerns Lucy's visit to Walravens at the urging of Madame Beck. There, Lucy meets the strange, shriveled Madame Walravens and learns from Père Silas, M. Paul's confessor, that M. Paul long ago definitively lost his heart to Justine Marie, granddaughter of Madame Walravens. When her family rejected M. Paul's suit, Justine Marie joined a convent and, surprisingly, M. Paul responded by providing the old woman with financial support. Just when Lucy believes M. Paul's loyalties make it impossible for her to have him, she learns that the story of Justine Marie has been invented by Madame Beck and Père Silas. Under the influence of opium—which Madame Beck has used to drug her to keep her away from M. Paul before he departs—Lucy comes upon Madame Beck, Madame Walravens, M. Paul, and Père Silas in the park, where they greet a girl named Justine Marie, M. Paul's goddaughter.

sanctity, confirm her power, and spread the reign of her tyrant "Church."[2]

It is tempting to cite Lucy's even more vitriolic attacks on priests for their "dreadful viciousness, sickening tyranny and black impiety,"[3] but the clergy is only one reason Lucy prefers a "Babylonish furnace" to a Roman Church. The rituals and trappings, the "swarming tapers," "swinging censers," "flowers and tinsel," "chanting," "superstitions," and "monkish extravagances"—all form a "painted and meretricious face" that obscures the *real* face of God—not to mention, the sinner's simple relationship *to* God. The culmination of Lucy's diatribe, scattered throughout the pages of the novel, comes in her declaration that "God is not with Rome."[4]

Of course, for all Lucy's moral earnestness, her excessive protests against the Roman Church must direct our attention to the fascination, albeit fearful, of a young Protestant woman who suddenly finds herself immersed in a strange Catholic world—sleeping in a nun's dormitory under a crucifix among "little Jesuit" students; subjected to mysterious apparitions of "the NUN"; attracted to a Catholic church where she finds herself in a confessional, a position she spends an inordinate portion of her narrative trying to justify; and finally, enamored of a man who calls himself a "lay-Jesuit." This thinly disguised fascination with Catholicism has a crucial function in the psychological liberation of Lucy Snowe and of Brontë herself, whose real-life experiences in Brussels inspired the creation of *Villette.*

THE TYRANNY OF REASON AND IMAGINATION

IF *VILLETTE* IS the story of Lucy Snowe's search for an authentic self, as Tony Tanner and other critics argue, then this effort most often finds expression in the language of mind and heart.[5] Many critics have

---

[2] Brontë, *Villette,* 514–15.
[3] Brontë, *Villette,* 184.
[4] Brontë, *Villette,* 515.
[5] For variations on this theme, see the following publications.

discussed the repressed Lucy's struggle toward emotional release, and such a struggle certainly exists. Lucy claims that she is "too prosaic to idealize,"[6] "not of an artistic temperament,"[7] and a "mere looker-on at life."[8] She claims even to have "liked peace so well, and sought stimulus so little, that when the latter came I almost felt it a disturbance...."[9] Yet we find her lonely and hopeless unto death, longing for the fullness of life experienced by Ginevra Fanshawe, wondering at a passionate performance of the actress in the role of Queen Vashti and at the sensuality of a painting of Cleopatra. Lucy does struggle in choosing between detachment and emotional engagement, reason and imagination (Lucy often uses "imagination" and "feeling" interchangeably). But on a deeper level her struggle is between self and the external forces seeking to annihilate self. As she conceptualizes them throughout the novel, *both* Reason and Imagination are such external forces, though she shows little awareness of their similarity.

Lucy discusses these forces most explicitly in her narrative about Graham's letters in chapter 21, where, at first glance, she does appear to cast Reason as villain and Imagination as savior. Here, she personifies Reason as a wizened woman who offers extended advice against hoping for the young doctor's affections, expressed in the letters he has promised

---

Nina Auerbach, "Charlotte Brontë: The Two Countries," *University of Toronto Quarterly* 42 (Summer 1973): 328–42. Rosemary Clarke-Beattie, "Fables of Rebellion: Anti-Catholicism in the Structure of *Villette*," *ELH*, 53 (Winter 1986): 821–47. Sandra Gilbert and Susan Gubar, *The Madwoman in the Attic* (New Haven: Yale University Press, 1979). Robert B. Heilman, "Charlotte Brontë's 'New' Gothic," in *From Jane Austen to Joseph Conrad*, ed. by Robert C. Rathburn and Martin Steinmann, Jr. (Minneapolis: University of Minnesota Press, 1958). Andrew D. Hook, "Charlotte Brontë, the Imagination, and *Villette*," in *The Brontës: A Collection of Critical Essays*, ed. Ian Gregor (Englewood Cliffs: Prentice, 1970). E. D. H. Johnson, "'Daring the Dread Glance': Charlotte Brontë's Treatment of the Supernatural in *Villette*," *Nineteenth-Century Fiction* 20 (1966): 325–36. Margot Peters, *Charlotte Brontë: Style in the Novel* (Milwaukee: University of Wisconsin Press, 1973).
  [6] Brontë, *Villette*, 95.
  [7] Brontë, *Villette*, 122.
  [8] Brontë, *Villette*, 211.
  [9] Brontë, *Villette*, 62.

to write. "Laying on my shoulder a withered hand, and frostily touching my ear with the chill blue lips of eld," Reason says, "Hope no delight of heart—no indulgence of intellect: grant no expansion to feeling."[10] When Lucy protests, Reason explains the basis for discouraging her ward: the limitations imposed by social status and her history. She must not forget her "inferiority" before Graham, nor the fact that "pain, privation, penury stamp your language...."[11] Unable to prevent her hopes and affections, Lucy continues to resist, crying, "But if I feel, may I *never* express?" Reason retorts, "*Never!*"

In the passage following this dialogue, Lucy underscores the oppressive nature of Reason and turns to Imagination for solace:

This hag, this Reason, would not let me look up, or smile, or hope: she could not rest unless I were altogether crushed, cowed, broken-in, and broken-down. According to her, I was born only to work for a piece of bread, to await the pains of death, and steadily through all life to despond. Reason might be right; yet no wonder we are glad at times to defy her, to rush from under her rod and give a truant hour to Imagination—*her* soft, bright foe, *our* sweet Help, our divine Hope.[12]

Lucy continues her narrative with a lengthy paean to Imagination, a "kinder Power" than the demonic "stepmother" Reason—indeed the "spirit," the "good angel" who rescues her from Reason's "ill-usage: her stint, her chill, her barren board, her icy bed, her savage, ceaseless blows..." She associates Imagination with "the perfume of flowers," "the fragrance of trees," "breezes pure," and finally praises her as a goddess:

Divine, compassionate, succourable influence! When I bend the knee to other than God, it shall be at thy white and winged feet, beautiful on mountain or on plain. Temples have been reared to the Sun—altars dedicated to the Moon. Oh, greater glory! To

---

[10] Brontë, *Villette,* 307.
[11] Brontë, *Villette,* 307
[12] Brontë, *Villette,* 308.

thee neither hands build, nor lips consecrate; but hearts, through ages, are faithful to thy worship. A dwelling thou hast, too wide for walls, too high for dome—a temple whose floors are space—rites whose mysteries transpire in presence, to the kindling, the harmony of worlds.

Sovereign complete! thou hadst, for endurance, thy great army of martyrs; for achievement, thy chosen band of worthies. Deity unquestioned, thine essence foils decay![13]

But soon, Lucy's very apotheosis of Imagination becomes proof of its status as a force external to the self, and consequently destructive of it. Reason personified destroys Lucy's spirit or essence (the longing subject who converses with the hag) by calling her attention to the shackles of social position and circumstances. Imagination deified destroys her spirit by bypassing or transcending it, offering Lucy a world of beauty to contemplate, a world where she temporarily forgets not only painful limitations, but also her self. How appropriate that Imagination answers Lucy's prayer by bidding her to fall asleep. When she awakens, her ecstasy has vanished and pain has returned. Later in the chapter, acknowledging her mistake in praising Imagination, she refers to its fruit as "a dream," "an image of the brain," "one of those shadowy chances...on which humanity starves but cannot live...a mess of that manna I drearily eulogized awhile ago—which, indeed, at first melts on the lips with an unspeakable and preternatural sweetness, but which, in the end, our souls fully surely loathe."[14]

THE TYRANNY OF CATHOLICISM

THROUGHOUT VILLETTE, LUCY not only transfers to the Roman Catholic Church the attributes she has assigned to Reason and Imagination; she also explicitly connects these attributes for the first time. Like the tyrannical Reason who denies Lucy "indulgences of intellect," the hierarchy of the Church is determined to impose "spiritual restraint" on

---

[13] Brontë, *Villette*, 308.
[14] Brontë, *Villette*, 318.

individuals, ensuring that "[e]ach mind was being reared in slavery."[15] Just as Reason warns Lucy to check her aspirations by remembering her "inferiority" (to Graham, but also implicitly to Reason), the "tyrant Church" warns her children of their duty to "serve Rome, prove her sanctity, confirm her power, and spread [her]...reign."[16] Just as Reason reminds Lucy that "pain, privation, penury stamp your language," so the Church increases the burden of the poor, the orphan, and the sick, making sure that even lowly school girls realize they are stamped by pain. Young Isabelle demonstrates this when she relates the painful destiny revealed to her by her priest: "*Pour assurer votre salut là-haut, on ferait bien de vous brûler toute vive ici-bas.*"[17]

Whenever Lucy brings up the subject of the Church's tyranny in her narrative, she usually does so in order to explain why it permitted "large sensual indulgence"[18] for the faithful: as an effort to "hide chains with flowers." Certainly this indulgence takes the form of festivities, eating, and drinking ("'Eat, drink, and live!' she [the Church] says. 'Look after your bodies; leave your souls to me,'"[19]), but Lucy often describes it as an indulgence of the imagination. One example of such indulgence at Madam Beck's establishment is the reading of the horrific legends of the saints, characterized by Lucy as sensational "figments" and "monkish extravagances" that instilled in the students a fear of the Church. Generally, for Lucy extravagant indulgence of the imagination takes the form of Church rituals, articles of veneration, and pageantry, like the garish procession M. Paul directs her to observe from a balcony: "[A] mingled procession of the church and the army—priest with relics, and soldiers with weapons, an obese and aged archbishop, habited in cambric

---

[15] Brontë, *Villette*, 195.
[16] Brontë, *Villette*, 515.
[17] Brontë, *Villette*, 148. "To ensure your salvation up above, they would do well to burn you alive down here" (translation provided by Ed. Mark Lilly in "Notes" [601] to *Villette*).
[18] Brontë, *Villette*, 195.
[19] Brontë, *Villette*, 196.

and lace, looking strangely like a gray daw in bird-of-paradise plumage, and a band of young girls fantastically robed and garlanded...."[20]

Despite Lucy's venomous attack on the Catholic Church's two forces of oppression, she herself experiences their seductive powers. The attraction to the Church's sensuality actually begins before Lucy ever arrives in Villette. When she goes to London, before deciding to cross to the Continent, Lucy reports that she has no "poetic first impressions" of the city, having neither "time nor mood for them" because her "position rose on me like a ghost. Anomalous; desolate, almost blank of hope."[21] But suddenly, in this city she has referred to as "a Babylon"—the word she later associates with the Catholic Church—she finds herself under the shadow of St. Paul's dome and gains a sense of assurance that she "could go forward." In fact, she feels so tranquil that she falls asleep. Surveying "THE DOME" upon awakening, she feels as if she "were at last about to taste life."[22] Elated, she walks to Paternoster-row, enters St. Paul's, and climbs to the dome to survey the city, descending with "a still ecstasy of freedom and enjoyment."[23]

The exotic "vastness and strangeness" of the Babylon before her provides an interpretive context for the specific features Lucy describes. What clearly moves her about London are its High-Church qualities: the "solemn" dome of the Anglican church, the "mighty tone" of its bell, the "classic" Paternoster-row.[24] Her attraction to these things in London foreshadows the compulsion she experiences as she wanders despondently through the streets of Villette: "[t]he bells of a church arrested me in passing; they seemed to call me in to the *salut*, and I went

---

[20] Brontë, *Villette*, 516.

[21] Brontë, *Villette*, 106–107.

[22] Brontë, *Villette*, 108.

[23] Brontë, *Villette*, 109.

[24] Although Brontë saw the Roman Church as epitomizing the seductive formalism Lucy describes here, she saw the High Anglican Church as its aspiring rival. The opening of her novel *Shirley* shows how closely she associates Romanists and High Church Tractarians, whom she calls "the present successors of the Apostles, disciples of Dr. Pusey and tools of the Propaganda" (quoted in Arthur Pollard, "The Brontës and Their Father's Faith," *Essays and Studies* 37 [1984]: 58).

[into the]...old solemn church, its pervading gloom not gilded but purpled by light shed through stained glass."[25]

Lucy's actions in the old church confirm the efficacy of such "monkish extravagances" in subjugating the individual to the authority of Rome's "agents," as she calls them in chapter 34. Kneeling with other worshippers, she proceeds to the confessional— "mechanically obedient" to the bidding of another penitent—and entrusts her secrets to a priest who correctly identifies her attraction to the sensual extravagances of Catholic ceremony: "You were made for our faith: depend upon it, our faith alone could heal and help you—Protestantism is altogether too dry, cold, prosaic for you."[26] The older narrator Lucy jokes about the power the priest has over the young Lucy; had she taken him up on his invitation to visit his home, she "might just now, instead of writing this heretic narrative, be counting [her] beads in the cell of a certain Carmelite convent on the Boulevard of Crecy in Villette."[27] Not surprisingly, she links his power to his kindness. As far as the young Lucy is concerned, however, nothing less than a genuine attraction to Catholic ritual, to its ability to help her mystically transcend painful circumstances, explains why a Protestant repelled by the Romish religion finds herself in perhaps the most Catholic of positions: kneeling before a priest in the confessional. It is also noteworthy that Lucy never considers going to a Protestant Church during her despondency. In fact, she mentions attending a Protestant church only once in the novel and reports that afterwards she felt "weary."

Having emphasized Lucy's attraction to things Catholic, I must now acknowledge that the excessive justifications she supplies to defend herself belie nothing more than just that—mere attraction. Lucy is never in danger of losing her Protestant faith; she hardly needs to have it tested in a society that embodies Catholic sensibility. Why, then, does Brontë choose such a setting for Lucy's search for a sense of her own authority as a free agent—that is to say, for her true self?

---

[25] Brontë, *Villette*, 232–33.
[26] Brontë, *Villette*, 234.
[27] Brontë, *Villette*, 235.

In *Villette*, Catholicism functions as a vehicle whereby Lucy is able to project onto an institution and its representatives the oppressive ways in which she conceives her position in the world—namely, as a pawn of abstract forces. Until she understands that what she calls Reason and Imagination are both self-destructive concepts created by internalizing the oppressive voices of real people around her, she can have very limited control of her own life. Her immersion in a Catholic world allows her to escape the hell of a neurotic introspection and confront some of her true opponents.[28]

Lucy links all three of her antagonists—Madam Beck, Père Silas, and M. Paul—to the oppressive elements of Roman Catholicism, which she often associates with Jesuit tactics. Madame Beck, the "little Jesuit," trains the girls at her establishment to spy on Lucy, to report "in Catholic ears whatever the Protestant teacher said."[29] Perpetual vigilance of Lucy's every movement, often so careless that Lucy must discover and feel restricted by it, is the chief means whereby Madame Beck tyrannizes, as determined as the hag Reason to squelch Lucy's affections for Graham. But ultimately, her control takes the form of fictions as dramatic as those of the goddess Imagination. She sends her to the fairytale residence of Madame Walravens, where she is "awestruck" when Père Silas leads her to a cell "more like an oratory than a boudoir, a very solemn little chamber, looking as if it were a place...dedicated to relics and remembrance."[30] Lisping a prayer like an incantation while a "yellow electric light" from the sky creates a halo around his bald head, he recounts to her the romantic story of the nun Justine Marie and M. Paul. When this appeal to her imagination does not keep Lucy from pursuing her beloved Paul, Madame Beck tries to induce opium fantasies to make her forget him. Ironically, when the opium disposes Lucy to Imagination's call, it is one that takes her into the night, to a "strange vision of Villette" that

---

[28] In the only other extensive treatment I have found of the role of Catholicism in *Villette*, Clark-Beattie's "Fables of Reflection" perceives the Roman Church as providing a similar vehicle for Lucy, but like Eagleton as well as Gilbert and Gubar, she identifies English social structures as the primary forces against which Lucy rebels.

[29] Brontë, *Villette*, 147.

[30] Brontë, *Villette*, 483.

both discloses the very real "secret junta" determined to take M. Paul from her and hardens her own resolve to fight for him.

Little needs to be said of Jesuit Père Silas's obvious efforts to control Lucy through both an authoritative voice like that of Reason—"depend upon it, our faith alone could heal and help you"—and the weaving of visions like those of seductive Imagination, not only at Madame Walravens's home, but in the lilac religious pamphlet he has M. Paul plant in her desk. Equally obvious are the efforts of the self-proclaimed "lay-Jesuit" M. Paul to lord his authority over Lucy and to capture her imagination, especially in the "Apple of Discord" chapter, in which he tries to tempt her with "the Papal ritual and ceremonial."[31]

While Lucy cannot banish Reason and Imagination so long as they remain abstractions, she can when they become incarnate in these representatives of Catholicism, as though only flesh-and-blood foes of her own cherished faith can make her see her danger with immediacy and drive her to rally her own soul against its destroyers. She resists them all, her assertion that "God is not with Rome" serving as the ultimate declaration of independence. Once she has defied them as Catholic representatives, she can also defy them as people seeking to restrict her freedom and happiness. She breaks loose from the control of Madame Beck, stands up to M. Paul, boldly declares her love for him, and finally, strikes out to set up her own school. In the end, she answers Reason's efforts to confine her to uncontrollable circumstances with her own resourcefulness, albeit with the financial assistance of Paul.[32] She replaces the ineffectual, fleeting dreams of Imagination with the "real, solid joy" she first experiences after receiving a letter from Graham—"the wild savoury mess of the hunter, nourishing and salubrious meat, forest-fed or desert-reared, fresh, healthful, and life-sustaining."[33]

---

[31] Brontë, *Villette*, 515.

[32] My concern is with the new sense of liberation or autonomy Lucy experiences in standing up for herself, as well as, with her actions toward financial independence. For a discussion of her continued subjection to social constraints, see Eagleton's essay.

[33] Brontë, *Villette*, 318.

BRONTË'S SELF-ASSERTION

LIKE LUCY SNOWE, Brontë knew the tyranny of her own compulsions both to restrain her individuality and to escape confining circumstances in the world of imagination. As a young woman under the care of a stern aunt, she learned her thoughts should be focused on Christian obligations appropriate for a young woman, especially her duty to assist her family financially—frequently as a teacher or governess, positions she loathed. Flights of imagination and the fictional writing inspired by them were to be shunned as self-indulgent and morally dangerous distractions.[34] Still, she could not help the "dreams that absorb me, and the fiery imagination that at times eats me up...," as she confessed to her friend Ellen Nussey, whose moral character she believed she could never successfully emulate.[35] In her biography of Brontë, Winifred Gérin characterizes her conflict as a double tyranny: "Rebel as she often would, she recognized the validity of the rival claims, and submitted to the dual tyranny. The urge to create was admittedly the dearest and strongest of tyrannic powers, the service of which brought her such delight that its excess rebuked her, and delivered her back into the thralldom of that *other* tyrant, Conscience."[36] Yet the tyranny in the foreground of her mind as she wrote *Villette* was of a different brand, one for which Catholicism no doubt proved as much an existential symbol for Brontë the writer as a vehicle for Lucy the protagonist in their struggles for selfhood.

For several years following her return from Belgium, Brontë was immobilized by her infatuation with Constantin Heger, master of the *pensionnat* where she had studied and taught during 1841 and 1842. This fact, hidden in the interest of propriety by Elizabeth Gaskell in her *Life of Charlotte Brontë*, published shortly after her death, is demonstrated by

---

[34] For a discussion of the extent to which both Brontë and Robert Southey—to whom she wrote for vocational guidance—saw moral dangers in a strong imagination, see Hook's "Charlotte Brontë."

[35] Quoted in Elizabeth Gaskell, *The Life of Charlotte Brontë*, 1857 (London: Penguin, 1975) 161.

[36] Winifred Gérin, *Charlotte Brontë: The Evolution of Genius* (Oxford: Clarendon University Press, 1967) 35.

Gérin in her biography. Gérin cites Brontë's correspondence to Heger in which she confessed she was "the slave to a dominant and fixed idea,"[37] an obsession which could have borne no fruit, Gérin argues, because the happily married Heger never reciprocated her feelings. So enthralled, Brontë found herself unable to write. She also took seriously Heger's advice against a literary career for women and resigned herself to teaching, for her the worst kind of bondage. According to Gérin, her "subservience to the spirit of another"[38] finally inspired *Villette*, a story of gaining autonomy, albeit through an acceptance of the loneliness autonomy entails. But it is this very loneliness that Brontë comes to see as her destiny, Gérin argues, an acceptance of which is essentially a move toward a freeing self-acceptance and self-reliance.

Naturally unwilling to give expression to such a discovery in *Villette* by recounting the true circumstances that gave rise to it, Brontë turned to another means of expression, one that must have suggested itself immediately, considering the setting of her story and her own attraction to the confessional:[39] the seductive power of Catholicism. The Roman Church, with which she so strongly identified Heger,[40] embodied his double hold on her as protective teacher to whose judgments she readily submitted and as the inspiration for romantic fantasies. Thus, Lucy Snowe's attraction to the dogmatic Père Silas and to the mystique of Catholic ritual can be seen as an expression of Brontë's own attraction to Heger, both an authority under whom she might subjugate her will and an occasion for dreams in which she could lose herself, as she did in the world she created for her Byronic character Zamorna.[41] Lucy's claim that

---

[37] Gérin, *Charlotte Brontë*, 256.

[38] Gérin, *Charlotte Brontë*, 259.

[39] Gérin cites the letter in which Brontë describes her trip to the confessional when she was distraught over her love for Heger (241–42). This experience is the basis for the similar scene during Lucy's gloomy holiday.

[40] See Gérin's description of Heger and the correspondence she cites of Brontë's own portrayal of him (206–207).

[41] Zamorna emerged in Brontë's juvenilia, which began with stories about her brother Branwell's wooden soldiers. Zamorna came to play a central role in her fantasies about the imaginary kingdom of Angria.

"God is not with Rome," then, corresponds to Brontë's relinquishment of her fantasies about Heger after two years of pining away for him.[42]

Thus, Catholicism has a two-fold function in Villette: as a catalyst for the heroine's final self-assertion, it serves an artistic purpose; as a source of personal symbols for the author, it serves the purpose of a much needed self-expression and, indeed, self-definition. For both protagonist and author, the Roman Church effectively incorporates the double-tyranny of external authority and romantic spells and, in doing so, proves paradoxically sacramental in mediating rebirth.

---

[42] The symbolic nature of Catholicism for Brontë in Villette is underscored by the paucity of references to it (six brief passages) in her first novel, The Professor, also set in Belgium. Writing it while still under the spell of Heger, she avoided the issue of submission and thus had no need for a symbol of its dangers. Her choice of a male protagonist engaged as a professor in a pensionnat for boys suggests her need to steer clear of personal struggles.

6

"BLIGHTED" BY A "UPAS-SHADOW": CATHOLICISM, GENDER, AND SENSUALITY IN *WESTWARD HO!*

IN "WHAT, THEN, Does Doctor Newman Mean?" Reverend Charles Kingsley lambastes John Henry Newman, defector to Rome, for promoting practices of "priestcraft" and "chicanery" in "the Medieval Church."[1] Kingsley's deeply felt anti-Catholicism, vented on no individual as much as on Newman, suffuses his sermons, correspondence, and fiction, as well as essays like this one.[2] Yet his most

---

[1] Quoted in *The Victorian Mind*, ed. Gerald Kauvar and Gerald Sorensen (New York: Putnam, 1969) 199. The full title of the article, which appeared in *Macmillan's Magazine*, is "'What, Then, Does Dr. Newman Mean?': A Reply to a Pamphlet Lately Published by Dr. Newman." The essay prompted the writing of *Apologia pro Vita Sua*, in which Newman explains his reasons for converting to Roman Catholicism.

[2] In a village sermon which shares its subject with *Westward Ho!*, for example, Kingsley praised English heroes of Elizabethan days who defended "the Gospel and the Bible against the Pope of Rome" (Quoted on p. 111 of Allan John Hartley's *The Novels of Charles Kingsley: A Christian Social Interpretation* [Folkstone: Hour Glass Press, 1977]). Some of his harshest judgments on Roman Catholicism can be found in letters he wrote to discourage corespondents from converting to the "Romish" religion. See, for example, a letter written in 1849 in which he rails against Catholicism's "anile sophistry," "inferior deities," and "prurient celibates" (Fanny Kingsley, ed., *Charles Kingsley: His Letters and*

sustained and vivid attack on the "Romish" Church remains his novel *Westward Ho!*[3]

Published in 1855 and intended as an instrument to rally patriotism during the Crimean War, *Westward Ho!* recounts the battle of Elizabethan England against Spain for dominion in the New World and in defense of English shores against the attack of the Spanish Armada.[4]

Memories of His Life, 2 vols., [New York: J. F. Taylor, 1899] 1:175–78). Creative works permeated by anti-Catholic sentiment include the play *The Saint's Tragedy* (1848) and the novels *Yeast* (1848) and *Hypatia* (1852).

[3] Robert Martin calls *Westward Ho!* Kingsley's "most vehemently anti-Roman novel" (*The Dust of Combat,* London: Faber and Faber, 1959, 174).

[4] Charles Kingsley, *Westward Ho!* 1855, 2 vols. (New York: J. F. Taylor, 1899). *Westward Ho!*'s rather involved plot can be summarized as follows. After sailing around the world with Sir Francis Drake, young Amyas Leigh returns to his home of Bideford to find an England infiltrated by Jesuits plotting with the Spanish to take over Ireland. Amyas's cousin Eustace, a despicable Catholic, appears to be in league with his Jesuit teachers. Eustace shares with Amyas and Amyas's brother Frank an attraction to beautiful Rose Salterne. Failing in his suit for Rose, Eustace joins his Jesuit friends. Amyas and Frank vow to relinquish Rose, each to the other. When war breaks out in Ireland, Rose learns from the witch Lucy Passmore that her future husband might be a foreign nobleman.

At this point, Salvation Yeo returns from the New World and tells the story of his travels with John Oxenham, who was captured by the Spanish and hanged. Oxenham's affair in South America with a Spanish nobleman's wife produced a daughter, whom Yeo vowed to protect. But he was apprehended by inquisitors and sent to the galleys. Having escaped, Yeo wants to return to the New World to carry out his promise. First, however, he joins Amyas and the English forces in driving the Spanish from Ireland. The Leigh brothers agree that Amyas will eventually marry Rose; however, upon learning that many of Bideford's young men love her, the two siblings create the Brotherhood of the Rose, whose members vow not to pursue her during the course of the war.

Successful in Ireland, the English take as hostages the Spanish nobleman Don Guzman Maria Magdalena Sotomayer de Soto. When Amyas sends the nobleman to Bideford to await ransom, Guzman secretly wins the heart of Rose and they elope to La Guayra, where he has secured à post as governor. Along with Yeo, his brother Frank, and members of the Brotherhood of the Rose, Amyas pursues Guzman to Caracas, where they learn that Guzman truly loves Rose. They are attacked by Guzman's men when Eustace, also in Caracas,

The novel's narrator presents this conflict as a religious war between the Protestant angel of truth and justice and the Catholic pawn of Satan, spewing a series of epithets at the Church of Rome, including "cruel," "heathen," "devilish,"[5] and "blighted" by a "Upas-shadow."[6] He characterizes the Pope as a tyrant and the Jesuits as perverse and conniving "rogues"[7] who corrupt youths with "base and vulgar...teaching"[8] and transport cargoes of "bulls, dispensations, secret correspondences, seditious tracts, and so forth"[9] across England, bastion of Protestant liberty. He also defends the Catholic penal laws, which "never troubled anyone who did not make conspiracy and rebellion an integral doctrine of his religious creed," and in fact, never troubled even traitors such as these "unless, fired with the glory of martyrdom, they bullied the long-suffering of Elizabeth and her council into giving them their deserts, and, like poor Father Southwell in after years, insisted on being hanged, whether Burleigh liked or not."[10]

---

convinces Guzman that Rose will leave him for the Leighs. Amyas escapes but Frank is captured.

After three years of searching for El Dorado, Amyas and his crew plan to steal a Spanish ship and return to England. With the help of an Indian tribe, they slay a troupe of Spanish slave drivers, freeing their slaves and departing with their treasure. Accompanying them is a beautiful Indian maiden, Ayacanora, whom Yeo eventually recognizes as Oxenham's daughter. The English take a Spanish ship, freeing its prisoners, one of whom is Lucy Passmore. Lucy tells Amyas that Frank and Rose died at the hands of the Inquisition.

Back in England, Amyas eagerly joins English forces against the Armada in hopes of killing Don Guzman, for whom he is consumed with hatred. In a stormy sea battle, demon-like Amyas pursues Guzman's ship, but a rocky shore smashes it, depriving Amyas of his revenge. When a bolt of lightning kills Yeo and blinds Amyas, the hero sees the event as a sign from God. Consequently, he repents of his obsessive hatred for Guzman and of his resistance to loving the half-Spanish Ayacanora, who clearly loves him.

[5] Kingsley, *Westward*, 1:3.
[6] Kingsley, *Westward*, 1:82.
[7] Kingsley, *Westward*, 1:92.
[8] Kingsley, *Westward*, 1:97.
[9] Kingsley, *Westward*, 1:93.
[10] Kingsley, *Westward*, 1:77.

The novel reserves its most venomous attacks for Spaniards, who are, after all, the concrete representatives of Romish tyranny, the flesh-and-blood antagonists of *Westward Ho!* In the mind of the admirable character Sir Richard Grenville, the "devilries of the Spaniards...enemies of God and man"[11] justify England's plunder of Spain's West Indian booty. Sir Richard declares to Devon's brave men that the treasure will be used in "building up the weal of the Reformed Churches throughout the world, and the liberties of all nations, against a tyranny more foul and rapacious than that of Nero or Caligula."[12] The foulness of the Spanish is expressed in their demonic rituals and relics, as well as their idolatrous worship of saints. Their rapaciousness extends beyond pillaging villages and enslaving Indians to the slaughter of native infants in the name of faith. Salvation Yeo, faithful servant of the novel's hero, Amyas Leigh, provides an especially graphic account of a West Indian massacre:

> [O]ne [Spaniard], catching the pretty babe out of my arms, calls for water and a priest (for they had their shavelings with them), and no sooner was it christened than, catching the babe by the heels, he dashed out its brains—oh! gentlemen, gentlemen!—against the ground, as if it had been a kitten; and so did they to several more innocents that night, after they had christened them; saying it was best for them to go to heaven while they were still sure thereof.[13]

In this fiendishness, the Spanish soldiers only follow the example of their ecclesiastical leaders, the bloodthirsty inquisitors who torture and kill the hero's brother, Frank Leigh, as well as Rose Salterne, the Devon maid who has eloped to South America with the Spanish aristocrat Don Guzman.

Undoubtedly, Kingsley accurately represents both the sentiments of many English patriots living during Elizabeth's reign and the heinous nature of the Spanish Inquisition, but *Westward Ho!*'s portrait of

---

[11] Kingsley, *Westward,* 1:18.
[12] Kingsley, *Westward,* 1:19.
[13] Kingsley, *Westward,* 1:231.

Catholics and Catholicism in general is undeniably skewed, as several Kingsley scholars attest.[14] Like Brontë, Kingsley writes in the wake of the Papal Aggression of 1850.[15] *Westward Ho!, Villette,* and many other

---

[14] Una Pope-Hennessey confirms *Westward Ho!*'s anti-Catholic bias in her discussion of Kingsley's review of *History of England* by Froude: "So accustomed had he become in *Westward Ho!* to using violent and depreciatory language about them [Catholic priests] and to coupling the profession of Catholicism with squalor of conduct and ferocious cruelty, that it must have seemed a very harmless thing to him to say in his review that Romish priests in general disregarded truth" (*Canon Charles Kingsley: A Biography,* London: Chatto and Windus, 1948, 212–13).

Susan Chitty, a more recent biographer, identifies Kingsley's views on Catholicism as one of the many biases making *Westward Ho!* unappealing to adults today: "Lacking as we do Kingsley's conviction that England alone has the privilege of 'replenishing the earth and subduing it for God and the Queen,' and that all Catholics are 'Jesuitical plotters' and all negroes 'ant-eating apes,' we cannot view their slaughter with the enthusiasm expected of us. To us, but evidently not to Kingsley, the extermination of seven hundred Spaniards in Ireland [depicted in the novel] is somewhat repugnant" (*The Beast and the Monk,* London: Hodder and Stoughton, 1974, 171).

Allan John Hartley is a noteworthy apologist for Kingsley's treatment of Catholics in *Westward Ho!* He admits that "*Westward Ho!* teems with defamatory remarks about Roman Catholics," that "[t]hey are accused of casuistry and vilified as liars and schemers," but insists that "theological polemic is not Kingsley's concern in this novel. The circumstances in which he wrote it were such as to enable him to rise above personal animosity" (*The Novels of Charles Kingsley: A Christian Social Interpretation,* Folkstone: Hour Glass Press, 1977, 114). The logic of such an argument puzzles me. On the basis of the examples I've cited from Kingsley's writings, I would also take issue with Hartley's conclusion that "Kingsley was less opposed to Roman Catholicism than to that which had come to represent it: Jesuitry and the Spanish Inquisition" (Ibid.).

[15] According to Martin, "If the Crimean War was the immediate stimulus to writing the book, surely a secondary one was the fright England had taken in 1850 over 'Papal Aggression' when Wiseman was named Archbishop of Westminster by the Pope. In 1851 the 'Ecclesiastical Titles Bill' was passed, forbidding Roman Catholics to establish bishoprics in England. The bill was never enforced, but it was evidence of the hysterical fear felt by some English Protestants, among them, of course, Kingsley" (175).

novels of the 1850s act as vicious addenda to the Ecclesiastical Titles Bill, a sanction against the Catholic Church.

Like many of its literary counterparts, *Westward Ho!* derides a standard list of Catholic features, seen in some of the above examples: blind obedience to the Pope, religious scrupulosity, the use of relics and other forms of superstition, and—perhaps the favorite target—the Jesuits.[16] But of all the Catholic evils depicted by Kingsley, two especially engage his imagination, revealing both his creativity and complexity: the Marian cult and the Roman Church's attitude toward carnal pleasures.

THE MARIAN CULT IN WESTWARD HO!

Over and over again in *Westward Ho!*, English heroes and the narrator himself condemn Catholics for their worship of the Virgin Mary. In the novel's opening chapter, John Oxenham ends his account of English bravery with a diatribe against the Virgin cult of the Spaniards: "They pray to a woman, the idolatrous rascals! and no wonder they fight like women."[17] When a friar credits "Mary, the fount of mercies" with Amyas's successful trip down the Magdalena River, the hero "bluntly" replies, "We have done well enough without her as yet."[18] The narrator mocks the boasting servants of Mary as they prepare the Armada:

> [The Spanish were] blessed by the pope, and sanctified with holy water and prayer to the service of "God and his Mother." Yes, they [English commanders] would fall, and England with them. The proud islanders, who had dared to rebel against St. Peter,

---

[16] According to Maison, "From the best-selling literature of the day we see that the Jesuit loomed large in Protestant imagination as a villain of the blackest dye, a spy, a secret agent, suave, supercilious and satanically unscrupulous, laying his cunning plots for the submission of England to 'Jesuitocracy,' wheedling rich widows, forcing his converts to change their wills in favour of his Order, to kneel in penitence almost naked for hours through chilly winter nights and to leave their families for life at a minute's notice" (169).

[17] Kingsley, *Westward*, 1:6.

[18] Kingsley, *Westward*, 2:274.

and to cast off the worship of "Mary," should bow their necks once more under the yoke of the Gospel.[19]

Oxenham indicates that English scorn for the Marian cult is inspired just as much—if not more so—by the inferiority of a female deity and her womanish worshippers as by idolatry itself. In *Westward Ho!* a man can possess no quality worse than womanishness. A case in point is Eustace Leigh, whose lack of virility renders him the most despicable character in the novel. When the athletic Amyas offers his "lion's paw" to his cousin, "gripping [his hand] with a great round fist," Eustace responds by "pinching hard" Amyas's hand "with white, straight fingers." He counters Amyas's direct gaze and "heartiest of smiles" with an obsequious glance and handshake.[20] Eustace fears his cousin because "he knew Amyas could have killed him with a blow; and there are natures, who, instead of rejoicing in the strength of men of greater prowess than themselves, look at such with irritation, dread, at last, spite; expecting, perhaps, that the stronger will do to them what they feel they might have done in his place."[21] While such sentiments are crushed by "brave men, though they be very sparrows," they thrive in the heart of "cowards" like Eustace. Only such a craven weakling could prey on the fair Rose Salterne, as Eustace does, causing her final destruction when he plants seeds of suspicion in the mind of her husband, Don Guzman.

Jesuit tutors Campion and Parsons bear the blame for Eustace's effete character, yet all the novel's celibates are "vowed not to be men."[22] In a passage describing Frank's character, the narrator goes so far as to suggest that womanishness is inherent in Catholic sensibility itself. Though ultimately a noble martyr of the Inquisition, Frank pales beside his strapping brother. He is a sensitive scholar, whose complexion "shamed with its whiteness that of all fair ladies around,"[23] one "as delicately

---

[19] Kingsley, *Westward*, 2:343.

[20] Kingsley, *Westward*, 1:80.

[21] Kingsley, *Westward*, 1:80–81.

[22] Kingsley, *Westward*, 2:44. These words belong to Frank Leigh, but reflect the sentiments of the narrator.

[23] Kingsley, *Westward*, 1:58.

beautiful as his brother was huge and strong."[24] Not only does Frank find the romantic Philip Sidney "lovely and loving as ever,"[25] but he falls under the spell of "the frescoes of the Vatican" and "the luscious strains" of Palestrina's music "beneath the dome of St. Peter's."[26] These effeminate qualities seem to explain Frank's sickliness and even the weakness revealed in his pathetic sobbing on his mother's lap when he learns that Amyas, too, loves Rose Salterne.

Naturally, Amyas's primary rival, Don Guzman Maria Magdalena de Soto, is himself contaminated by the womanishness contaminating his name. He is introduced as "tall and graceful…golden-haired and fair-skinned, with hands as small and white as a woman's."[27] Manly Amyas's initial reaction to Guzman is predictable: "In spite of his beauty and his carriage, Amyas shrank from him instinctively." As the narrator ironically notes, a man marked by such effeminate traits champions "our Lady and the choir of saints…[whose] divine protection…enables the Catholic cavalier single-handed to chase a thousand Paynims."[28] He does his best to make good this claim, finally threatening England's sacred shores in the Spanish Armada—and only after stealing away Devon's most precious possession, Rose Salterne, to whom the town's men have pledged their devotion.

The novel's assault on the Marian cult and the womanishness it encourages echoes sentiments Kingsley expressed throughout his life. In an 1851 letter, he denounced Rome for robbing its faithful of manly qualities "by substituting a Virgin Mary, who is to *nurse* them like infants, for a Father in whom they are men and brothers."[29] Kingsley emphasized the need for Christian men to be strong, both morally and physically, a belief central to what came to be called "muscular Christianity."[30] He

---

[24] Kingsley, *Westward*, 1:38.

[25] Kingsley, *Westward*, 1:38.

[26] Kingsley, *Westward*, 1:36.

[27] Kingsley, *Westward*, 1:296.

[28] Kingsley, *Westward*, 1:318.

[29] *Letters*, Kingsley ed., 1:221.

[30] According to Chitty, this term was probably first used in reference to Kingsley by a writer for the *Saturday Review* in 1858. For a fascinating discussion of muscular Christianity in light of recent cultural and gender theory, cf. Donald

elaborated on his belief in a letter written to his future wife, Fanny, during their engagement:

> There has always seemed to me something impious in the neglect of personal health, strength, and beauty, which the religious, and sometimes clergymen of this day affect...I could not do half the little good I do do here, if it were not for that strength and activity which some consider coarse and degrading...How merciful God has been in turning all the strength and hardihood I gained in snipe shooting and hunting, and rowing, and jack-fishing in those magnificent fens to His work.[31]

He ends his letter by decrying "effeminate ascetics" and exhorting the virile priest whom men can "look up to" as "their superior, if he chose to exert his power, in physical as well as intellectual skill."[32] Indeed, he declares Christ himself a "strong *man*" in a later letter meant to dissuade a youth from converting to Catholicism: in contrast to the "indulgent virgin," Christ is "stern because loving" and punishes "as a man would do it, '*mighty* to save.'"[33]

To some extent, Kingsley might have seen muscular Christianity as an aspect of Christian Socialism, which he strongly advocated as a young clergyman. His deep concern for the plight of the poor and factory laborers precipitated his brave, if somewhat rash, declaration: "I am a Church of England parson...and a Chartist!"[34] He believed a minister must roll up his sleeves and fight for the humane treatment of those on the lowest rung of the social ladder. At the same time, his grave aversion to effeminate portrayals of God and his near fanatical zeal in deriding

---

E. Hall's *Muscular Christianity: Embodying the Victorian Age* (Cambridge: Cambridge University Press, 1994). Chapter 4 of the study is devoted to Kingsley.

[31] *Letters,* Kingsley ed., 1:63.

[32] *Letters,* Kingsley ed., 1:64.

[33] *Letters,* Kingsley ed., 1:228.

[34] Quoted in Brenda Colloms, *Charles Kingsley: The Lion of Eversley* (London: Constable, 1975) 116. Colloms describes here the Chartist meeting in which Kingsley made this declaration.

"Mariolatry"[35] suggest that Kingsley is driven by his insecurities as much as by his vision of Christian activism. We can gain insight into these insecurities by considering the woman worship practiced by Kingsley's heroes in *Westward Ho!*

For the most part, the role of the novel's English women is the fairly nominal one of "angel in the house," a Victorian conceptualization that both deifies women and renders them ineffectual in matters of the world.[36] This kind of woman worship is consistent with the perimeters Kingsley earnestly drew around manly romantic love and around gender roles.[37] However, *Westward Ho!*'s heroic Leigh brothers practice a form of woman worship incongruent with Kingsley's ideals. Desiring to join Amyas's crusade to rescue Rose, Frank "looked forward to asking the queen's permission for his voyage with the most abject despondency and terror."[38] When Amyas grows irritated with him, Frank retorts, "You cannot comprehend the pain of parting from her." In his interview with the queen, he demonstrates the extent of his anxiety, weeping and falling to his knees to ask for mercy when the jealous Elizabeth upbraids him for wanting to desert her for another woman. Since Kingsley presents England's struggle against Spain as a high moral cause, Elizabeth seems less concerned about inspiring manly virtue than servile devotion to her. Faced with her jealousy and pettiness (which led her to withhold knighthood from Frank because of his decision), Frank only increases his obeisance. "Had I my will," he announces to Amyas, "there should be in every realm not a salique, but an anti-salique law: whereby no kings, but only queens should rule mankind."[39] Though his own feelings for Elizabeth do not run so deep, Amyas concedes, "There's some sense in

---

[35] Kingsley uses this term on several occasions. For example, see his letter from February 5, 1851 (1: 228).

[36] The epithet is taken from the title of a popular Victorian poem by Coventry Patmore glorifying the role of women in domestic affairs.

[37] Kingsley sees "woman worship," along with "Christian art" and "chivalry," as "witnesses" or symbols of spiritual reality (*Letters*, 1:162). For him, assigning women a spiritual role meant elevating conjugal relations to the level of sacrament.

[38] Kingsley, *Westward*, 2:13.

[39] Kingsley, *Westward*, 2:15.

that...I'd run a mile for a woman when I would not walk a yard for a man."[40]

Amyas lives up to this claim, not so much in his final surrender to Ayacanora, daughter of John Oxenham and a Spanish woman, as in his total submission to the woman who wills this marriage, his mother. When Frank tells Amyas he wishes to accompany him on his voyage west, Amyas is concerned less about encouraging Frank's manly duties than about avoiding his mother's disapproval. He constantly keeps Mrs. Leigh before his mind's eye during his three-year sojourn and, on returning to Bideford, submits himself to her will rather than pursuing England's interests in America. When she blesses his union with Ayacanora, forged at her direction, one gets the feeling that Mrs. Leigh will act as the third and most powerful party within the marriage: "[F]ear not to take her to your heart again; for it is your mother who has laid her there."[41]

Perhaps more telling than the submission of Kingsley's heroes to women is the narrator's fascination with the way in which the chief antagonist combines feminine and manly qualities without surrendering his nobleness. Pretty courtier Don Guzman, the enemy of England and abductor of Rose Salterne, is both graceful and strong, eloquent and outspoken, schooled and experienced in battle, beautiful and athletic, refined and daring. As a character who incorporates traits identified by Kingsley as womanish and manly, he attracts both women and men. He captures the hearts of country maidens, especially that of Rose, who finds him a mixture of Frank and Amyas in his graceful manliness. He is admired by his captors, including Amyas, who is intrigued by the Don's charms and stories of El Dorado. The narrator himself defends Guzman, emphasizing the sincerity of his love for Rose and the injustice of Amyas's demonization of Guzman after the Spanish Inquisition executes Frank. Kingsley goes so far as to open his hero's eyes by the end of the tale—ironically, by blinding him—so that Amyas can see Guzman as a spiritual brother whom he has wronged.

What does this vindication of Guzman—at odds with his role as villain—suggest about Kingsley's own struggles, and what purpose does

[40] Kingsley, *Westward*, 1:15.
[41] Kingsley, *Westward*, 2:455.

Catholicism serve in his effort to resolve them? Kingsley lived up to his own standards of manliness as a husband and father, a sportsman, and a lover of hiking and the outdoors. He also resisted the sort of emotionalism and introspection he believed to be not only unmanly, but also hazardous to one's faith. However, resistance does not change one's nature, in his case "delicate, nervous, and painfully sensitive,"[42] qualities aggravated by his awkwardness and severe stammering. Nor can it eliminate chronic depression and nervous breakdowns or recurring religious doubts, Kingsley's lifelong vulnerabilities. Certainly futile would have been any effort to resist his emotional dependency on Fanny, which at times approached the kind of woman worship ascribed to Frank and Amyas Leigh. Justin McCarthy, a student at Cambridge during Kingsley's appointment there, attributed the professor's temperamental nature to the strong feminine element of his character: "despite his rough voice and vigorous manner, he was as feminine in his likes and dislikes, his impulses and prejudices, as Harriet Martineau was masculine in her intellect and George Sand in her emotions."[43] Another student of Kingsley's, John Martineau, noted, "For all his man's strength there was a deep vein of the *woman* in him."[44] And John Blackwood, editor of *Blackwood's Magazine,* once remarked, "With all his blustering, would-be manliness, I do not look upon Kingsley as a man of power and substance at all."[45]

In *Westward Ho!* Kingsley safely projects the "womanishness" in himself onto outsider, Catholic characters and then derides them. As the novel's chief Catholic, Don Guzman shares in this derision. However, in his case, it is perfunctory, emphasizing his status as outsider so that Kingsley can project onto him qualities that he dares not aspire to himself. Guzman allows Kingsley to explore the possibility of combining masculine and feminine traits in a man, rather than stubbornly clinging to his facile notion that they must be mutually exclusive. By ultimately

---

[42] *Letters,* Kingsley, ed., 1:6. Fanny makes this observation about Kingley's nature.

[43] Quoted in Pope-Henessey, *Canon,* 3.

[44] Quoted in Chitty, *The Beast,* 124.

[45] Quoted in Martin, *The Dust of Combat,* 181.

vindicating Guzman in the novel, Kingsley suggests fictively a model that could ameliorate his own insecurities. And, by making Guzman the defeated enemy, he ensures that his readers—and, perhaps, he himself—do not take such a model too seriously.

Specifically in terms of Catholicism, Guzman also allows Kingsley to provide a fairer, more reasonable picture of the Roman Church. Catholicism as embodied in Guzman belies its effete portrayal in the novel's other Catholic characters and makes explicit what Kingsley suggests at the margins of his tale: the Church in general possesses both masculine and feminine attributes. Catholicism incorporates patriarchy and a frequently nurturing priesthood, dogma and mysticism, military assertion, and ascetic withdrawal from the world. Kingsley's dogmatism will not permit such an admission, probably not even to himself, but what he cannot do in terms of an institution he scorns, he *can* do in terms of an individual. Just as he has his narrator acknowledge in passing the patriotism and virtue of many of England's Catholics during Elizabethan times, Kingsley can also present a noble picture of a very Catholic individual. Taking the next rational step, admitting the complexity of the Catholic Church, is beyond him. As Margaret Thorp concludes, "Kingsley's was an immature, a boy's imagination. He did not recreate for himself scenes in a past age, he pictured Charles Kingsley moving in those scenes and wrote accordingly."[46] No wonder George Eliot said of *Westward Ho!*, "Kingsley sees, feels and paints vividly, but he theorises illogically and moralises absurdly."[47] To Kingsley's credit, however, Don Guzman represents a step toward objectivity.

CATHOLICISM AND THE FLESH

A related conflict that finds expression in *Westward Ho!* is between spirit and flesh. As we have seen, Kingsley derides the asceticism practiced by Jesuits Parsons and Campion; it is a sort of unmanly rejection of natural—that is to say, God-given—impulses to live fully, to love, and if need be, to fight passionately for the glory of God. His play *The Saint's*

---

[46] Margaret Farrand Thorp, *Charles Kingsley, 1819–1875* (New York: Octagon Books, 1969 [rpt of Princeton edition, 1937]) 121.

[47] Quoted in Chitty, *The Beast,* 173.

Tragedy, begun as a biography of St. Elizabeth of Hungary, was an attack on such asceticism. The play recounts the story of a thirteenth-century woman, naturally good and full of life, who comes under the control of a fiendish monk after the death of her husband and begins a life of morbid, self-inflicted penance. In his letters as well as this drama, Kingsley not only scorns mawkish self-denial, but celebrates what he calls a "healthy materialism":

> Oh! will it not be better thus to wait for The Renewal, and learn to love all things, all men—not as spirits only, not with "a love for poor souls" as the cant saying is (that unappreciable, loveless abstraction), but—as men and women, of body, soul, and spirit, each being made one, and therefore all to be loved? Is it not better thus to love intellect as well as spirit, and matter as well as intellect, and dumb animals, and trees, and rocks, and sun, and stars, that our joy and glory may be fuller, more all-embracing, when they are restored, and the moan which the earth makes day and night to God, has ceased for ever? Better far, than to make ourselves sham wings, and try to fly, and drop fluttering down, disgusted with our proper element, yet bound to it, poor selfish isolated mystics![48]

Long before writing this advice to a young man considering a conversion to Roman Catholicism, Kingsley offered similar counsel to his then fiancée, Fanny, whom he believed suffered from a morbid temperament encouraged by Puseyite asceticism.[49] He urged her to "study nature" instead, to "extract every line of beauty, every association, every moral reflection, every inexpressible feeling from it."[50] Such study includes "the human figure, both as intrinsically beautiful and as

---

[48] *Letters,* Kingsley ed., 1:89.

[49] Before marrying Kingsley, Fanny had considered joining a Puseyite sisterhood. Many of Kingsley's first letters to her were intended to dissuade her from such a move. His *Life of St. Elizabeth of Hungary*—an earlier, unfinished prose version of *The Saint's Tragedy*—was planned to be a wedding gift for Fanny.

[50] *Letters,* Kingsley, ed., 1:68.

expressing mind." Though perhaps surprisingly bold, his view on marriage is a natural extension of such thinking: "[T]hese desires, which men call carnal, are truly most spiritual, most beloved by Him [the Lord], and...He Himself, when we are fit for our bliss, will work what the world might call a miracle, if necessary, to join us and those whom we love."[51]

In a letter to Fanny, Kingsley even goes so far as to say, "When you go to bed tonight, forget that you ever wore a garment, and open your lips for my kisses and spread out each limb that I may lie between your breasts all night (Canticles, I, 13)," and "At a quarter past eleven lie down, clasp your arms and every limb around me, and with me repeat the *Te Deum* aloud."[52] He saw in "those thrilling writhings" of sexual union a foreshadowing of "a union which shall be perfect" in heaven.[53]

Needless to say, nothing so erotic finds its place in a Victorian adventure tale like *Westward Ho!* In fact, the closest the novel comes to sensuality can be found in suggestive descriptions of Ayacanora, the half-clad "nymph" whose fiery beauty tempts Amyas to abandon civilization and escape with her to the exotic forests of South America. However, *Westward Ho!* does convey Kingsley's delight in the sensuousness of creation. Lush descriptions of the New World abound, one of the most tantalizing appearing in the chapter on Barbados. It is dawn and "the level rays glittered on smooth stems of the palm-trees, and threw rainbows across the foam upon the coral-reefs, and gilded lonely uplands far away."[54] In this "primeval orchard," Amyas's men

crawled from place to place plucking greedily the violet grapes of the creeping shore vine, and staining their mouths and blistering their lips with the prickly pears...[They retrieved] acid junipa-apples, luscious guavas, and crowned ananas, queen of all the fruits, which they had found by hundreds on the broiling ledges of the low tufa-cliffs; and then all, sitting on the sandy turf, defiant of galliwasps and jackspaniards, and all the weapons of

---

[51] *Letters*, Kingsley, ed., 1:71.
[52] Quoted in Chitty, *The Beast*, 80.
[53] Quoted in Chitty, *The Beast*, 81.
[54] Kingsley, *Westward*, 2:28.

the insect host, partook of the equal banquet, while old blue land-crabs sat in their house-doors and brandished their fists in defiance at the invaders, and solemn cranes stood in the water on the shoals with their heads on one side, and meditated how long it was since they had seen bipeds without feathers breaking the solitude of their isle.[55]

While such feasts for the senses recur throughout *Westward Ho!*, the novel, paradoxically, also suggests Kingsley's attraction to sensibilities he deems "monkish." One example is the affectionate portrayal of Frank, whose ascetic leanings make him see the beauties of nature as "phantoms" reflecting the "real world" of heaven.[56] At times, Frank's contemplative Christianity—as "bloodless" as the "delicate fingers of the courtier"[57]—even appears to be a viable alternative to Amyas's muscular Christianity. Mrs. Leigh suggests this, asserting that her sons will be equally blessed, despite the distinctions in them discerned by Amyas, who says, "My blessing, I suppose, will be like Esau's, to live by my sword; while Jacob here, the spiritual man, inherits the kingdom of heaven, an angel's crown."[58] Kingsley grants this equal blessing to Frank and Amyas in a way that turns Amyas's categories on their heads; for, besides succeeding in the world of human affairs by his defeat of the Armada, Amyas receives the gift of spiritual awakening, and Frank's detachment from the material world allows him to die a hero's death, surrendering his own life for love of faith and country.

Kingsley also reveals his ascetic impulses in the lusty Amyas himself. The hero's typical theology is captured in his response to Frank's contemplative spirituality: "God made all these things [the beauties of nature]...what's good enough to please God, is good enough to please you and me."[59] However, when two of his crew members appeal to this theology to justify their remaining behind in the tropical paradise, his

---

[55] Kingsley, *Westward*, 2:29.
[56] Kingsley, *Westward*, 2:30.
[57] Kingsley, *Westward*, 2:7.
[58] Kingsley, *Westward*, 2:11.
[59] Kingsley, *Westward*, 2:30–31.

righteous anger flares. He denounces them for "living thus the life of a beast,"[60] something he himself has had to resist, as we see in the chapter's title: "How Amyas Was Tempted of the Devil."

Westward Ho!'s positive depictions of both pleasure and self-denial reflect their place in Kingsley's life. He delighted in sensuousness—pleasure in God's creation—as his letters to Fanny indicate. He also reveals his eroticism in those letters, as we have seen, and especially in his drawings discovered in Fanny's diary of a nude, voluptuous maiden. (In one illustration the woman is even engaged in sexual intercourse with her lover!)[61] Chitty argues that the same illustrations indicate Kingsley's sense of guilt for indulging his fantasies, since in almost all the sketches the woman is undergoing torture. At the head of each chapter, for example, the woman lies crucified, and the book's frontispiece is an especially graphic drawing of Elizabeth's mother undergoing genital impalement. And this apparent morbidity was not confined to the drawings. As spiritual preparation for his wedding day, Kingsley fasted, slept on the floor, and rolled naked in thorns until he bled. For the first month of his marriage, at Kingsley's insistence, Charles and Fanny abstained from sex.

Kingsley defended his "Popish raptures and visions" brought on by "self-torture"[62] as preparations for more perfect sexual consummation in the future, but Chitty suggests that he deluded himself. During his college days at Cambridge, when he had temporarily abandoned religion and caroused with his schoolmates, he engaged in sex, perhaps with a prostitute. Before he married Fanny three years later, he confessed his impurity, which he felt made him unworthy of her and which could be purged through his monkish penances. In one letter to her, he confesses he even contemplated entering a monastery in France, where he would have "gone barefoot into the chapel at matins (midnight) and there confessed every sin of my whole life before the monks and offered my

---

[60] Kingsley, *Westward*, 1:200.

[61] Chitty, *The Beast*. Chitty was the first biographer to bring to light the strange mixture of eroticism and asceticism in Kingsley's character. Chitty drew on documents recently released by family members, consisting of approximately three hundred of Kingsley's love letters to Fanny, as well as Fanny's diary, which contained Kingsley's erotic drawings.

[62] Quoted in Chitty, *The Beast*, 75.

naked body to be scourged by them."[63] But I question Chitty's position. In openly acknowledging his ascetic impulses as well as his delight in pleasure, Kingsley was able to reconcile the two, as we have seen, by sanctifying nature, including human nature's sexual dimension. There is no reason to believe that Kingsley continued to be racked with guilt for his whole married life because of one sexual escapade during his youth. On the contrary, there is every indication that his erotic drawings and letters to Fanny brought him a sense of freedom and fulfillment that continued though his conjugal life. If we accept this, then it makes sense to accept even his monkish penances before his marriage as exactly what he claimed them to be: the means to encourage his appetite for a feast by fasting. Considering his muscular Christianity, he also might have viewed them as some kind of manly initiation rite. Even claiming Kingsley exhibits sadomasochistic tendencies does not require us to conclude that he was guilt-ridden or self-divided.

Westward Ho! might be seen as representing Kingsley's integration of the spiritual and carnal dimensions of his personality or, at least, as effectively expressing his ideal of their union. The opposite tendencies of Frank and Amyas, both heroic figures, are never disparaged by Kingsley's narrator because the characters do not take these tendencies to extremes. Frank's ascetic sensibility does not preclude enthusiastic involvement in a military mission, and Amyas's lustiness does not preclude godliness or, in the end, even an ecstatic experience.

The novel's Catholic characters are another story. On one hand, Kingsley depicts them as spiritual grotesques: the effete Campion and Parsons practice an unmanly celibacy and a misogyny encouraged by their twisted self-denial; Eustace's own religiosity and acts of mortification contribute to his vileness; and the perverse inquisitors burn

---

[63] Quoted in Chitty, The Beast, 59. He also acknowledged his own early attraction to Catholicism itself in the letter to a young man considering converting to the Roman religion: "Believe me, I can sympathize with you. I have been through it; I have longed for Rome, and boldly faced the consequences of joining Rome; and though I now have, thank God, cast'all wish of change behind me years ago as a great lying devil's temptation, yet I still long as ardently as ever to see in the Church of England much which only now exists, alas! in the Church of Rome" (Letters 1:175).

sinful Protestant flesh. On the other hand, as though one pole requires the other, Catholics in the novel are fiendish gluttons: Eustace's lust for Rose—seen in "a quiver in his voice and a fire in his eye, from which she shrank by instinct"—makes him hold her "the more fiercely" until she shrieks for help;[64] hungry for blood, Catholic soldiers bash babies against rocks; inquisitors derive sadistic pleasure from the torture they inflict; and the greedy Pope is eager to expand his coffers and his worldly dominion.

Unlike the portrayal of Catholic womanishness, the portrayal of Catholic Manicheanism is integrated into the novel's design.[65] Against the dangerous extremes of spirit and flesh represented by *Westward Ho!'s* Catholic characters, Kingsley juxtaposes his own integrative vision, expressed most eloquently in the following passage from the novel's final chapter:

> Yes, it is over; and the great Armada is vanquished. It is lulled for awhile, the everlasting war which is in heaven, the battle of Iran and Turan, of the children of light and of darkness, of Michael and his angels against Satan and his fiends; the battle which slowly and seldom, once in the course of many centuries, culminates and ripens into a day of judgment and becomes palpable and incarnate; no longer a mere spiritual fight, but one of flesh and blood, wherein simple men may choose their sides without mistake, and help God's cause not merely with prayer and pen, but with sharp shot and cold steel. A day of judgment

---

[64] Kingsley, *Westward*, 1:114.

[65] Manicheanism here refers to a tendency to polarize spirit and matter into elements of good and evil, with matter finding its quintessential expression in sexuality. Proponents of the system of Manes, a third-century Babylonian, believed that celibacy should be embraced by the enlightened elect. Strains of such dualism and elitism can be seen in the ethos' of both Puritanism and Evangelicalism, as well as in the asceticism of monastic life in the Roman Catholic Church, which has condemned Manicheanism from the time of its development.

has come, which has divided the light from the darkness, and the sheep from the goats, and tried each man's work by the fire.[66]

In this apocalyptical interpretation of history, Kingsley sees the battle against Spanish oppressors as the "palpable" and "incarnate" expression of a spiritual war. But rather than reducing the material world to its symbolic value, he understands engagement in it as the means to shape spiritual reality. Not only is it the "sharp shot and cold steel" or "each man's work" that determines one's personal spiritual status as sheep or goat, but also it is the collective action of England that "lulled for a while, the everlasting war."

This passage serves as an appropriate prelude to Amyas's great epiphany. Earlier in the novel, Amyas chides Frank for his transcendentalism, arguing that demeaning the material world by reducing it to a reflection of a better, spiritual world shows ingratitude to the Creator. Yet, after defeating the Armada, he becomes deeply convinced of the symbolic value of the material world. Seated in "narrow and untrodden cavern" beneath a "hideous" abyss where he could hear "the mysterious thunder and gurgle of the surge in the subterranean adit,"[67] the blind Amyas sees "the water and the sky; as plain as ever I saw them, till I thought my sight was come again."[68] Amyas continues recounting his vision to William Cary:

> But soon I knew it was not so; for I saw more than man could see; right over the ocean, as I live, and away to the Spanish Main. And I saw Barbados, and Grenada, and all the isles that we ever sailed by; and La Guayra in Caracas, and the Silla, and the house beneath it where she lived. And I saw him walking with her on the barbecue, and he loved her then. I saw what I saw; and he loved her; and I say he loves her still.[69]

---

[66] Kingsley, *Westward*, 2:419.
[67] Kingsley, *Westward*, 2:442.
[68] Kingsley, *Westward*, 2:444.
[69] Kingsley, *Westward*, 2:444.

Amyas's vision takes him to the wrecked Spanish galleon beneath the sea, where he finds Don Guzman in his cabin, prawns and crayfish swimming above the heads of him and his men. When Guzman asks Amyas to make peace with him, Amyas shakes his enemy's hand.

Encouraged by the sublime natural setting and consisting of vivid sensory impressions, this epiphany allows Amyas to enjoy spiritual communion with Guzman. The epiphany's ultimate value, however, is not as a mystical experience; rather, it is as a catalyst for action, removing his self-absorption and hatred so that he can once again carry out duties to family, friends, and country. Ultimately, the vision allows him to abandon celibacy and marry Ayacanora—having forgiven her for being half-Spanish—and perhaps to anticipate eagerly (at least, in the author's mind) the connubial pleasures that Kingsley himself praised.

In the final analysis, Catholicism in *Westward Ho!* serves two functions for Kingsley because it reflects two personal conflicts, only one of which he adequately resolved. Never at ease with his own feminine attributes, Kingsley turns Catholic characters into effeminate whipping boys before allowing himself imaginative freedom with Don Guzman. Even then the Don hardly affects the novel's direction. True, the blinded, bereft Amyas learns something from Guzman about feminine sensibilities, but a few pages do not bring his enemy back to life or weaken the novel's promotion of the manly hero and British chauvinism. As Robert Martin observes, "At the end of the book Amyas Leigh is struck blind by lightning because his vengeance becomes personal rather than national and religious, but Kingsley's sympathy is clearly with him in his hatred of all things Spanish and Roman."[70]

Conversely, the author's conscious efforts to reconcile spirit and flesh are reflected in the coherent, albeit unsoundly applied, theology of sexuality in *Westward Ho!* Very deliberately, Kingsley juxtaposes Catholicism's disordered views toward sensuality—seen in ascetic and depraved characters—and his own vision of spirit and flesh in harmony. One may certainly object to the role Kingsley assigns to Catholicism;

---

[70] Martin, *Dust,* 177.

however, it becomes an effective foil for enlightening his readers—and, very likely, for reminding himself—of the dangers of Manicheanism.

7

CRUCIFIXES AND MADONNAS: CATHOLICISM AND THE VALIDATION OF SUFFERING IN *ROMOLA*

DURING THE OXFORD Movement, an evangelical Mary Ann Evans decried the Tractarians for their dangerous admiration of Rome, contending that they

evince by their compliments to Rome, as a dear though erring Sister, and [by] their attempts to give a romish colour to our ordinances, with a very confused and unscriptural statement of the great doctrine of justification, a disposition rather to fraternize with the members of a church carrying on her brow the prophetical epithets applied by St. John to the Scarlet beast, the Mystery of iniquity, than with pious non-conformists. It is true they disclaim all this, and that their opinions are seconded by the extensive learning, the laborious zeal, and the deep devotion of those who propagate them, but a reference to facts will convince us that such has generally been the character of heretical teachers. Satan is too crafty to commit his cause into the hands of those who have nothing to recommend them to approbation."[1]

---

[1] George Eliot, *The George Eliot Letters*, ed. Gordon S. Haight, 9 vols. (New Haven: Yale University Press, 1954–1956) 1:26.

Of course, the young woman who wrote this letter to the pious mentor of her youth, Maria Lewis, was actually on the verge of renouncing Evangelicalism and the Christian faith altogether—along with every other kind of theism, for that matter.[2] And in time, under the pen name of George Eliot, she would be condemning those who adopted her former intolerance for Roman Catholicism.

In her 1855 review of *Westward Ho!*, for example, Eliot denounced Kingsley's facile depiction of Protestantism and Catholicism as embodiments of good and evil, arguing that "Mr. Kingsley's ethics seem to resemble too closely those of his bug-bears the Dominicans [of the Inquisition], when he implies that it is a holy work for the 'Ayes' to hunt down the 'Noes' like so many beasts of prey."[3] Her 1855 assessment of Dr. John Cumming's Evangelical teaching is even more pointed: in characterizing Catholicism as "the masterpiece of Satan," Cumming's doctrines evince "*the absence of genuine charity.*"[4] In such an estimation, she concurs with "a large body, both of thinkers and practical men,"[5] who see in Cumming's words the same falsehoods of which he accuses the Catholic Church, though such enlightened people explain these falsehoods in terms of Cumming's egotism rather than the Satanic influences he is so quick to cite in decrying the lies of Rome.

---

[2] Evans was born in 1819 to Anglican parents but attended the school of Nancy Wallington from 1828 to 1832, where she came under the influence of the Evangelical governess Maria Lewis, with whom she faithfully corresponded through her early adulthood. Her Evangelical views were reinforced at the Calvinistic school run by Mary and Rebecca Franklin, which she attended from 1832 to 1835. According to Gordon S. Haight, Evans's Evangelical fervor had gradually waned with reading that challenged her religious beliefs, but her acquaintance with agnostics Charles and Caroline Bray in 1841 "crystallized her rejection of orthodoxy" (*George Eliot: A Biography*, Oxford: Oxford University Press, 1968, 39). She never abandoned an agnosticism eventually shaped by various positivist theories and never again affiliated herself with any religious institution.

[3] George Eliot, *The Essays of George Eliot*, ed. Thomas Pinney (New York: Columbia University Press, 1963) 131.

[4] Eliot, *Essays*, 179.

[5] Eliot, *Essays*, 186.

As an adherent of positivism's religion of humanity, particularly the brand elaborated by Ludwig Feuerbach,[6] Eliot championed "genuine charity" as the highest virtue. In this ideal, which she shared with Christianity—be it of Protestant or Catholic expression—she was able to salvage essential elements of her religious heritage and to express them within her fiction. In his essay "Religion in the Novels of George Eliot," Svaglic explains, "the basic inspiration which gave direction to all her works and led her to make of her novels a plea for human solidarity was Christianity. Even though she came to reject historical Christianity long before the appearance of *Scenes of Clerical Life* in 1857, she maintained to the end ethical idealism it had taught her...."[7] Accordingly, some of Eliot's most noble protagonists, like the Reverend Edgar Tryan in "Janet's Repentance" and Dinah Morris in *Adam Bede*, are exemplary Christians.

Theoretically, given Eliot's interest in the moral rather than the doctrinal aspects of Christianity, the fact that such protagonists are Protestants and not Catholics would appear to be either incidental or purely a matter of writing about the familiar. But the truth is, Eliot maintained her bias in favor of Christian sects that emphasized their non-conformist, Protestant identities in a climate of increasing Catholicism, both Roman and Anglican. If, as Svaglic argues, Eliot saw Dissent as "more actively benevolent than the Established Church of her childhood,"[8] she surely saw it as superior in that capacity to the Roman

---

[6] The positivism in this discussion is a philosophical movement similar to empiricism and naturalism. It should not be confused with logical positivism. Evans translated Feuerbach's *Das Wesen des Christenthums* in 1854. As Haight notes, Evans was strongly drawn to Feuerbach's "daring conception of love: 'Love is God himself, and apart from it there is no God...not a visionary, imaginary love—no! a real love, a love which has flesh and blood, which vibrates as an almighty force through all living.'" She agreed whole-heartedly with Feuerbach's distinction between "self-interested love" and "the true human love," which "impels the sacrifice of self to another'" (*George Eliot: A Biography*, 137) (internal quotes are from Evans's translation of Feuerbach, *The Essence of Christianity*).

[7] Martin J. Svaglic, "Religion in the Novels of George Eliot," 1954, in *A Century of George Eliot Criticism*, ed. Gordon S. Haight (Boston: Houghton Mifflin, 1965) 286.

[8] Svaglic, "Religion," 289.

Church, too. Despite her pleas for tolerance of Catholicism, she regarded its authoritarian papacy as oppressive and supported the Republican cause in Italy.[9] During her travels to Italy, she found Romish rituals "a melancholy, hollow business,"[10] surely a poor substitute in Eliot's mind for the benevolent practices with which Dissenting churches occupied themselves.

The strongest of Eliot's judgments against Catholicism's moral enervation is found in *Romola* (1862–1863), the only one of Eliot's novels featuring Catholic characters in a Catholic setting.[11] Though the events of

---

[9] Eliot greatly admired Italian Patriot Giuseppi Mazzini, whose aim, as Haight notes, was the "[d]estruction of the Papacy as a spiritual and temporal power" (*Letters*, 2:15n).

Her fears of social anarchy, however, kept her from contributing to the fund Mazzini had established to carry out his radical causes. Cf. Frederick Karl, *George Eliot: Voice of a Century. A Biography* (New York: Norton, 1995) 391.

[10] Eliot, *Letters*, 3:228.

[11] George Eliot, *Romola*, 1862–1863 (London: Penguin, 1980). *Romola* is the story of a young Florentine woman who moves from submission to male authorities to disillusionment and a new sense of duty to humanity. The daughter of a blind scholar, Romola learns at her father's knee and absorbs the humanist values rejected by her brother Dino, a monk whose superstitious faith evokes Romola's pity for him. Romola promises her father always to safeguard the remarkable library he has collected, but both she and her father inadvertently prevent her from keeping that promise by welcoming Tito Melema, a handsome young Greek, into their home. A self-absorbed opportunist, Tito has abandoned his adoptive father, Baldassare, to slavery for the sake of money, and when he enters faction-torn Florence, he conveniently sides with whichever party will benefit him at the moment. Not long after marrying Romola, Tito loses her trust and love by selling her father's library.

The contentious atmosphere in Florence is ever in the background of Romola's story, as is the dramatic preaching of Savonarola, whose popular following is enormous. Romola herself is devoted to Savonarola, who decries the greed and lust for power dominating the political scene. His influence over her is so great that when he stops her on the road during her flight from Tito, urging her to stay true to her marriage vows, she heeds his advice and returns to Florence. However, upon her discovery that Tito has formed a marriage-like bond with a peasant named Tessa after seducing her, she abandons him for good. Tito meets his death at the hand of Baldassare, who has escaped from his captors. When Savonarola allows her godfather to go to the scaffold to advance

Romola take place during the Renaissance, the superstition, blind obedience, and excessive moroseness depicted in the novel's pages reflect her perceptions of popular Catholic piety as it was still practiced when Eliot visited Italy in 1860 and 1861, before writing *Romola*. In the person of Dino, brother of the novel's title character, Eliot blames these unenlightened features of Catholicism for the destruction of a sense of duty derived from pure, unselfish love:

> There was an unconquerable repulsion for her [Romola] in that monkish aspect [of her brother]; it seemed to her the brand of the dastardly undutifulness which had left her father desolate—of the groveling superstition which could give such undutifulness the name of piety. Her father, whose proud sincerity and simplicity of life had made him one of the few frank pagans of his time, had brought her up with a silent ignoring of the claims the Church could have to regulate the belief and action of beings with a cultivated reason. The Church, in her mind, belonged to that actual life of the mixed multitude from which they had always lived apart, and she had no ideas that could render her brother's course an object of any other feeling than incurious, indignant contempt.[12]

In light of Eliot's positivist tenets, one can soundly interpret *Romola* as the calculated condemnation of unenlightened Catholicism in favor of a Comtean view of society and the universe. According to Bullen, for example, Romola's moral development corresponds to the Comtean theory of society's moral evolution, which understands Catholicism as an immature stage, superseded by the agnostic, humanist ideals of positivism.[13]

---

the cause of his own party, Romola rebukes him and comes to a new awareness of her duty to the plague-stricken masses around her. '

[12] Eliot, *Romola*, 209–10.

[13] Cf. Bernard J. Paris, "George Eliot's Religion of Humanity," *ELH* 29 (1962): 418–43.

However, such an interpretation ignores an important role that Eliot assigns to Catholicism in *Romola*, a role by which the popish religion actually helps promote her positivist vision. For, while the novel highlights Rome's ethical failures vis-à-vis a Comtean scheme, it also suggests Catholicism's theological superiority to that of Evangelicalism when it comes to the potential for engaging the imagination and thereby moving the heart to act from love. Unlike the emphasis of austere Evangelicalism, which envisioned a Christ released from the bonds of history and promising a spiritual existence, the emphasis of Catholicism's incarnational theology—as I have noted in the discussion of Dickens in chapter 3—is on a Christ intimately involved with the material world into which he was born, a world of the senses, a world of experience. According to such theology, in his incarnation Christ validated human flesh, and in his sacramental presence within the Church, he continues to validate it in rituals that appeal to the senses, rituals that puritanical Dissenters found repugnant.

Ironically, incarnational theology resembles positivism in its emphasis on human experience. It is no wonder that Comte's *Philosophie positive* presents the Religion of Humanity as a purified form of Catholicism, one without a corrupt institution and without a distorted view of the highest good as a transcendent God. However, Comte's new religion lacked the aesthetic and symbolic expressions of human experience so psychologically important to Eliot and so powerfully present in Catholic culture. The Catholic faithful can enjoy these things intimately through concrete depictions of Christ and the saints, rather than through abstract, oftentimes baffling language about the sacred.

Eliot expresses her fascination for such humanization in *Romola*. In the same breath she uses to mock the Florentines' superstitious treatment of San Giovanni's image on their coins as a guarantee of prosperity, she describes with admiration the procession on his feast day, in which the saints themselves, through the medium of vivid effigies, "seemed...to have brought their piece of the heavens down into the narrow streets, and to pass slowly through them."[14] She goes on to wonder at the material components of this religious experience:

---

[14] Eliot, *Romola*, 131.

The clouds were made of good woven stuff, the saints and
cherubs were unglorified mortals supported by firm bars, and
those mysterious giants were really men of very steady brain,
balancing themselves on stilts, and enlarged, like Greek
tragedians, by huge masks and stuffed shoulders; but he was a
miserably unimaginative Florentine who thought only of
that—nay, somewhat impious, for in the images of sacred things
was there not some of the virtue of sacred things themselves?[15]

While Catholicism's demand for blind obedience to a sometimes bar-
baric hierarchy earns Eliot's condemnation, Catholicism's incarnational
perspective explains Eliot's positive view of church authority as embodied
in Savonarola. Although Romola at first rejects the "right of priests and
monks to interfere with my actions,"[16] she ultimately bends to
Savonarola's will, not from fear or ignorance, but because she discerns in
it the embodiment of Divine Law, which of course for Eliot is altruism.[17]
His authoritative glance is sacramental, as it were, a visible sign of the
Divine presence. "Such a glance," Eliot confesses, "is half the vocation of
the priest or spiritual guide of men."[18] While Romola ultimately rejects
his advice to remain with her husband and eventually loses her
confidence in Savonarola himself, she does not doubt the higher law of
duty he embodies. On the contrary, she sees it more clearly than ever,
experiencing a "new baptism," and returns to nurse Florence's sick.
Considering the new life Savonarola has brought to her, she asks, "Who,
in all her experience, could demand the same gratitude from her as he?"[19]

But it is incarnational theology's treatment of suffering that
particularly interests Eliot in *Romola*. According to this theology, Christ
validated suffering through his passion and death, even transforming it
into the means for redeeming humanity. Through their own suffering,

---

[15] Eliot, *Romola*, 132.
[16] Eliot, *Romola*, 429.
[17] Cf. Paris, "Religion of Humanity."
[18] Eliot, *Romola*, 429.
[19] Eliot, *Romola*, 652.

believers participate mystically in that of Christ. The sacraments ritualize and religious icons represent such a salvific mystical union. As Romola suggests, such an approach sometimes yields repulsive art—"hideous smoked Madonnas; fleshless saints in mosaic...[and] skinclad skeletons hanging on crosses..."[20]—but it also offers great potential for affirming suffering as an inevitable dimension of sacrificial love. It explains, perhaps, Eliot's attraction to à Kempis during her father's sickness. It certainly emerges as *Romola*'s central theme, which Eliot explores through the crucifix, a dominant symbol in the novel.

Savonarola introduces this symbol. Raising his own crucifix from the pulpit, he graphically describes the forms of torture endured by Christ. However, he applies them to himself now: "Take me," he calls to heaven, "stretch me on thy cross...let the thorns press my brow, and let my sweat be anguish."[21] Although "envy and hatred" have allowed political turmoil and tyranny to thrive in Florence, Savonarola is persistent in seeking lasting peace, freedom, and prosperity. Still, his emotional focus is on the bliss of embracing the pain of one's own circumstances. In his case, that bliss comes with accepting his exposure to the powerful Medici party. In the case of the hardened Baldassare— who is so moved by Savonarola's evocation of the crucified image that, sobbing, he "clutched his own palms, driving his long nails into them"[22]—that bliss validates years of slavery, illness, and imprisonment, all followed by a cruel betrayal.

By the end of the novel, Romola adopts Savonarola's perspective on love, first returning to her betrayer and then assisting the plague-stricken villagers, the destitute Florentines, and even her husband's mistress and illegitimate children. But what captures Eliot's imagination is the process by which Romola comes to accept her own brand of pain and the central role the crucifix plays in this process. Despite her bias against mawkish piety, Romola is powerfully drawn to this symbol, at first without understanding why. She kneels in "strange awe"[23] before Dino's deathbed and accepts the crucifix from Savonarola, an act that "appeared to relieve

---

[20] Eliot, *Romola*, 77.

[21] Eliot, *Romola*, 293–94.

[22] Eliot, *Romola*, 295.

[23] Eliot, *Romola*, 216.

the tension in her mind."[24] Eliot elaborates on Romola's inexplicable fascination in chapter 36, in which Romola admires her brother's love for the crucifix: "If there were much more of such experience as [Dino's] in the world, she would like to understand it—would even like to learn the thoughts of men who sank in ecstasy before the pictured agonies of martyrdom. There seemed to be something more than madness in that supreme fellowship with suffering."[25]

This passage indicates, however, that as much as the crucifix's power moves Romola, she still resists identifying herself with men like Dino who experience "ecstasy" before such tortured images, and she does this for two reasons. First, she senses that Dino has missed the point of the crucifix. In describing to Tito her encounter with Savonarola and her dying brother, she recounts a revealing meditation: "Last night I looked at the crucifix a long while, and tried to see that it would help him, until at last it seemed to me by the lamplight as if the suffering face shed pity."[26] The connection she discerns here between suffering and love is one that Dino has failed to appreciate, which Eliot makes clear in her judgment against Dino following the deathbed scene. While he dedicated his life to self-renunciation, he abandoned "the simple questions of filial and brotherly affection"[27] by keeping from Romola facts that might have prevented her unhappy marriage. But the more important reason for Romola's reluctance to identify with those awestruck by the crucifix is that she is unwilling to confront her own suffering. When Dino dies, she tries to evade her grief by allowing Tito to lock the crucifix in a triptych, described by him as "a little shrine, which is to hide away from you forever that remembrancer of sadness."[28] And when Tito betrays her by selling the library, she disguises herself as a nun and flees her beloved Florence rather than facing the hurt she experiences in his presence.

---

[24] Eliot, *Romola*, 217.
[25] Eliot, *Romola*, 396.
[26] Eliot, *Romola*, 237.
[27] Eliot, *Romola*, 218.
[28] Eliot, *Romola*, 259.

Before going, she removes the crucifix from its "tabernacle"—but "without looking at it"[29]—and hides it under her mantle.

The nun's disguise reveals the destructive consequences of hiding the crucifix and the truth it represents. Becoming the very things she abhors, Romola actually seeks the "rude sensations" caused by the "harsh sleeves" and "hard girdle of rope" of the habit because "they were in keeping with her new scorn of that thing called pleasure which made men base."[30] This artificial martyrdom is an inadequate substitute for the duty-derived suffering Romola is called to endure as Tito's wife. The fruit of Romola's flight from the world is a notable loss of "tenderness" and "keen fellow-feeling." It is no coincidence that in her new attire Romola resembles Dino, who has also misunderstood the message of the cross by seeking a life of penance that is redundant for one whose duties as a son and brother would have carried their own proper sacrifices.

Only when Savonarola stops her on the road and makes her look at the crucifix does Romola come to understand that, like the good it accompanies, authentic suffering is "not a thing of choice."[31] Authentic suffering, like that of the crucified Christ, both accompanies the duties determined by one's station in life and has value as an offering. In Romola's case, she must embrace her "marriage-sorrows." Savonarola describes such a self-defining offering with particularly sadistic fervor: "The iron is sharp—I know, I know—it rends the tender flesh."[32] But he promises that it also produces ecstasy: "The draught is bitterness on the lips. But there is rapture in the cup."

One could argue that Romola ultimately rejects her "new fellowship" with suffering because she goes on to abandon her husband and reject the authority of the one who teaches her to bear her marriage-sorrows. But she abandons her husband only because she believes her station in life has changed since Tito is pledged to another, and although she becomes disillusioned with Savonarola, she does not reject his doctrine of suffering, primarily because her pain is too overwhelming to ignore.

---

[29] Eliot, *Romola*, 398.
[30] Eliot, *Romola*, 390.
[31] Eliot, *Romola*, 432.
[32] Eliot, *Romola*, 436.

Bearing the loss of her love for Tito and her disappointment in a flawed Savonarola, she confronts a level of agony beyond all her previous experiences:

> Romola felt orphaned in those wide spaces of sea and sky. She read no message of love for her in that far-off symbolic writing of the heavens, and with a great sob she wished that she might be gliding into death...Presently she felt that she was in the grave, but not resting there: she was touching the hands of the beloved dead beside her, and trying to wake them.[33]

Then, when she flees Florence and labors in the plague-stricken village, Romola rediscovers her calling because, once again, she embraces her sorrow. Admittedly, she now seems to doubt the value of suffering and to seek only its relief when others endure it;[34] however, her own suffering yields a renewed tenderness toward Tito and a decision to return to Florence where she might be of use to him: "There was still a thread of pain within her, testifying to those words of Fra Girolamo, that she could not cease to be a wife. Could anything utterly cease for her that had once mingled itself with the current of her heart's blood?"[35] She chastises herself for once more trying to escape the pains of the world, for trying to "shake the dust from off her feet."[36] Despite the errors of the man who taught her to seek authentic suffering, she realizes that "there had been a great inspiration in him which had waked a new life in her."[37] This "new life," mentioned earlier, is owed to suffering for, as Romola advises young Lillo, by embracing one's disagreeable lot, one develops a strength of character that heals in times of calamity. Conversely, when one pursues pleasures and disaster comes, one experiences "the one form

---

[33] Eliot, *Romola*, 590.

[34] Romola says "If everything else is doubtful, this suffering that I can help is certain; if the glory of the cross is an illusion, the sorrow is only the truer." (Eliot, *Romola*, 650.)

[35] Eliot, *Romola*, 651.

[36] Eliot, *Romola*, 652.

[37] Eliot, *Romola*, 652.

of sorrow that has no balm in it, and that may well make a man say, 'It would have been better for me if I had never been born.'"[38]

Romola finally becomes such a paradigmatic sorrow-bearer that Eliot assigns her the role of *Mater Dolorosa*, the suffering Madonna of popular Catholic piety epitomized in the *Stabat Mater*. This Medieval lyric, which dwells on the agony of the Virgin Mary at the foot of the cross, bids the sorrowful mother to "[b]ihold thy child wyth gladde mood," because his death has redeemed humanity.[39] In countless prayers and hymns the sorrowful Virgin embraces her pain, and as a spiritual mother of all believers, she also embraces her children in their pain. Through Savonarola, Eliot gives Romola the same mission. Echoing the words of Luke's Gospel about Mary, Savonarola acknowledges that "the sword has pierced your soul,"[40] but reprimands Romola for seeking to avoid those in need when she cannot bear her own sorrow:

> [Y]ou think nothing of the sorrow and the wrong that are within the walls of the city where you dwell: you would leave your place empty, when it ought to be filled with your pity and your labour. If there is wickedness in the streets, your steps should shine with the light of purity; if there is a cry of anguish, you, my daughter, because you know the meaning of the cry, should be there to still it. My beloved daughter, sorrow has come to teach you a new worship: the sign of it hangs before you.[41]

When famine threatens the city, the Florentines long for the image of the *Madonna dell' Impruneta* to be carried in procession, for perhaps "that Mother, rich in sorrows and therefore in mercy, would plead for the suffering city."[42] The image is brought forth, but hidden behind a veil. Eliot pointedly names this chapter "The Unseen Madonna," while she

---

[38] Eliot, *Romola*, 675.

[39] *One Hundred Middle English Lyrics*, ed. Robert D. Stevick (Indianapolis: Bobbs-Merrill, 1964) 29.

[40] Eliot, *Romola*, 434.

[41] Eliot, *Romola*, 435.

[42] Eliot, *Romola*, 445.

names the next one describing Romola's work among the sick, "The Visible Madonna," as if to emphasize that a "Mother rich in sorrows" belongs in the world, not in a locked tabernacle. Romola's patients bless her "in much the same tone as that in which they had a few minutes before praised and thanked the unseen Madonna,"[43] and Romola herself acknowledges her role as sorrowful mother: "Florence had had need of her, and the more her own sorrow pressed upon her, the more gladness she felt in the memories, stretching through the two long years, of hours and moments in which she had lightened the burden of life to others."[44]

While Romola is tempted to abandon her role after she learns of Tito's infidelity, she resumes it in the plague-stricken village and finally among the needy Florentines, including Tessa, who asks Romola "whether she could be the Holy Madonna herself."[45] When Romola humbly answers, "Not exactly, my Tessa; only one of the saints," she perhaps is indicating that the role of the Madonna belongs not exclusively to her, but to all who will turn in their sorrow to the needs of others.

Eliot's interest in validating pain should not surprise us. When Mary Anne was five, her sick mother sent her away to a boarding school where she pined for her brother Isaac and was traumatized by nocturnal fears. When she rejected Christianity as a young adult, the father she worshipped vilified her, going so far as to banish her from his house. Her thirties were dominated by a "need to be loved."[46] Even when she finally found love in George Lewes, after experiencing rejection by Herbert Spencer because he found her homely, she had to endure the anxiety caused by her irregular relationship with him, resulting in violent headaches and fits of depression. Perhaps the factor most responsible for Eliot's emotional pain was the division in her as an intellectual woman[47]

---

[43] Eliot, *Romola*, 462.
[44] Eliot, *Romola*, 463.
[45] Eliot, *Romola*, 546.
[46] Haight, *George Eliot*, chap. 5.
[47] See Deirdre David's excellent discussion of Eliot's conflicts as an intellectual woman in "George Eliot: The Authority of a Woman Intellectual," part 3 of *Intellectual Women and Victorian Patriarchy* (Ithaca: Cornell University Press, 1987).

and a fundamentally religious person in an age of social and religious upheaval. As biographer Frederick Karl writes,

> Despite the elegance and even self-confidence of her pose, she was a deeply divided woman, a deeply divided thinker, and, as part of this, an artist desperately trying to hold together many disparate and even contradictory forces. What helps to make Eliot the voice of the century is that recognition, projected from herself, of the uncertainties, the destabilization, the wobbling center in Victorian life. Added to this was her realization of the ambiguous, even precarious, role of women. In those areas which later became the prerogative of feminists, she was caught between the daring of her private life and her difficulty in putting that daring into public policy, or public statements. But far more than even this, she was deeply divided as a person, full of contradictory impulses. Profoundly religious when growing up, she moved toward a rationalism and secularity that never completely replaced her earlier Calvinism. Her humanitarian impulses, her avowed humanism, her earnestness as to individual duty and discipline were all calculated responses to a religious or spiritual life she could no longer experience; and yet the substitutes proved unsatisfactory.[48]

On a trip to Germany in 1858, Eliot fled from the Protestant St. Sebald's Church at Nuremberg where a lifeless service was being conducted, only to linger at the Frauenkirche during mass. She recounts in her journal the ecstasy she experienced there:

> How the music that stirs all one's devout emotions blends everything into harmony,—makes one feel part of one whole, which one loves all alike, losing the sense of a separate self. Nothing could be more wretched as art than the painted Saint Veronica opposite me, holding out the sad face on her miraculous handkerchief. Yet it touched me deeply, and the

---

[48] Karl, *George Eliot,* xi–xii.

thought of the Man of Sorrows seemed a very close thing—not a faint heresy.[49]

She recorded a similar experience on beholding Raphael's Sistine Madonna in Munich: "a sort of awe, as if I were suddenly in the presence of some glorious being, made my heart swell too much for me to remain comfortably."[50] Given the pain Eliot experienced in her lifetime, it is no wonder that at least some of the somber rituals and religious art of Catholicism attracted her. Neither is it any wonder she identified enough with a religion that exalted sorrow, for all her rejection of its dogma, to make its sensibilities the focus of a major novel.

---

[49] Haight, *George Eliot*, 256. From Eliot's journal entry for 14 April 1858.
[50] Haight, *George Eliot*, 264. From Eliot's journal entry for 20 July 1858.

CONCLUSION

AS THE EIGHT novels addressed by this study vividly demonstrate, authors of fiction helped promote anti-Catholic discourse in nineteenth-century Britain. Indeed, given the "imaging and metaphorizing" power of fiction, as Kinney describes it, and the popularity of these novels, their authors were arguably more influential in shaping such discourse than were the authors of sectarian and mainstream journals, parliamentary speeches, sermons, and petitions. How better to inspire hatred for the dark, vile, foreign oppressor Rome than through dramatic battle tales of Protestant against Catholic? The "manly" Protestant heroes of Scott and Kingsley save free and righteous England from the ploys of Catholic fops and effeminate priests. The independent and enlightened heroines of Trollope, Brontë, and Eliot—all Protestant in spirit, if not in name—resist insidious Jesuitical conspirators. Through the tales flash powerful tropes, like Scott's leviathan—stuck with the harpoons of reformers—and Trollope's multi-eyed Jesuit spider. Abounding are unforgettable scenes, like Lucy Snowe's prostration before the evil Père Silas in the shadows of the confessional and Beatrice's rape by the demon-priest Tripalda. Add to these fictional elements incisive narrative diatribes—like Romola's against "groveling superstition" and Lucy Snowe's against "the dreadful viciousness, sickening tyranny and black impiety" of the Roman clergy—and the result is undisputed victory over the popular Protestant imagination. These novels strikingly dramatize the many evils ascribed to Rome in nonfictional discourse: superstition, idolatry, deceit, sexual impotence or license, corruption, oppression, debauchery, and treason.

However, unlike nonfictional discourse of the day, these novels also explore the imaginatively rich possibilities of Catholic culture. In several cases, this culture corrects deficiencies in Protestantism. Scott discovers in Catholicism's appreciation for revelry, irreverence, and humor a remedy for the dry Calvinism of his childhood. Shelley discovers in Scholasticism a model for the intelligent faith she sees lacking in the Evangelicalism of her day. In the Catholic aesthetic, Kingsley finds the counterpart of his muscular Christianity, and both Dickens and Eliot find an affirmation of a sorrow deemed morbid by enlightened and Evangelical Protestantism. An attraction to Catholicism's incarnational theology, attributed to Dickens in chapter 3, was also shared by Scott, Kingsley, and Eliot, novelists who longed to proclaim the sacredness of humanity in all its lusty materiality. In all these cases, the novelists exploit Catholicism for its ability to integrate what many expressions of Protestantism tended to polarize: sacred and secular, spirit and flesh, revelation and historicity.

Brontë, too, was drawn to the sensuality of Catholic culture, but with Lucy Snowe's "God is not with Rome," she ultimately renounces it, allowing it no final place in the protagonist's puritanical sensibilities. Perhaps more than any other novel studied here, *Villette* reduces Catholicism to anti-model. It is a perfect tool for liberating the protagonist and the author from forces that rendered vulnerable the sensitive and intelligent women of their day. Catholicism provided a somewhat similar tool for the other female authors in this study. Unlike Brontë, however, Shelley, Trollope, and Eliot exhibit no defensiveness in their attraction to Catholicism, choosing instead to revise its deficiencies rather than simply using it as anti-model and casting it aside. In *Valperga*, Shelley celebrates the imaginative power of Dante's Catholic mysticism, but reminds her readers that the difference between a ruined Beatrice and a morally triumphant Euthanasia is the power of reason also celebrated by Dante. By appropriating scholastic ideals for themselves, women like Euthanasia can assume authority denied them by a patriarchal society and church. In exploring the true nature of duty in *Father Eustace*, Trollope teaches her female readers to admire the single-mindedness, zeal, and discipline of her Jesuits, even as she warns them against tyrants who practice such duty without love. A similar dynamic takes place in

Eliot's *Romola* when the heroine borrows from Savonarola his noble willingness to suffer but only for a cause that liberates her from his grip.

Denunciation, appropriation, exploration, and revision—the novels of this study include all of these projects. Rome inspired the sort of complex and contradictory responses multi-layered novels are uniquely suited to register, and because such responses flourished, so did novels that could give them expression. The result was a culture's troubled reunion with Catholicism—not the indigenous Catholicism from the days of Chaucer and Malory, but a displaced Catholicism returning home. "Britain's Roman Catholic Revival" describes a Protestant literary movement of re-assimilation as much as it does the rebirth of Roman Catholicism itself on English soil.

BIBLIOGRAPHY
OF WORKS CITED

Alighieri, Dante. *The Divine Comedy of Dante Alighieri*. 3 volumes. Translated by John D. Sinclair. New York: Oxford University Press, 1939.

Altick, Richard D. *Victorian People and Ideas. A Companion for Modern Reader of Victorian Literature.* New York: Norton, 1973.

Andrews, Malcolm. "Introduction." In *The Old Curiosity Shop*, by Charles Dickens. London: Penguin, 1972.

Aquinas, Thomas. *Introduction to St. Thomas Aquinas*. Edited by Anton Pegis. New York: Random House, 1945.

———. *On the Truth of the Catholic Faith. Summa Contra Gentile.* Translated by Anton Pegis. Garden City: Doubleday, 1955.

Armstrong, Anthony. *The Church of England, the Methodists, and Society, 1700–1850.* Totowa NJ: Rowan and Littlefield, 1973.

Auerbach, Nina. "Charlotte Brontë. The Two Countries," *University of Toronto Quarterly* 42 (Summer 1973): 328–42.

Bagehot, Walter. "The Waverley Novels." 1858. In *Critical Essays on Sir Walter Scott. The Waverley Novels.* Edited by Harry E. Shaw. New York: G. K. Hall, 1996.

Baker, Joseph Ellis. *The Novel and the Oxford Movement. 1932.* New York: Russell and Russell, 1965.

Blumberg, Jane. *Mary Shelley's Early Novels. This Child of Imagination and Misery.* Iowa City: University of Iowa Press, 1993.

Brontë, Charlotte. *Villette.* 1853. London: Penguin, 1979.

Brown, David. *Walter Scott and the Historical Imagination.* London: Routledge and Kegan Paul, 1979.

Bullen, J. B. "George Eliot's *Romola* As a Positivist Allegory," *Review of English Studies* 26 (1975): 425–35.

Butt, John, and Kathleen Tillotson. *Dickens at Work*. London: Methuen, 1957.

Charles Kingsley, His Letters, and Memories of His Life. Edited by Fanny Kingsley. 2 volumes. New York: J. F. Taylor, 1899.

Chitty, Susan. *The Beast and the Monk*. London: Hodder and Stoughton, 1974.

The Christian Faith. In *The Doctrinal Documents of the Catholic Church*. Edited by S. J. Dupuis and J. Neuner. Dublin: The Mercier Press, 1976.

Clarke-Beattie, Rosemary. "Fables of Rebellion. Anti-Catholicism in the Structure of *Villette*," *ELH*, 53 (Winter 1986): 821–47.

Cohen, Jane R. *Charles Dickens and His Original Illustrators*. Columbus: Ohio State University Press, 1980.

Coleridge, Samuel. *From Biblographia Literaria*. In *Norton Anthology of English Literature*. Edited by M. H. Abrams. Volume 2. 5th edition. New York: Norton, 1986.

Colloms, Brenda. *Charles Kingsley: The Lion of Eversley*. London: Constable, 1975.

Curran, Stuart. "Women readers, women writers." In *The Cambridge Companion to British Romanticism*. Edited by Stuart Curran. Cambridge: Cambridge University Press, 1993.

Daiches, David. "Scott's Achievement As a Novelist." 1951. In *Walter Scott: Modern Judgements*. Edited by D. D. Devlin. London: Macmillan, 1968.

David, Deirdre. *Intellectual Women and Victorian Patriarchy. Harriet Martineau, Elizabeth Barrett Browning, George Eliot*. Ithaca: Cornell University Press, 1987.

Dickens, Charles. *Barnaby Rudge*. 1841. In *The Oxford Illustrated Dickens*. Oxford: Oxford University Press, 1954.

———. *A Child's History of England*. 1851–1853. In *The Oxford Illustrated Dickens*. Oxford: Oxford University Press, 1958.

———. *Letters from Charles Dickens to Angela Burdett-Coutts, 1841–1865*. Edited by Edgar Johnson. London: Jonathan Cape, 1953.

———. *The Letters of Charles Dickens*, 1820-1867, vols. 1–11. Edited by Madeline House, et al. The Pilgrim Edition. Oxford: Clarendon, 1965-1999.

———. *Miscellaneous Papers, Plays, and Poems*. Edited by B. W. Matz. Centenary Edition. 36 volumes. London: Chapman and Hall, 1911.

———. *The Old Curiosity Shop*. 1840–1841. In *The Oxford Illustrated Dickens*. Oxford: Oxford University Press, 1951.

———. *Pictures from Italy*. 1846. Edited by David Paroissien. New York: Coward, McCann, and Geoghegan, 1974.

Eagleton, Terry. *Myths of Power: A Marxist Study of the Brontës*. London: MacMillan, 1975.

Edwards, Francis. *The Jesuits in England from 1580 to the Present Day*. Tumbridge Wells, Kent, England: Burns and Oates, 1985.

Eliot, George. *The Essays of George Eliot*. Edited by Thomas Pinney. New York: Columbia University Press, 1963.

———. *The George Eliot Letters*. Edited by Gordon S. Haight. 9 volumes. New Haven: Yale University Press, 1954–1956.

———. *Romola*. 1862–1863. London: Penguin, 1980.

Ferris, Ina. "Story-Telling and the Subversion of Literary Form in Walter Scott's Fiction." 1985. In *Critical Essays on Sir Walter Scott. The Waverley Novels*. Edited by Harry E. Shaw. New York: G. K. Hall, 1996.

Franchot, Jenny. *Roads to Rome. The Antebellum Protestant Encounter with Catholicism*. Berkley: University of California Press, 1994.

Gaskell, Elizabeth. *The Life of Charlotte Brontë*. 1857. London: Penguin, 1975.

Gérin, Winifred. *Charlotte Brontë. The Evolution of Genius*. Oxford: Clarendon University Press, 1967.

Gilbert, Alan D. *Religion and Society in Industrial England. Church, Chapel, and Social Change, 1740–1914*. London: Longman, 1976.

Gilbert, Sandra, and Susan Gubar. *The Madwoman in the Attic*. New Haven: Yale University Press, 1979.

Green, Garrett. *Imagining God: Theology and the Religious Imagination*. Grand Rapids: Eerdmans, 1989.

Haight, Gordon S. *George Eliot. A Biography*. Oxford: Oxford University Press, 1968.

Hall, Donald E. *Muscular Christianity: Embodying the Victorian Age*. Cambridge: Cambridge University Press, 1994.

Hartley, Allan John. *The Novels of Charles Kingsley. A Christian Social Interpretation*. Folkstone: Hour Glass Press, 1977.

Heilman, Robert B. "Charlotte Brontë's 'New' Gothic." In *From Jane Austen to Joseph Conrad*. Edited by Robert C. Rathburn and Martin Steinmann, Jr. Minneapolis: University of Minnesota Press, 1958.

Heineman, Helen. *Frances Trollope*. Boston: Twayne, 1984.

———. *Mrs. Trollope. The Triumphant Feminine in the Nineteenth Century*. Athens: Ohio University Press, 1979.

———. *Restless Angels. The Friendship of Six Victorian Women.* Athens: Ohio University Press, 1983.

Hook, Andrew D. "Charlotte Brontë, the Imagination, and *Villette.*" In *The Brontës. A Collection of Critical Essays.* Edited by Ian Gregor. Englewood Cliffs: Prentice, 1970.

Houghton, Walter E. *The Victorian Frame of Mind, 1830–1870.* New Haven: Yale University Press, 1957.

House, Humphrey. *The Dickens World.* London: Oxford University Press, 1941.

Johnson, Edgar. *Charles Dickens. His Tragedy and Triumph.* 2 volumes. New York: Simon and Schuster, 1952.

———. *Sir Walter Scott. The Great Unknown.* 2 volumes. New York: Macmillan, 1970.

Johnson, E. D. H. "'Daring the Dread Glance.' Charolotte Brontë's Treatment of the Supernatural in *Villette.*" *Nineteenth-Century Fiction* 20 (1966): 325–36.

Kant, Immanuel. *Foundations of the Metaphysics of Morals.* 1785. Translated by Lewis White Beck. Indianapolis: Bobbs-Merrill, 1959.

Karl, Frederick R. *George Eliot. Voice of a Century. A Biography.* New York: Norton, 1995.

Kingsley, Charles. *Westward Ho!* 1855. 2 volumes. New York: J. F. Taylor, 1899.

Kinney, Arthur. "Is Literary History Still Possible?" *Ben Johnson Journal* 2 (1995): 199–222.

Krueger, Christine L. *The Reader's Repentance. Women Preachers, Women Writers, and Nineteenth-Century Social Discourse.* Chicago: Chicago University Press, 1992.

Lackey, Lionel. "*The Monastery* and *The Abbot.* Scott's Religious Dialectics," *Studies in the Novel* 19/1 (1987) 46–65.

Lockhart, John. *Memoirs of Sir Walter Scott.* 1837–1838. 10 volumes. Edinburgh: Charles Black, 1882.

Looten, Tricia. *Lost Saints: Silence, Gender, and Victorian Literary Canonization.* Charlottesville: University of Virginia Press, 1996.

Maison, Margaret M. *The Victorian Vision. Studies in the Religious Novel.* New York: Sheed and Ward, 1961.

Marcus, Steven. *Dickens from Pickwick to Dombey.* New York: Norton, 1965.

Martin, Robert. *The Dust of Combat.* London: Faber and Faber, 1959.

Mellor, Anne K. *Mary Shelley. Her Life, Her Fiction, Her Monsters*. New Brunswick: Rutgers University Press, 1988.

————. "Why Women Didn't Like Romanticism." In *The Romantics and Us.*

Essays on Literature and Culture. Edited by Gene W. Ruoff. New Brunswick: Rutgers University Press, 1990.

Neville-Sington, Pamela. *Fanny Trollope. The Life and Adventures of a Clever Woman*. New York: Viking, 1998.

Norman, Edward R. *Anti-Catholicism in Victorian England*. London: George Allen and Unwin, 1968.

One Hundred Middle English Lyrics. Edited by Robert D. Stevick. Indianapolis: Bobbs-Merrill, 1964.

The Oxford Movement. Edited by Eugene R. Fairweather. New York: Oxford University Press, 1964.

Page, Norman. *A Dickens Companion*. London: Macmillan, 1984.

Paris, Bernard J. "George Eliot's Religion of Humanity," *ELH* 29 (1962) 418–43.

Paroissien, David. "*Pictures from Italy* and Its Original Illustrator," *Dickensian* 67 (1971): 87–90.

Parsons, Coleman. *Witchcraft and Demonology in Scott's Fiction. With Chapters on the Supernatural in Scottish Literature*. Edinburgh: Oliver and Boyd, 1964.

Patmore, Conventry. *The Angel in the House*. 1854–1862. London: George Bell and Son, 1885.

Paz, D. G. *Popular Anti-Catholicism in Mid-Victorian England*. Stanford: Stanford University Press, 1992.

Peters, Margot. *Charolotte Brontë. Style in the Novel*. Milwaukee: University of Wisconsin Press, 1973.

Pollard, Arthur. "The Brontës and Their Father's Faith." *Essays and Studies* 37 (1984): 46–61.

Pope-Henessey, Una. *Canon Charles Kingsley. A Biography*. London: Chatto and Windus, 1948.

Raleigh, John Henry. "What Scott Meant to the Victorians." 1963. In *Critical Essays on Sir Walter Scott. The Waverley Novels*. Edited by Harry E. Shaw. New York: G. K. Hall, 1996.

The Renaissance in England. Non-Dramatic Prose and Verse of the Sixteenth Century. Edited by Hyder Rollins and Herschel Baker. Lexington: D. C. Heath, 1954.

Rieger, James. "Shelley's Paterin Beatrice," *Studies in Romanticism* 4 (1965): 169–84.

Robertson, Fiona. *Legitimate Histories. Scott, Gothic, and the Authorities of Fiction.* Oxford: Clarendon, 1994.

Sanders, Andrew. *Charles Dickens Resurrectionist.* New York: St. Martin's, 1982.

Scott, Sir Walter. *The Abbot.* 1820. New Abbotsford Edition. 2 volumes. Boston: Dana Estes, 1900.

———. *The Journal of Sir Walter Scott.* Edited by W. E. K. Anderson. Oxford: Clarendon, 1972.

———. *The Monastery.* 1820. New Abbotsford Edition. 2 volumes. Boston: Dana Estes, 1900.

Shatto, Susan. *The Companion to Bleak House.* London: Unwin Hyman, 1988.

Shelley, Mary Wollstonecraft. *Collected Tales and Stories.* Edited by Charles E. Robinson. London: Johns Hopkins University Press, 1976.

———. *The Journals of Mary Shelley, 1814–1844.* Edited by Paula R. Feldman and Diana Scott-Kilvert. 2 volumes. Oxford: Clarendon, 1987.

———. *The Letters of Mary Wollstonecraft Shelley.* Edited by Betty T. Bennett. 3 volumes. London: Johns Hopkins University Press, 1980–1988.

———. *Rambles in Germany and Italy in 1840, 1842, and 1843.* London: Edward Moxon, 1844.

———. *Valperga.* [Or] *The Life and Adventures of Castruccio, Prince of Lucca.* 1823. London: George Routledge, 1857.

Shelley, Percy Bysshe. *Shelley's Prose and Poetry.* Edited by Donald H. Reiman and Sharon B. Powers. New York: Norton, 1977.

———. *The Poetical Works of Percy Bysshe Shelley.* Edited by Mary Wollstonecraft Shelley. 1839. 4 volumes. London: Edward Moxon, 1854.

Spark, Muriel. *Child of Light. A Reassessment of Mary Wollstonecraft Shelley.* Hadleigh, Essex: Tower Bridge, 1951.

Sunstein, Emily. *Mary Shelley. Romance and Reality.* Boston: Little, 1989.

Svaglic, Martin J. "Religion in the Novels of George Eliot." 1954. In *A Century of George Eliot Criticism.* Edited by Gordon S. Haight. Boston: Houghton Mifflin, 1965.

Tanner, Tony. "Introduction." In *Villette,* by Charlotte Brontë. London: Penguin, 1979.

Tarr, Mary Muriel. *Catholicism in Gothic Fiction. A Study of the Nature and Function of Catholic Materials in Gothic Fiction in England*

(1762–1820). Ph.D. dissertation, Catholic University of America, 1946. Catholic University of America Press, 1946.

Thorp, Margaret Farrand. *Charles Kingsley, 1819–1875*. New York: Octagon Books, 1969 [Reprint of Princeton edition, 1937].

Trollope, Anthony. *An Autobiography*. Oxford: Blackwell, 1919.

Trollope, Frances Eleanor. *Frances Trollope. Her Life and Literary Work*. London: Richard Bentley, 1895.

Trollope, Frances Milton. *Domestic Manners of the Americans*. 1832. Dover NH: Alan Sutton, 1984.

———. *Father Eustace. A Tale of the Jesuits*. London: Henry Colburn, 1847. New York: Garland Publishing, Reprint 1975.

———. *The Vicar of Wrexhill*. London: Richard Bentley, 1837. New York: Garland Publishing, Reprint 1975.

Trollope, Thomas Adolphus. *What I Remember*. New York: Harper, 1888.

The Victorian Mind. Edited by Gerald Kauvar and Gerald Sorensen. New York: Putnam, 1969.

Walling, William. *Mary Shelley*. New York: Twayne, 1972.

Wallis, Frank H. *Popular Anti-Catholicism in Mid-Victorian Britain. Texts and Studies in Religion*. Volume 60. Lewiston: Edwin Mellen Press, 1993.

Welsh, Alexander. *City of Dickens*. Cambridge: Harvard University Press, 1971.

Wilt, Judith. *Secret Leaves. The Novels of Walter Scott*. Chicago: University of Chicago Press, 1985.